Computers and Talk
in the Primary Classroom

THE LANGUAGE AND EDUCATION LIBRARY

Series Editor
Professor David Corson, *The Ontario Institute for Studies in Education,
252 Bloor St. West, Toronto, Ontario, Canada M5S 1V6*

Other Books in the Series
Competing and Consensual Voices
    PATRICK COSTELLO and SALLY MITCHELL (eds)
Critical Theory and Classroom Talk
    ROBERT YOUNG
Language Policies in English-Dominant Countries
    MICHAEL HERRIMAN and BARBARA BURNABY (eds)
Language Policy Across the Curriculum
    DAVID CORSON
Language, Minority Education and Gender
    DAVID CORSON
Learning about Punctuation
    NIGEL HALL and ANNE ROBINSON (eds)
Making Multicultural Education Work
    STEPHEN MAY
School to Work Transition in Japan
    KAORI OKANO
Studies in Immersion Education
    ELAINE M. DAY and STAN M. SHAPSON
Reading Acquisition Processes
    G. B. THOMPSON, W. E. TUNMER and T. NICHOLSON (eds)
Worlds of Literacy
    M. HAMILTON, D. BARTON and R. IVANIC (eds)

Other Books of Interest
Children Talking: The Development of Pragmatic Competence
    LINDA THOMPSON (ed.)
The Guided Construction of Knowledge
    NEIL MERCER
Literacy, Language and Community Publishing
    JANE MACE (ed.)

The Open University Readers
Language and Literacy in Social Practice
    JANET MAYBIN (ed.)
Language, Literacy and Learning in Educational Practice
    BARRY STIERER and JANET MAYBIN (eds)
Media Texts: Authors and Readers
    DAVID GRADDOL and OLIVER BOYD-BARRETT (eds)
Researching Language and Literacy in Social Context
    DAVID GRADDOL, JANET MAYBIN and BARRY STIERER (eds)

Please contact us for the latest book information:
Multilingual Matters Ltd, Frankfurt Lodge, Clevedon Hall,
Victoria Road, Clevedon, BS21 7HH, England

Language and Education Library 12
Series Editor: Professor David J. Corson
The Ontario Institute for Studies in Education

Computers and Talk in the Primary Classroom

Edited by
Rupert Wegerif and Peter Scrimshaw

MULTILINGUAL MATTERS LTD
Clevedon • Philadelphia • Toronto • Sydney • Johannesburg

Library of Congress Cataloging in Publication Data

Computers and Talk in the Primary Classroom
Edited by Rupert Wegerif and Peter Scrimshaw
The Language and Education Library: 12
Includes bibliographical references and index
1. Interaction analysis in education. 2. Oral communication–computer-assisted
instruction–Great Britain. 3. Education, elementary–Computer-assisted
instruction–Great Britain. 4. Sociolinguistics–Great Britain.
I. Wegerif, Rupert. II. Scrimshaw, Peter. III. Series.
LB1034.C65   1997
370'.1'4–dc21   97-10084

British Library Cataloguing in Publication Data

A CIP catalogue record for this book is available from the British Library.

ISBN 1-85359-391-5 (hbk)
ISBN 1-85359-395-8 (pbk)

Multilingual Matters Ltd

UK: Frankfurt Lodge, Clevedon Hall, Victoria Road, Clevedon BS21 7HH.
USA: 1900 Frost Road, Suite 101, Bristol, PA 19007, USA.
Canada: OISE, 712 Gordon Baker Road, Toronto, Ontario, Canada M2H 3R7.
Australia: P.O. Box 586, Artamon, NSW, Australia.
South Africa: PO Box 1080, Northcliffe 2115, Johannesburg, South Africa.

Typeset by Bookcraft, Stroud, UK.
Printed and bound in Great Britain by WBC Book Manufacturers Ltd.

Contents

Acknowledgements

The research discussed in this book was made possible only by the willing co-operation and support of the heads, teachers and children of the following schools: Brampton Infants, Cavell First, Chapel Break First, Cloverhill First, Old Stratford Primary, Oakway Junior, Bignold Middle, George White Middle, Greenleys Middle and Watling Way Middle. We are very grateful to them all and to the many unnamed schools who took part in the CD-ROM in Primary Schools project. In accordance with the agreement with the schools, names of individual children have been changed, and the schools and classrooms in which particular studies were carried out are not identified.

Some of the chapters in this book were based on, or contain material from, previously published articles. Grateful acknowledgement is made to the publishers who granted permission for these articles to be reproduced. Blackwells are thanked for permission to print Chapter 9, a version of which first appeared as Collaborative learning and directive software in the *Journal of Computer Assisted Learning* (1996, 12 (1), 22–32). Elsevier are thanked for permission to print Chapter 2 and Chapter 16, both of which contain some material from a longer article first published as 'How do Teachers Help Children to Learn? An Analysis of Teachers' Interventions in Computer-based Activities' in *Learning and Instruction in 1993* (Vol. 2, 339–55), and Elsevier are also thanked for permission to reproduce some figures in Chapter 18 which first appeared in an article titled 'Using Computers to Help Coach Exploratory Talk Across the Curriculum', in *Computers and Education* (1996, 28 (1), 51–60)

The Spoken Language and New Technology (SLANT) project, funded by the Economic and Social Research Council (ESRC) of the United Kingdom, supported the research reported on in several chapters of this book. The ESRC also funded the doctoral research on improving interactions around computers reported by Madeline Watson in Chapter 16. Madeline Watson's research benefited as well from a student bursary awarded by the National Council for Educational Technology. The Department for Education and Employment funded, and the National Council for Educational Technology commissioned, the evaluation of CD-ROM use in primary classrooms referred to by Janet Collins in Chapter 12. The Engineering and Physical Sciences Research Council (EPSRC) of the United Kingdom funded the doctoral research of Rupert Wegerif, some of the results of which are presented in Chapter 17. We are very grateful for the support of these funding bodies.

Finally, we would like to thank John Elliott. Although it was not possible for him to make a formal contribution to this book, as co-director of the SLANT project he was a major source of advice, help and encouragement to the research team.

Contributors

Janet Collins is a Lecturer in the School of Education at the Open University. She is author of *The Quiet Child*, published by Cassell. Before moving into full-time university research Janet was a primary school teacher with 12 years experience.

Lyn Dawes is a teacher-researcher at a middle school in Buckinghamshire who worked with the Spoken Language and New Technology project. Lyn has published a number of articles for professional journals on the teaching of talking skills.

Eunice Fisher is a Senior Lecturer in Psychology in the faculty of Humanities and Social Sciences at Nene College. She was the Senior Research Associate on the Spoken Language and New Technology project.

Neil Mercer is a Professor and Director of the Centre for Language and Communications in the School of Education at the Open University and was co-director of the Spoken Language and New Technology project. He is the author, with Derek Edwards, of *Common Knowledge: The Development of Understanding in the Classroom* and of *The Guided Construction of Knowledge: Talk Between Teachers and Learners in the Classroom*.

Gary Perkins is a teacher-researcher at a middle school in Buckinghamshire who worked with the Spoken Language and New Technology project.

Terry Phillips is a lecturer in Education at the University of East Anglia and was a member of the Spoken Language and New Technology project research team. He has published numerous articles on children's talk and is an editor of *Oracy Matters*.

Peter Scrimshaw is a Senior Lecturer in the School of Education at the Open University. He has written or edited a number of books on curriculum evaluations, with a special emphasis on the role of IT in schools including: *Language, Classrooms and Computers*.

Joan Swann is a Senior Lecturer in the Centre for Language and Communications in the School of Education at the Open University and author of *Girls, Boys and Language.*

Alison Syred-Paul is a teacher-researcher in a primary school in the north of England who worked with Janet Collins and others on the CD-ROM in primary schools evaluation.

Madeline Watson first became involved in these issues as a teacher–researcher in a middle school in Buckinghamshire. She is now a full-time doctoral student in the Centre for Language and Communications in the School of Education at the Open University with awards from both the Economic and Social Research Council and the National Council for Educational Technology.

Rupert Wegerif is a Research Fellow in the Centre for Language and Communications in the School of Education at the Open University.

A Note on Transcriptions

The names of all the children used in transcriptions of classroom talk have been changed. Transcripts are punctuated to make them as readable as possible. The following conventions, or a sub-set of them, are used throughout:

/	a short pause of less than one second
(2)	a pause of about two seconds
=	where one speaker follows another with no noticeable pause
[[	overlapping utterances
(...)	a section of unintelligible speech

A commentary or function coding is sometimes placed in a right-hand column. In some chapters brief comments on actions, such as writing or clicking with the mouse, are put in parentheses within the transcript. Some further transcription conventions are used in particular chapters. Where this is the case explanations are provided in the text.

Chapter 1

Introduction: Computers in the Classroom Context

RUPERT WEGERIF AND PETER SCRIMSHAW

Background

Computers are becoming an established part of primary education in many countries of the world. In Britain most primary classrooms now have reliable access to at least one computer (DFE, 1995) and politicians of all political persuasions can be heard calling for many more computers in classrooms as if their mere presence was a panacea guaranteed to cure all educational problems. But in fact there remains considerable uncertainty and debate among teachers and educationalists over how best to use computers in the classroom. Some surveys report that computers in schools are underused. Teachers, already burdened with many demands, do not always find it easy to fit the computer into their teaching (Underwood & Underwood, 1990: 16). This book explores the contentious and increasingly important issue of how computers are being used in primary classrooms and how they could be used. It approaches this issue from the perspective of spoken language because we believe that this is the most important medium for classroom education.

In Britain, as in many other countries, computers in primary schools are mainly used by more than one child at a time. This appears as an efficient use of a relatively scarce resource. Teachers, when asked, also justify the use of group work at computers as a support for peer learning and the development of communication skills (Crook, 1994). A number of studies have reported on the potential of computers to support educationally valuable small-group work (Light, 1993; Light et al., 1994; Howe et al., 1996; Hoyles et al., 1994;) and the work of Scardemalia and colleagues (Scardemalia et al., 1989; Scardemalia & Bereiter, 1991) has shown how local computer networks can provide a powerful resource for peer learning. However, there has been little research reported, until now, on the quality of children's talk around standalone computers in ordinary classrooms.

This book is an account of research which attempted to fill this gap.

The chapters in this book are based upon a number of classroom research projects and evaluations carried out in the Centre for Language and Communications at the Open University, in some cases in collaboration with colleagues from the University of East Anglia. The Spoken Language and New Technology (SLANT) project was a naturalistic study observing and recording the talk of groups of children engaged in normal activities at the computer using a range of educational software available in many schools. Through an open-ended observational approach which did not narrow down possible explanations and outcomes in advance, the project team sought to discover the main factors influencing the quality of children's talk at computers and so influencing the quality of their learning. The investigation of children's talk around computers continued through subsequent research projects, looking at the use of CD-ROMs in primary schools and exploring ways in which teachers could improve both the quality of children's talk around computers and the use of computers within the curriculum.

The Importance of Talk

The significance we give in this book to talk perhaps needs to be explained and justified further. There is a bias in the way we normally describe communication towards what can be called a transmission model. On this apparently common-sense model it appears easy to distinguish the senders of messages, people, from the messages, what is said, and both of these things from the medium that is used, the language. It is perhaps because of this apparently common-sense, but in fact highly misleading, model that the language used in classrooms remained almost invisible to educational research for so long. Psychologists and educationalists both focused on either the development of people or the development of content with often little reference to the language used. The sociocultural approach largely shared by the contributors to this book takes it as a given that language is the essential medium of learning. An important reference point for the application of a sociocultural approach to classroom discourse is the book *Common Knowledge* (Edwards & Mercer, 1987)which describes how talk in classrooms between teachers and learners leads to the development of shared understanding. In *Common Knowledge* education is described as the process of being guided into the appropriate use of educated language, and understanding itself is described as a discursive achievement primarily realised in and through the talk of learners. From this sociocultural perspective the central question about the role of computers is how they fit into, alter and support the talk between teachers and learners that carries the development of understanding in the classroom.

The sociocultural position developed in *Common Knowledge* and carried forward by the authors of this book owes a great deal to the work of Vygotsky (Vygotsky, 1978, 1986, 1991; van der Veer & Valsinger, 1994). Vygotsky's theory of development gives a central role to language and to 'socialisation' through education (Wertsch, 1985b). The significance of key Vygotskian and neo-Vygotskian concepts such as the Zone of Proximal Development (ZPD) and 'scaffolding' for the study of classroom discourse is recognised. However, these Vygotskian concepts appear to reflect a focus on an individual child's development in the context of being taught by an adult. It is difficult to see how these concepts can be applied unchanged to understand the educational role of peer talk. The chapters of Section 1 describe the development of a theoretical framework for understanding collaborative learning. While Vygotsky described talk as a tool, 'a mediational means', supporting individual intellectual development many of the chapters in this book go further to take the quality of talk itself as an aim of education. This is reflected in the development of a new kind of analytic framework for investigating peer talk. Essentially this is a characterisation of the main 'types of talk' or, following Mercer (Mercer, 1995), 'social modes of thinking' available to children working together. This framework, influenced by both genre analysis (Halliday, 1978; Martin, 1984) and by recent philosophy of language (Habermas, 1970, 1979a,b, 1990, 1991a,b, 1993) offers a way of investigating the cognitive dimension of peer talk. One of the types of talk characterised, 'exploratory talk', appears to offer a situated description of 'reasoning' – a type of talk which is of central concern in education. The significance of this 'exploratory talk' to education is an important theme of the book as a whole.

The Importance of Context

The significance given to context is one of the features that distinguishes the sociocultural from other approaches in psychology and education. Despite the laudable work of Cole and his colleagues (for example, Newman *et al.*, 1989); Crook (1987, 1991, 1994)and Scardemalia and colleagues (Scardemalia *et al.*, 1989; Scardemalia & Bereiter, 1991), much research on the educational role of computers has treated and continues to treat the computer as if it were a self-sufficient teaching machine which could have a determinate effect on learners independent of the larger educational context in which it is used. (To demonstrate the truth of this point it is only necessary to flick through 1996 issues of the major journals in this area, such as the *Journal of Computer-Assisted Learning, Computers and Education* and *AI in Education* which have many accounts of software development and evaluation unrelated to classroom teaching practice.) Our claim that learning is not a mechanical process but a discursive process foregrounds the importance of the continuing conversations going on in the classroom both between the teacher and learners and between the learners themselves. It is these conversations and the communicative climate of the classroom that shape children's expectations as they approach the twin challenges of both working at the computer and working together with others. It is also this larger discursive context, particularly the way activities are integrated into the curriculum, that will determine whether or not experiences at the computer contribute to any continuing development of understanding or competence.

Context as we are using it here, refers to anything that appears within or has an impact upon the talk of children as they work together at computers. A shared belief in the importance of context leads the authors in this book to explore a number of themes which reach beyond the immediate interaction between children and computer screen. One of the most important of these is the role of the teacher in shaping learning experiences at the computer. There is a shared interest in how teachers set up group work at the computer, how they intervene during such work and how they contextualise the work after the event in terms of their teaching aims and the official curriculum. The significance of the expectations of children as they approach the computer and how these interact with the software is another broad theme that runs through the book. Gender too emerges as an important factor in shaping the expectations of children. Research has shown that gender affects not only the way children feel about computers (Culley, 1988), and the way children interact with each other (Underwood, 1994) but also their response to differently illustrated computer interfaces (Light *et al.*, 1994).

Our view of context is not passive. The approach to discourse analysis developed in the first section of the book focuses on how talk constructs context. The expectations of children, their roles, and what they learn are all shaped by the talk of the teacher in setting up exercises and by the way that the children talk together. Our sociocultural approach suggests that the construction of knowledge together is the construction of a shared linguistic context through talk. The talk of children together around computers is looked at in two ways: both from the point of view of how this talk constructs context and from the point of view of how elements of context impact upon this talk. In the book there is a move from descriptions of the talk of children and its double relationship to context, to an account of how active measures were taken by teachers and researchers working together to change the context and to change the way in which context was constructed by the talk of the children. That is to say how measures were taken to shape children's expectations, their roles as participants in collaborations and so the quality of their learning.

Methods for Researching Classroom Discourse

The question of how to go about researching classroom talk is a major, if often implicit, theme running through all the chapters of this book. Issues here range from the choice of underlying paradigm to the small, but often very important, details of how to present transcript evidence. The concept of action research had a large impact on the research described in this book. Supporters of the action research model advocate that teachers themselves become involved in critical reflection on teaching in their own classrooms. The engaged perspective of practitioners is, it is argued, particularly valuable in being able to relate research to improved practice. A number of chapters in this book are jointly written by university researchers and class teachers. This illustrates the research partnership model in which researchers and teachers work closely together to their mutual advantage. We claim that this approach potentially combines the strengths of action research with the strengths of academic research, bringing together theory grounded in a wide reading of background literature and the implementation of improved classroom practice grounded on the specific expertise of experienced teachers. We hope that the advantages of this research partnership model are reflected in the book as a whole.

The impact of the sociocultural perspective has already been described in our emphasis on the importance of talk and the importance of context. However, taking a sociocultural perspective is not narrowly prescriptive of research methods. In the studies reported here we find not only descriptive and qualitative research but also the use of quantified evaluations and, in one case, an experimental design with systematic comparisons between different conditions. The elaboration of an interpretative framework based on types of talk in the first section of the book stems from a desire to generalise between sequences of talk in a way that does not lead to the loss of context associated with more established coding schemes (Wegerif & Mercer, 1996; Wegerif & Mercer, in press). This reflects a tension between the desire to present talk accurately in its full context and the need to be able to generalise from particular incidents to draw conclusions which other researchers will find convincing and useful and so will be able to take up and build upon. The different styles of research described in these chapters and the different degrees of detail in the presentation of transcripts represent different individual responses to this tension. A related challenge faced by researchers working within a sociocultural paradigm but also concerned with the issue of educational evaluation, is how to integrate quantitative measures, where these are appropriate, with qualitative research in such a way that the context is neither lost nor distorted. A number of different solutions to this challenge are exemplified in this book in what is clearly a continuing debate.

Overview of the Book

Language, Classrooms and Computers (Scrimshaw, 1993) concluded with a chapter on 'Researching the Electronic Classroom' which emphasised the need to develop better theory of the role of computers in the classroom in order to improve practice. The aim, the authors proposed, must be to:

> create a theory of computer assisted learning visibly relevant to the improvement of practice; and correspondingly, a practice that was informed by, and critically responsive to that theory. (Mercer & Scrimshaw, 1993: 189)

In Figure 1.1 the circular relationship between practice, research and theory is drawn out including within it both cycles in the development and evaluation of software and in the development and evaluation of new ways of working with computers in the classroom.

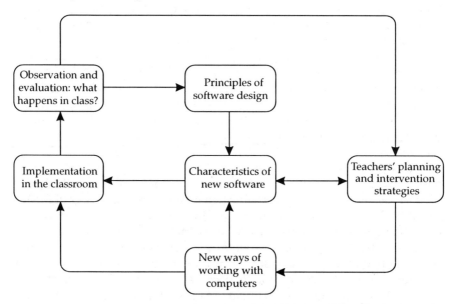

Figure 1.1   A creativity cycle for improving computer-based learning and teaching (from Scrimshaw, 1993: 186)

The structure of this book follows from and gives substance to these aims. The book begins with a section emphasising theory, moves on to a section containing studies of classroom talk around computers which both applied and developed that theory, and ends with a section focusing on showing how this research contributed to improving classroom practice.

The first section consists of an extended discussion of the educational significance of classroom talk, especially children's talk together, and how this can be characterised and researched. A theoretical framework can be seen emerging through the dialogue of these chapters, which are presented in the order of their writing. In Chapter 2, Neil Mercer and Eunice Fisher present the work of Vygotsky. They expand upon the significance and value of key concepts in this approach but also point out the limitations of current neo-Vygotskian theory with respect to the peer learning that is so important to the use of computers in primary classrooms. In the following chapter Eunice Fisher explores the particular characteristics of pupil–pupil talk and characterises three distinct types of pupil–pupil talk which have educational significance. In Chapter 4 Eunice returns to and expands upon her earlier understanding of exploratory talk through a comparison of the talk of children at computers in primary classrooms to the talk of students in higher education and to the talk of an academic research team. She argues from her data that exploratory talk develops over time, both over the time scale of a seminar or meeting and over the time scale of an academic career. In Chapter 5 Rupert Wegerif and Neil Mercer close Section 1 by summarising what has been learnt from the previous chapters and by outlining a new dialogical framework for the analysis of classroom talk which combines a typology of the main social modes of thinking available in peer talk with a schema of levels of analysis to help in applying the 'types of talk' framework to studies of classroom discourse.

In the second section of the book various elements from the theoretical framework developed in the first section are applied to studies of classroom talk around computers. These studies focus on factors that influence the quality of children's talk together at the computer including issues of teaching methods, gender difference and of software design. In Chapter 6 Terry Phillips and Peter Scrimshaw look at adventure games and explore how their design impacts upon children's talk. Eunice Fisher considers a range of software in Chapter 7 and argues that educationally valuable discussion is most likely to occur with the more open-ended software such as word-processors than with more directive software. In Chapter 8 Rupert Wegerif responds to the claim made by Fisher. He develops a quantitative method to explore this claim further and he finds that it is not entirely accurate because of a very interesting category of computer-group interaction in which exploratory talk between pupils appears to occur within a directive computer–pupil interchange. The educational significance of this type of exchange is brought out. In Chapter 9 Peter Scrimshaw and Gary Perkins investigate a 12-minute session of talk at a word-processing package exploring the factors that influenced the style of talk of the children with a particular focus on their expectations of working together and of working at the computer. In the next chapter Joan Swann discusses the same session to explore the value of an alternative reading from a gender perspective, demonstrating in the process how it is possible to read the same transcript of a session productively in more than one way. In Chapter 11 Madeline Watson continues the focus on gender, returning to a transcript session used by both Eunice Fisher and Rupert Wegerif as a good illustration of exploratory talk in order to show how the gendered discourse styles of the different participants contributed to this reading. Janet Collins and Alison Syred-Paul, in Chapter 12, apply the framework of analysis developed in earlier chapters, which was based on data gathered around relatively small educational programs, to new studies of the use of CD-ROMs in classroom. They point to the value of cumulative talk for groups of children negotiating large databases together and also to the significant impact of software design features. In the last chapter of the section, Rupert Wegerif surveys the recordings of children working together at computers taken by the SLANT project to produce a summary of the different factors influencing the incidence of exploratory talk among groups of children working together around the computer.

The final section of the book focuses on the role of the teacher in using computers effectively in the classroom. The theme of this section is how research can be applied to improve classroom practice. Teacher-researcher Lyn Dawes describes how researching the quality of talk among children working together on the computer led her to develop a program to teach language awareness and improve communication strategies. Neil Mercer and Eunice Fisher then explore the ways in which teachers intervene in children146s activities at the computer and how their interventions could be improved. In Chapter 16, Madeline Watson gives an account of how the literature on classroom interventions and the findings of research, in particular the awareness of the gender effects she describes in her earlier chapter, fed into the development of a teaching strategy which improved the way children relate to each other in groups around the computer. In the final chapter of the book Rupert Wegerif and Lyn Dawes report on an intervention study that built upon the findings of the research reported in earlier chapters. This intervention combined the kind of coaching in 'exploratory talk' described by Lyn Dawes in Chapter 14 with the use of software specially designed to support the kind of educational exchanges between computers and children described by Rupert Wegerif in Chapter 8. This study illustrates the central message of our book: the potential for a dynamic and positive relationship between theory, research and improving classroom practice.

Section 1

Talk Matters

Chapter 2

The Importance of Talk

NEIL MERCER AND EUNICE FISHER

In this chapter, adapted from an article published in **Learning and Instruction** *in 1992, Neil Mercer and Eunice Fisher make a case for the educational importance of classroom talk. Using the work of the Russian researcher Vygotsky as a starting point, they suggest that a sociocultural approach to classroom activities enables us to develop an integrated theory of teaching and learning that provides practising teachers with an applicable theoretical framework. They pick out the concepts of the 'zone of proximal development', 'scaffolding' and 'context' as central to understanding the teaching and learning process. However, they also point to the fact that the first two of these key concepts for neo-Vygotskian theory are based on the teacher–student relationship and they raise the need for sociocultural theory to help us understand collaborative learning where the interaction is between equals.*

Introduction

Spoken language is at the heart of the psychological study of teaching and learning not simply because language is the principal means of communication between teachers and learners, but also for other more subtle reasons. One is that language is a vital means by which we represent our own thoughts to ourselves. Vygotsky (1978) described language as a psychological tool, something each of us uses to make sense of experience. A second reason is that language is also our prime cultural tool – the thing we use to share experience and so collectively, jointly, make sense of it. The continuous, cumulative, contextualisation of events and the creation of a 'common knowledge' through discourse are the very essence of education as a cultural and psychological process.

Some Central Features of the Neo-Vygotskian Perspective

Vygotsky proposed that learning occurs first in a social or inter-psychological context, prior to its becoming internalised or individualised

13

within an intra-psychological category (Vygotsky, 1978: 57). We will use the term 'neo-Vygotskian' to refer to a theoretical approach to the study of learning and cognitive development which draws heavily, though not exclusively or literally, on the work of Vygotsky (Mercer, 1992, 1994). Others have called it 'cultural psychology' (Crook, 1991), 'sociocognitive-developmental theory' (Smith, 1989) and 'sociohistorical theory' (Newman *et al.*, 1989; Rogoff, 1990). The essence of this approach is to treat learning and cognitive development as culturally based, not just culturally influenced, and as social rather than individualised processes. It highlights communicative aspects of learning, whereby knowledge is shared and understandings are constructed in culturally formed settings.

Compared with other theories of learning and cognition, the neo-Vygotskian approach has certain attractive features for researchers who are concerned with the use of computers for learning and instruction in schools.

Firstly, most theories of learning and cognitive development have focused on the individual to the extent that cultural and interactional factors in learning and development are marginalised or even ignored. In recent years, critical attention has focused on the inherent 'individualism' of Piagetian theory, and on the marginal role attributed to language, culture and social interaction in the empirical research of Piaget and his followers (see e.g.; Edwards & Mercer, 1987; Mercer, 1992; Walkerdine, 1984). In research into computer-based learning, the influence of Piagetian ideas has been particularly strong. This is well exemplified by the work of Papert (1980), who promotes a radical 'discovery-learning' approach to learning through LOGO, in which the child's relationship with a human teacher is supplanted by an individualised computer-based learning environment.

Other more recently developed approaches to cognitive development share the same individualistic emphasis. For example, much 'cognitive science' (e.g. Simon, 1980, 1981), is based on a narrow, individualistic definition of learning and this is reflected in its applications to the use of computers in education (e.g. O'Shea & Self, 1983). In contrast, because neo-Vygotskian theory gives a central and prominent place to communicative and cultural factors, it seems better suited to the needs of researchers who wish to study learning and instruction in social context, and also to those concerned with the implementation and design of software for classroom use. In particular, it offers interesting possibilities for theoretical development in the study of 'situated learning' with computers, especially if such research focuses on children's problem-solving practice in schools (Lave, 1992), learning through directed peer collaboration (Scardamalia *et al.*,

1989; Scardamalia & Bereiter, 1991) and the process of learning through 'cognitive apprenticeship' (Collins *et al.*, 1990).

Secondly, neo-Vygotskian theory offers both a theory of learning and a theory of instruction. In all societies, talk is the prime medium for sharing knowledge, and one through which adults influence the representations of reality which children eventually adopt. Neo-Vygotskian theory deals directly with this essential feature of learning and instruction in school. It encourages the view that to communicate with others through speech is to engage in a social mode of thinking.

We therefore believe that a neo-Vygotskian framework offers a suitable basis for an educationally relevant theory of learning and instruction. However, its principal concepts (the Zone of Proximal Development and 'scaffolding'; discussed below) have not yet been properly defined for classroom research. Although the concepts are now in common use in discussions of educational processes, they were developed in observational research on parent–child interactions (Bruner, 1978; see also Wertsch, 1985a,b; Wood, *et al.*, 1976), and only subsequently applied to educational settings by drawing analogies between learners at home and in school and between the supportive activities of parents and teachers (e.g. Bruner, 1985, 1986). Some educational researchers have therefore suggested that the concepts themselves cannot map on well to the pedagogic realities of classroom education. David McNamara (personal communication) comments that:

> The theory implies that each child's 'scaffold' or ZPD is different and that the teacher must treat each child's learning individually – this is probably an unrealistic aspiration as far as most teachers and most classes are concerned.

Smith (1989) points to the lack of relevant empirical work illustrating the theory's explanatory value. While we accept the grounds for these criticisms, we see them as a stimulus for research rather than as a reason to abandon the neo-Vygotskian framework. For all its current weaknesses, it represents the only available theoretical perspective which is potentially capable of handling teaching and learning as culturally based, 'situated' activity. Through the research presented in this book we hope to advance further its empirical validity and educational relevance.

Three Key Concepts in the Neo-Vygotskian Framework

The essential psychological asymmetry of the teaching and learning relationship may be said to be represented in the neo-Vygotskian concepts of the Zone of Proximal Development and scaffolding. (Also relevant is the concept of appropriation, which we will not deal with in this chapter. See Mercer, 1992). To these we must add the significance of variations in the situations in which learning and teaching occur. This is embodied in the concept of context.

The Zone of Proximal Development (ZPD)

The Zone of Proximal Development (ZPD) is defined as:

> The distance between the actual developmental level as determined by independent problem solving and the level of potential development as determined through problem solving under adult guidance or in collaboration with more able peers. (Vygotsky, 1978: 86)

We believe that the concept represents two basic and essential aspects of human development. One is that learning with assistance or instruction is a common and important feature of human mental development. The second is that the limits of a person's learning or problem-solving ability can be expanded by providing the right kind of assistance or instruction.

Within a neo-Vygotskian framework, learning and problem solving are seen as context-bound processes, so that the level of understanding achieved by individuals in specific settings is recognised to be, in part at least, a function of those settings as dynamic contexts for cognitive activity (Crook, 1991). Thus, what appear to be variations in the ability of a child to solve 'the same' problem across different experimental settings (for example, as described by Donaldson, 1978) might best be explained in terms of variations between the implicit contextual frameworks surrounding those tasks. As Newman, *et* al., (1989) argue, a great deal of psychological research is flawed because researchers have naively accepted that experimental tasks can be defined independently of the inter-subjective contexts in which they are performed.

References to the ZPD are increasingly common in developmental and educational research; but it seems to us that there is a danger that the term is used as little more than a fashionable alternative to Piagetian terminology or the concept of IQ for describing individual differences in attainment or potential. In our view, such usages miss the essence of the concept, and lose its radical implications for the study of learning. The limits of the ZPD for any particular child on any particular task will be established in the course of an activity, and one key factor in establishing those limits will be the quality of the supportive interventions of a teacher. That is, the ZPD is not an attribute of a child (in the sense that, say, IQ is considered to be) but rather an attribute of an event. It is the product of a particular, situated, pedagogical relationship. Through establishing a ZPD, a teacher or researcher may gain valuable insights into how a child may be encouraged to progress. But children do not carry their ZPDs with them when they leave a classroom, and a new task with a different teacher may generate quite different 'zones' for the same group of children.

It may be that the ZPD should not be envisaged as a delimited area which can be measured at any one time. Indeed, Vygotsky's interpretation of it suggests that it is so entirely context dependent, defined in part by the teacher's instruction ('instruction creates the zone of proximal development' Vygotsky, 1934a: 450, quoted in Wertsch, 1985b), that we must regard each individual as having an ever-changing series of zones relating to each cognitive activity. Perhaps we might borrow a concept from the so-called 'hard' sciences and postulate a probability similar to that offered by the concept of the half life of atomic elements. Because physicists are unable (even in this most exact of sciences!) to predict the rate of decay of any one atom, they have developed the notion of a half life which is the length of time it would take for half the population of atoms of any one element to decay. Thus, being unable to predict the behaviour of a specific atom does not deter physicists from making usable predictions about the population of atoms. Similarly, being unable to predict a child's ZPD at any one moment should not prevent us from using it as a useful guide to their possible development over a series of activities. It might then be possible to judge a task according to the following three-part typology:

(1)   Tasks which fall beyond the child's ZPD – tasks on which, even with teacher support, the child is unable to make any independent moves - i.e. an almost zero success rate.

(2)   Tasks within the ZPD – tasks on which, with teacher support, the child can sometimes succeed. These would range from those on which she can succeed with major help, but making some independent moves right through to those on which she can succeed unaided some of the time (50%?), but on which some teacher support is still required.

(3)   Tasks which are below the level of ZPD – tasks on which the child can succeed unaided, say 90% or more of the time.

In everyday classroom practice, numerical calculations as suggested above might well prove impractical; but where special diagnosis is required owing to a child's learning difficulties, an approach such as this could well be useful. As Brown and Ferrara (reported in Wertsch, 1985b) suggest, the testing of ZPD would require a detailed task analysis so that suitable tasks and 'probes' to uncover progress can be developed. However, they report on experimental work which, through the use of prompts to help children complete tasks, discriminated between fast and slow learners and between children who were able to transfer their new learning over a wide range of tasks as opposed to those who had only a narrow transfer range. They found that while these abilities bore positive relationships to age and IQ, (approximately two-thirds of the children had task performances which could be predicted from their IQ) they maintain that tests such as these, using 'graduated aids' to uncover readiness in the children, would make possible a reliable and early identification of those children who are learning disabled.

As Brown and Ferrara (reported in Wertsch, 1985b) suggest, a second educational implication of the ZPD is the emphasis it gives to instruction which aims at the upper limits of the child's ability. Even where it is impossible to undertake the detailed analyses suggested above in order to estimate ZPD, we suggest that a concept which focuses attention ahead of the child's competence and encourages an approach which seeks out new activities which the child can attempt with help, rather than building simply on the child's known achievements, could lead to an important shift of emphasis for some teachers.

Scaffolding

This brings us to the second concept, that of 'scaffolding'. In the context of parental tutoring, Bruner (1978) uses the term to refer to steps taken by an adult to reduce the degrees of freedom in carrying out some task so that a child can concentrate on the difficult skill he or she is in the process of acquiring. It represents the kind and quality of cognitive support which an adult can provide for a child's learning – a form of 'vicarious consciousness' (as Bruner also put it) which anticipates the child's own developing understanding. As such, it clearly relates to the concept of the Zone of Proximal Development. We and our associates, involved in both educational research and the in-service training of teachers, have found the concept of 'scaffolding' a very useful tool in analysing and understanding teachers' pedagogic strategies (see, for example: Fisher, 1991; Maybin et al., 1992; Mercer, 1991). Teachers too seem to find the concept very appealing, perhaps because it resonates with their own intuitive conceptions of what it means to intervene successfully in children's learning. It has also begun to appear in studies of computer-based learning. However, it has been used without being operationally defined for the classroom, and so is used loosely and given a variety of covert interpretations. For example, Hoyles et al., (1991: 219), in their study of pupil discussion in computer-based learning, say: 'We refer to scaffolding as "hooks" available in any setting which assist pupils in overcoming significant obstacles in the generalisation process'; while Emihovich and Miller (1988), in a study of young children being instructed in the use of LOGO, employ the term only to refer to teachers' express guidance, through talk, to the children. Bruner's own application of it to the relationship between teacher and pupil (Bruner, 1985) is achieved simply by drawing an analogy between the discourse of parental tutoring and that of classroom teaching. If we start from the position that the concept of 'scaffolding' is potentially applicable to classroom education, the essential problem is to decide what counts as 'scaffolding' and what is merely 'help'. Is 'scaffolding' a description of a particular kind of teacher behaviour (whatever its outcome for the pupil), or a label that can be applied to any kind of teacher intervention which is followed by learning success for a pupil? Maybin *et al.*, (1992: 188) offer the following hypothetical formulation:

> 'Scaffolding' is not just any assistance which helps a learner accomplish a task. It is help which will enable a learner to accomplish a task which they would not have been quite able to manage on their own, and it is help which is intended to bring the learner closer to a state of competence which will enable them eventually to complete such a task on their own. To know whether or not some help counts as 'scaffolding', we would need to have at the very least some evidence of a teacher wishing to enable a child to develop a specific skill, grasp a particular concept or achieve a particular level of understanding. A more stringent criterion would be to require some evidence of a learner successfully accomplishing the task with the teacher's help. An even more stringent interpretation would be to require some evidence of a learner having achieved some greater level of independent competence as a result of the scaffolding experience (that is, demonstrating their increased competence or improved level of understanding in dealing independently with some subsequent problem).

Contexts

Research in the neo-Vygotskian tradition has stressed the context-specific nature of learning (Cole, 1985; Crook, 1987; Edwards, 1991). It has also been shown that children may be able to accomplish activities within familiar or supportive contexts which they cannot do in unfamiliar or unsupported situations (Donaldson, 1978; Mercer & Fisher, 1992). What is more, even when children seem to have learned what their teachers have taught them, there are often large and fundamental differences between their understanding of particular concepts and that of their teachers (Driver *et al.*, 1985). So if learning and teaching are socially situated the nature of the context within which they take place is central both to under-standing and improving them. On one level the concept of context is straightforward; educational activities take place in specific locations and among specific actors; these facts together identify the physical and social contexts as important. But a feature of the context is socially significant only if it is taken into account by one or more actors in some way, so some aspects of the situation may not qualify. Conversely, actors bring to situations their previous memories, whether shared or not, and these too may be referred to, thus extending the context back in time, and across into different locations.

The Role of Talk in Classroom Teaching and Learning

Thinking about classroom life in terms of these three concepts gives us a different perspective from which to see the educational importance of talk. Firstly, it provides information about the location of the ZPD. Secondly, it is the main medium through which teachers and other children scaffold learning. Thirdly, it is the commonest way that human beings have of evoking a spatially or temporally distant context, and much learning and teaching requires this evocation in order to link present experiences to past knowledge (Edwards & Mercer, 1987). The situationally specific nature of their learning, and the narrowness of their previous knowledge both conspire to lead children to conclusions which focus on particular rather than general and more fundamental aspects of the activity. It is only in attempting to reformulate and express their ideas that they may come to realise the inadequacy of them. For these reasons, activities which encourage a true sharing of ideas among essentially equal partners are likely to be a fruitful way of encouraging children to test out their assumptions and develop their thinking, and pupil–pupil discourse offers a potentially rich setting for pupils, teachers and researchers to look more closely at pupils' learning.

Limitations of the Current Neo-Vygotskian Framework

Having put the case for the neo-Vygotskian framework we want to point out its current limitations. Most of the empirical research on which neo-Vygotskian theory is based deals only with the supportive intervention of adults in the learning of *individual* children (i.e. through experimental learning tasks, or observations of parents and young children at home). Indeed it seems ironic that, while the model of learning and development which these concepts offer educational research is 'sociocultural' rather than 'individualistic', the development of the concepts themselves has not taken full account of the social and cultural realities of classrooms in which one adult is responsible for the learning of many children and in which (in British primary schools, at least) children commonly work in pairs or groups. It is not evident to us that the neo-Vygotskian concepts we have outlined are adequate to understanding the educational role of talk between children working together in classrooms. New concepts are needed if we are to understand peer learning.

Chapter 3

Educationally Important Types of Children's Talk

EUNICE FISHER

In this chapter, first published as an article in **Language and Education** *in 1993, Eunice Fisher locates pupil-pupil talk within classroom talk as a whole, comparing and contrasting it with teacher–pupil talk, which she suggests has quite different characteristics. She then considers whether some kinds of pupil talk are more educationally significant than others, and argues that exploratory talk has a distinctive and central role. This chapter contains the first published account of the three types of talk – disputational, cumulative and exploratory – which feature prominently throughout the rest of this book. This typology develops some sociocultural concepts for analysing peer learning and so begins to fill a gap in this area noted in Chapter 2. Here Fisher presents each type of talk through a description of the functions of utterances. Later, in Chapter 4, Fisher deepens this analysis by showing how features of exploratory talk develop over time.*

Introduction

A good deal is already known about the distinguishing features of teacher–pupil discourse. Teachers ask a lot of questions; they often initiate discourse topics and they attempt to control the content of classwork by a variety of discourse strategies such as feedback (Sinclair & Coulthard, 1975) and through elicits, reformulations, reconstructions and selected emphasis through repetition (Edwards & Mercer, 1987). We also know from this and other research that the pupil's role in these discourse processes is often one of mere respondent, where the skill of the exercise tends to be more related to 'finding out what the teacher wants to hear' than to any pursuit of understanding. This is not to say that pupils never take the leading or even an equal role in talking with their teachers; but merely to emphasise that the necessarily asymmetric relationship between them means that, when seeking out or formulating new ideas, there is a tendency for pupils (and perhaps teachers too) to see the teacher's ideas as the ones which should be accepted. Indeed, it may be that it is only through pretence (e.g. asking questions to which they know the answers) or through absenting themselves from the discourse entirely, that teachers can reduce the influence of their own greater knowledge of most topics which are discussed in school. As a result, some teachers seek to promote pupil–pupil discourse, though they do so through a wide variety of strategies with great diversity of results.

In this chapter some examples of pupil–pupil discourse will be examined in which peer groups develop their ideas. These are contrasted with teacher–pupil discourse as well as with some pupil–pupil discourse which fails to develop the pupils' ideas. The aim in so doing is to identify the differences in the three types of discourse and describe some of the factors which may have contributed to those differences. The implications of these discourse features for learning will also be discussed.

Although the examples given are drawn from a computer setting, much of what goes on and the discourse strategies used are applicable to group work and paired activities in other contexts, and it is these more general aspects that will be considered here. Exploratory talk provides the main focus of this chapter because, as Chapter 2 has indicated, talk which features argument and exploration through hypothesis and challenge may be more valuable for learning than talk which features automatic consensus or unproductive disputes.

Influences on Groups Working Together

Within the Spoken Language and New Technology (SLANT) project (described in Chapter 1) we have found that teachers often have explicit aims in grouping their pupils, not all of which are directly related to maximising the short-term outcomes of the topic in hand. These strategies have direct implications for the subsequent discourse, and the criteria by which they are implemented fall under the two broad headings of perceived ability and social factors.

Perceived ability

Teachers use their knowledge of pupils' ability and of their task expertise to group children, though they do not necessarily attempt to group 'like with like'. They may see one child as being able to offer some knowledge to the group which the others don't have, or they may choose children whose abilities they see as complementary. Sometimes teachers will designate a group leader, or a group reader, and sometimes they merely suggest that the children 'help each other' or that one helps the other with particular tasks.

Regardless of how the teacher perceives their abilities, the children will also have their own views on who is 'clever'. No doubt these views often do coincide with the teacher's, but however the children perceive their respective abilities is likely to affect the kind of contribution they make to the task. Consequently, while it may sometimes be effective for pupils of differing abilities to work together so that one can help the other with a specific difficulty, it can be counter-productive to put together pupils who see themselves as sharing little common ground. For example, disparate expertise at the keyboard or in reading can lead to one pupil doing the work and the other becoming disenchanted.

Social factors

Social factors, such as gender, also affect how groups work together, and may well interact with ability/perceived ability in a complicated way. The effects are also likely to vary with age.

Class teachers in primary schools generally seem to know their pupils well, but in spite of this, there were some examples within SLANT where teachers only appreciated how dominant one pupil was within a group when they subsequently viewed a video of the group working without the teacher. Because the product may be satisfactory, and perhaps more speedily produced when one child dominates a group, it may be difficult for teachers to appreciate within the normal classroom activity just how little others in the group have contributed. Asking the children afterwards who did what can also be misleading. In SLANT we have found instances where those who claim to have done most work were mistaken, and some who claimed not to have been allowed to make any decisions or key the computer had in fact dominated the activity!

Pupil-Pupil Talk

In this section, the contextual differences of teacher–pupil and pupil–pupil discourse will be discussed, and the features of pupil–pupil talk will be examined through selected examples.

If we wish to contrast teacher–pupil and pupil–pupil talk, bearing in mind teachers' strategies which seem to arise from their leadership role, and assuming for the moment an approximate equivalence between pupils, we might expect to find the following aspects of pupil–pupil talk, not common in teacher–pupil talk:

- No one consistent leader or initiator of exchanges.
- A lack of 'eliciting' and 'reformulating' which characterises teacher talk.

- Little attempt at summarising, other than where the activity demands it.

Instead, we might expect to find initiation of new exchanges by any and all members of the group. Questions that arise would be genuine attempts to solve problems rather than a testing of the other partner's knowledge. Discourse strategies which aim at clarifying the position and/or reinforcing the learning are also likely to be rare, owing to their direct relationship to the leadership role. This lack of an unchallengeable leader has other implications for the discourse. It places a responsibility on the participants to manage their exchanges if anarchy is to be avoided, so that a new set of classroom discourse rules might be expected to emerge. However, even five-year-olds are experienced in talking with their peers, and it may be that the strategies which serve them outside will also serve well inside the classroom.

Set out below are examples of pupil–pupil discourse. The analysis of this talk will aim at identifying the features which lead to the exploration and development of ideas through talk, as well as those which may inhibit or prevent discursive exploration.

Writing a Nativity story

In the first example, two year 2 pupils, Milly and Charles, have been asked to write their own version of the Nativity story, using Folio, together with a concept keyboard which their teacher has prepared so as to give them easy access to the more difficult words they may need to spell (for example, 'Bethlehem').

The school which these pupils attend has a population drawn almost exclusively from the nearby council estate, and a very high proportion of the children come from materially poor backgrounds. The school staff actively pursue a policy aimed at encouraging the resolution of difficulties through negotiation. This class has already done work earlier in the term 'talking about talk' in which they considered the differences between talk for a variety of purposes; for example, argument, chatter, screaming, discussing, telling stories. They are very used to group discussion, brainstorming and role- play activities.

The teacher has asked them to plan their story before they begin writing it (though they are already at the computer and are free to begin when they wish). She has also suggested that they should see themselves as ordinary people who happen to be in Bethlehem at the time of the Nativity.

Sequence 1: Planning the Nativity story

They begin, facing towards each other and sideways on to the computer. (Note: In all the following sequences of transcript the discourse is in the left column and a description of the function is in the right column in italics.)

C:	We could live in Bethlehem	*Initiates with proposition*
M:	Yes we'll live in Bethlehem right Then then we're That could be something like if we were playing out the back way And then they came across and some And then you heard some voices saying about it And we'd go out wouldn't we	*Accepts and extends*
C:	Right then	*Accepts*
M:	That would mean that we would go out	*Justifies*
C:	The front	*Extends + challenges*
M:	And see what was happening And then you'd see a person on a donkey And a woman next to him wouldn't yer?	*Extends*
C:	Yes	*Accepts*

In this sequence the children stick fairly closely to their brief and draw on their knowledge of the Nativity story, while making some effort to incorporate themselves into their version. Their discourse is characterised by an acceptance of what the other says, followed by an extension of their partner's proposition, although Charles makes a challenge to Milly's suggestion that they are 'playing out the back' by finishing one of her utterances with 'the front'. She ignores (accepts?) this suggestion and continues her extension of what has gone before. However, as they go a little further with their planning, they begin to challenge one another. The next sequence follows immediately:

Sequence 2: At the stable

M: So they were going to the   *Extends*
       stable

C: No   *Challenges + counter hypothesis*
       No pretend they were already
       in the stable

M: In the stable   *Accepts?*

C: And we just see this strange   *Extends*
       star
       And then we go and see what
       it is
       And say 'Why are all these
       people in the stable?'

M: Or we could   *Challenges + counter hypothesis*
       We could just wait and not see
       the star
       And then the shepherds could
       come

C: Yeh   *Accepts*

In each case the challenge is followed by an alternative hypothesis, but one which remains an extension of the discourse that has gone before.

In the examples above, the sequence opens with cumulative talk and there are many other examples of this type of discourse throughout this activity. The example is, in fact, an instance of a particular kind of cumulative talk (we called it cumulative text talk) that appeared in a number of the sessions where groups were using word processors to prepare collective stories or accounts.

Exploratory talk occurs in Sequence 2, where the children debate the issue of whether to be outside or inside the stable. Although Charles challenges Milly's proposition:

> No
> No pretend they were already in the stable

he only amends it rather than rejecting it outright and goes on to elaborate, in effect providing a justification for his alteration

> And we just see this strange star
> And then we go and see what it is

And say 'Why are all these people in the stable?'

Similarly, a little later when they are trying to 'write themselves a role' in the story, they continue to build on each other's ideas, even when they challenge the plausibility of some of the offerings.

Sequence 3: Incorporating themselves

C:	Pretend I'm out playing football	*Initiates with proposition*
M:	Yes *(pause)* No, they wouldn't have a football then because [Remember in Bethlehem 2000 years ago	*Accepts, rejects and justifies*
C:	Oh	
M:	What would they be doing They wouldn't have skipping ropes	*Hypothesises*
C:	I know what we can do	*Challenge*
M:	What?	*Question*
C:	They'd be doing	
M:	They'd be doing what?	*Question*
C:	They could be doing like things Some feeding their donkey they had in their back garden	*Counter hypothesis*
M:	Oh no We could put. They could…Their father could have drawed a hop-scotch so the girl was playing on the hop-scotch and the boy was]	*Counter hypothesis*
C:	[playing what?	*Question*
M:	Or they might just be sitting in the house reading a book or something	*Alternative counter hypothesis*
C:	I know. They're outside and they're getting suntanned	*Challenge + counter hypothesis*

M:	Yes 'cos Bethlehem's a hot place	*Acceptance + justification*

The children then go on to write their story which, although it does not incorporate quite the richness of the ideas they discussed, does include their main concern, i.e. how to represent their own presence in a way that is compatible with Bethlehem 2000 years ago, but characterised so that they can identify with it. They maintain their idea that they will be outside in the garden, where they see the wise men arriving at the stable and so go in to have a look for themselves.

In these examples, both children contribute ideas to the planning, and each seems to listen to the other's offering, even though they do not always agree. Later they run into difficulty with spelling, but they still tackle the problem in a reflective way, and although Milly seems to be more accurate with her spelling, they both offer insightful comments. For example, in their attempts to spell 'once':

Sequence 4: How to spell 'once'

M:	It is an 'o' and then it might be a 'u'	*Initiates with hypothesis*
C:	I think that's an 'h'	*Alternative hypothesis*
M:	No. When I look in a book I don't usually see an 'h' If you think about it. It's 'o' It's probably a 'u' next to it.	*Challenge + justification*

(They then ask the researcher how to spell 'once')

Sequence 5: 'Two' or 'to'

C:	Was to (he types in 'was') Shall I put the short 'to' or the long 'too'	*Question*
M:	Just the 't' 'o' 'w' I think (C types in 'to') Or is it?	*Response/hypothesis*
C:	't' 'o' or 't' 'o' 'w'	*Question*
M:	I think it's 'w' 'o'	*Alternative hypothesis*
C:	No. It's 't' 'o' 'w' or 't' 'o'	*Challenge*
M:	No. It must be 't' 'w' 'o'	*Challenge + proposition*

C:	*(Points to number keys)* That's one 'two'	*Proposition + attempt to clarify*
M:	That's number two. We want two for two children	*Proposition, challenge + alternative*
C:	That's two	*Repetition of proposition*
M:	That's 'to' *(points to 'to' on screen)* Just that	*Acceptance*

(They continue keying in text)

In this last sequence, Milly seems to have been distracted from the correct spelling by the fact that her original error (reversing 'o' and 'w') has resulted in 'to' being typed on to the screen. After an unsuccessful challenge, she accepts the mistaken spelling and they continue to write their story. There is no acrimony throughout the hour that they spend at the computer, and there are numerous challenges and extensions of ideas. However, as in the examples above, Milly is inclined to 'give way' after some discussion, and it does seem that at least part of their success is due to her (stereotypically female!) strategy.

The next example is taken from another pair of children, Hettie and Mark from the same class also writing a Nativity story in which they are participants, though they interpret their possible roles quite differently.

Sequence 6: Packing for the journey

H:	OK Let's start	*Initiates with instruction*
M:	They're packing. Or do you want to do them on the journey?	*Proposition/question*
II:	No I'll be Mary you be Joseph	*Challenge new proposition*
M:	No you were Mary last time though	*Challenge + justification*
H:	Well I can still be Mary	*Counter justification*
M:	Mary's saying (2). All right I'm Joseph and you're Mary	*Ignores then accepts proposal*

This rather negative beginning, in which almost every turn represents a challenge to the one above and in which there is little evidence of either partner attempting to build on the other's ideas, is an example of disputational talk. On this occasion, it sets the tone for a session which failed in that neither the teacher nor the children were satisfied with the process or outcome, and which finished in frustration. These children have shown at other times that they are capable of productive investigative discourse, but in this example they failed to resolve their power struggle (and the girl failed to 'give way'!) so that the whole session is affected. However, it may be that their attempt to role-play the principal characters was the origin of their problems in that Hettie, at least, seems to feel she should be individually responsible for Mary's lines, so making a shared responsibility difficult. There are several confusions in their discourse which appear to arise from this source.

Sequence 7: Rejecting a suggestion

M:	Mary you can get on the donkey	*Initiates with proposition*
H:	I can say what I want to say. You don't tell me what to say. All right	*Challenge/justification*
M:	It was only a suggestion	*Justification*
H:	I don't need any	*Proposition*

Other types of pupil–pupil discourse which fail to be collaborative include talk in which one pupil's ideas dominate and in which the other pupil(s) fail to extend, challenge or develop alternative proposals. Talk in which ideas are not made explicit or which are purely operational/directing also lacks collaborative elements. For example:

Pupil 1: Your go

(Press space bar)

Pupil 2: OK

Teachers, Pupils and Their Influence on Discourse

From the above it seems that pupil–pupil talk contains very different features from the teacher–pupil talk, described above. Most notably, it lacks the teacher strategies described by Edwards and Mercer (1987) though it does contain genuine questions or requests for information. As has been suggested, the teacher's responsibility in the classroom and the necessarily asymmetric relationship between teacher and pupils might be expected to affect teacher–pupil discourse in specific ways, not apparent in discourse between 'equals'. However, there are also wide-ranging differences within pupil–pupil talk, even in the same classroom or with similar activities. Some of these are likely to be the result of individual pupil differences and some may be due to the type of software being used. Although discourse strategies such as those often used by teachers are less frequent in pupil–pupil talk, teacher influence is none the less still very strong. In the next examples we will examine the discourse of a group of 11-year-old children in a class where the teacher, disappointed by her pupils' poor discourse skills, attempted to raise their awareness of appropriate strategies by means of explicit teaching and practice in discursive activities.

After some weeks of preparation, including talking about talk and about group responsibility, Peter, Adrian and Diana are working with an adventure game, Viking England. (The whole class has been studying the Vikings as part of their history project.) This program is designed to encourage the users to adopt the role of Viking raiders, and requires them to make a variety of interdependent choices in conducting their raids. In the sequence below, the children have already selected the equipment they wish to take on their journey and have chosen their route. They now have to organise a camp, and select from the following in order of importance:

A   Find food

B   Find grazing

C   Set up defences

D   Provide shelter

E   Hide the boats

F   Find slaves

Sequence 8: Organising a Viking Camp

D:	Place in order of importance (reads aloud from the screen)	*Initiates with instruction*
P:	Set up defences. I choose 'set up defences'. Then there's a place to hide behind	*Proposition and justification*
D:	Wait. Why do you want?	*Challenge seeks justification*
A:	Because then we're safe	*Justification*
P:	Because we're safe aren't we	*Justification*
D:	Yes, but suppose someone spots our boat?	*Challenge*
A:	Oh no.	

P:	OK what about defences? Say we get attacked and can't hide the boats? Then what would happen?	*Hypothesis, Justification + Challenge*
D:	What do we do if we run out of food	*Counter challenge*
P:	I'd say we put 'Find slaves' last. *(He has earlier suggested this is an important one)*	*Proposition*
D:	We can't find the slaves until we've raided sort of thing	*Accepts + Justification*
P:	Yeh	*Accepts proposition*
	I'd say D first, then E, then B and C A and F	*Question, seeking consensus*
	Which do you reckon we should go for then	
D:	I think we should do D first	*Accepts*
	['Cos	*Attempts justification*
P:	*(turning to Adrian)* [Do you agree with that	*Question + seeks consensus*
A:	Yes	*Accepts*
P:	But say we get attacked while hiding the boats	*Counter hypothesis*
D:	It shouldn't take that long to hide the boats though would it	*Justification*
P:	Well there's four of them.	*Counter justification*
	They're quite big	*Accepts*
	OK	
	Press D then	

(Adrian presses and they go on to discuss the rest of the sequence)

As in Sequences 1–4 above, these children use exploratory talk by making a series of hypotheses with justifications.

For example, in answer to Diana's renewed challenge about the risks of not hiding the boats first, Peter counters her with an hypothesis:

> OK what about defences
> Say we get attacked and can't hide the boats
> Then what would happen

This sophisticated countering is ultimately successful, though once again it is the girl who gives way. However, this is by no means always the case in this session. Although the group becomes increasingly excited as the session progresses, they never become aggressively confrontational.

They also use cumulative talk (rather than cumulative text talk, since here they are not composing) in which they pick up and add to previous statements, apparently accepting without challenge. Adrian, in Sequence 7, picks up Peter's suggestion of the need to hide by answering Diana's challenge with:

> Because then we're safe

and this is followed by a repetition from Peter. However, rather than being a means of drawing attention to key points, as are teacher's repetitions, these pupils' repetitions seem to serve a group cohesion function. They occur in much of our data and are most commonly used by the group member who contributes least to the decision making. In this group, repetitions are most often made by Adrian. Although he is probably as vocal as the others and also does most of the keyboard work, he is the weakest contributor in terms of ideas which are taken up. He has, in fact, been identified in the school as a 'problem' because of his aggressive behaviour, and his work is below average within the class. The teacher considered his inclusion in this group was a risk (especially in front of the camera), yet he remained involved with the task and the group throughout the session, and seems to have found a positive and satisfying way of taking part. The teacher had emphasised to the children the notion of group responsibility for failures as well as successes, and suggested to the pupils that abstaining from decision making did not absolve the abstainer from responsibility for failure. The children seemed to have taken this notion to heart, as is apparent from their discourse strategies. For example Diana's frequent use of 'Why' and Peter's use of 'What do you think' both serve to encourage other members of the group to reflect on the decision-taking process. This awareness of the group responsibility was also evident in their responses to a short questionnaire which was administered to the whole class by their teacher after the activity, in which there were several responses stipulating that responsibility lay with the whole group.

As with our earlier examples (Sequences 1–4) the discursive strategies that these pupils use are ones which have been explicitly encouraged by the teacher during the previous few weeks and also were restated by her at the beginning of this session. It is, in fact, of note that those sessions within these two classes which did not 'work as well' were set up (because of clashes between school timetables and research visits) in a more *ad hoc* fashion, with the teacher commenting at the time on the constraints which she felt. It is suggested that the outcome relates very directly to the prior work done in the class and to the instructions at the beginning of the activity.

Discussion

In the above it has been shown that pupil–pupil discourse differs from teacher–pupil discourse in that it frequently lacks those strategies reported by Edwards and Mercer (1987), which teachers use for directing the content of classroom talk. The range of features occurring in pupil–pupil discourse varies across and within groups, and seems to be dependent on several contextual factors including the nature of the task (and software), how the teacher 'sets up' the task and the pupils' perception of the task, as well as their skills and previous experience. As we have seen, the range and sequence of these features has implications for the progress of the task, and it seems likely, therefore, that they may also have more far-reaching effects on the pupils' intellectual and social development.

Within cognitive psychology there has been considerable debate as to the relationship of talk to thinking, for example see Cromer (1979) for a discussion of these issues. A less tortuous and perhaps more fruitful approach follows if, instead of attempting to understand how what is said might relate to cognitive representation, we adopt an approach suggested by Middleton and Edwards (1990) and examine how cognition is represented in conversation. This then allows us to examine talk as the best indicator we have (however inadequate) of the speakers' thinking.

Following this approach, we can now consider the potential for learning and understanding of the discourse features described in this chapter.

In the above sequences, the talk generally falls under one of three headings:

Disputational talk, which can be characterised as an initiation in various forms (e.g. proposition, hypothesis, instruction), followed by a challenge (either a direct rejection or a counter proposition/hypothesis). This results either in a lack of any clear resolution, or a resolution which does not build directly on the previous utterances.

Cumulative talk, in which initiations are accepted either without discussion or with additions or superficial amendments which do not develop previous ideas.

Exploratory talk, in which the initiation may be challenged and counter-challenged, but with hypotheses which are developments of that initiation.

Progress then rests on the joint acceptance of one of the suggestions, or of a modification of what has been put forward.

Exploratory talk offers a potential for learning not obvious in the other two types indicated here, and suggests that there is scope for pupil–pupil groups to go beyond mere drill and practice of already learned concepts. It is in exploratory talk, therefore, where we may hope to find evidence of pupils extending their learning within the Zone of Proximal Development (ZPD). It is usual to consider ZPD learning as that which takes place between individuals where one is more 'expert' than the other and, as Rogoff and Wertsch (1984: 5) suggest, ZPD development:

> involves joint consciousness of the participants, where two or more minds are collaborating on solving a problem. A corollary of this notion of intersubjectivity is that the participants do not have the same definition of the talk or of the problem to be solved. Through their interaction, the child's notion of what is to be done goes beyond itself, with the adult's support, and comes to approximate in some degree that of the more expert adult. [...] both participants play an important role in using the zone of proximal development, even in situations that are not directly conceived of as instruction by the participants.

Rogoff and Wertsch are referring to child–adult interaction, but other writers have been concerned with peer learning in groups which are asymmetrical (peer tutoring, for example see Foot *et al.*, 1990) or symmetrical (peer collaboration, for example see Doise & Mugny, 1984). What is of interest here is the notion of both participants playing an important role to enable learning which 'goes beyond itself'. Illustrated in the sequences above is one mechanism by which ZPD development might occur in a situation in which the participants have equal status and in which both are struggling to develop an idea. Their resulting concepts may perhaps still be ill-matched to those of the teacher or other 'expert', but in seeking solutions to their task and in orally formulating those solutions, it is suggested that the participants will at the very least develop their awareness of the major points at issue. They may also, through their joint resolution of the task in hand, move nearer to a workable or teacher-acceptable definition.

It should be remembered that in classroom peer-group learning contexts, pupils do not generally work without the support of a teacher, even though she may not be actively involved in the particular task. As Mercer and Fisher (1992) argue, where pupils work effectively to develop new skills it is likely that the teacher will have defined the task in such a way that it is (in her estimation) at a level which will be within the pupils' ZPD, and she will have provided the 'scaffolding' which will enable them to do things they otherwise would not be able to do. As has also been suggested above, the teacher's role in developing her pupils' discourse strategies may be crucial. In particular we have noted the efficacy of the pupils' commitment to group responsibility. It could be argued that this is comparable to an awareness of inter-subjectivity, and its role in the group's activity.

Pupil–pupil talk often lacks the eliciting and reformulating features of teacher–pupil talk, but has its own distinctive features, depending on the context in which it occurs and the discursive strategies which the pupils have been encouraged to use. Where the discourse leads to successful exploratory talk, it is characterised by challenges, hypotheses and justifications, with consensus being sought only after these have taken place. Where talk fails to be exploratory, it may be of a cumulative nature in which ideas are accepted unchallenged and without justification, or continuously disputational leading to a breakdown of communication within the group.

Chapter 4

Developments in Exploratory Talk and Academic Argument

EUNICE FISHER

In this chapter, Eunice Fisher sets the notion of classroom talk in a wider context by comparing it with talk in several educational settings. The talk of children working round computers in classrooms is compared with the classroom talk of students in higher education and also with talk recorded in research team meetings. Fisher argues that the dimension of time is important to understanding and to characterising exploratory talk. Focusing on the use of questions and challenges as a way into understanding what is happening in the talk, she shows that the nature and quantity of questions and challenges changes over time as discussions develop and changes also as the experience of participants grows. In this account of the complexity of exploratory talk found in different settings there is an implicit criticism of the account of exploratory talk Fisher gave in Chapter 3 which was written two years earlier. It should also be noted that her methodology has developed from the use of a functional coding to the use of a more fully interpretative account supported by a focus on key incidents.

Introduction

As in schools, peer group discussion is used in Higher Education, with the expectation that it will help students develop their understanding of the course content and improve their ability to communicate ideas. Researchers too use discussion to develop their research thinking. Given the extent of its use within schools, we might expect to see those who successfully progress into Higher Education, to be proficient in discursive techniques for exploring ideas. If this is so, it should be possible to identify and characterise aspects of discursive development. It will be argued that there is a developmental progression both within a discussion over time and across education (from the compulsory sector, to undergraduates, to researchers) in the use of two particularly important discourse strategies: questions and challenges.

Why Social Talk Skills Might not Help Classroom Discussion

Social conversation, as has been shown by Schegloff and his colleagues (Sacks *et al.*, 1974; Schegloff, 1982) is interactively developed through the of implicit rules, shared by speakers of a culture or subculture. The talk is 'locally managed' by the participants and usually communicates effectively, even though the contents may be incompletely specified. This is made possible because social conversation relies on shared knowledge and some shared expectations of the purpose of the talk. Institutional talk, including talk in educational contexts, is constrained by the particular rules of talk in that setting. Courtroom talk (Drew & Heritage, 1992), interviews (Button, 1992) and teacher–pupil talk (Edwards and Mercer, 1987) all assume that a particular specified professional of that institution will ask questions and that those questions will be answered within certain boundaries by the recipients. Generally there will be very strict limits on the kinds of questions those recipients will be allowed to ask back, and these are likely to be confined to issues of clarification. Teachers have professionally identifiable strategies, and usually ask questions to which they require not just a 'right' answer, but a particular 'right' answer (Edwards & Mercer, 1987). Successful respondents in classrooms are those who learn to play the relevant game and thus develop an appropriate 'communicative competence' (Hymes, 1972).

As suggested in Chapter 3, peer group talk in educational settings differs from teacher–pupil talk in the classroom. The 'ground rules' (Edwards & Mercer, 1987) for teacher–pupil talk are generally inappropriate amongst peers since they rely on one participant being endowed with power, with specialist knowledge and with the responsibility for structuring the conversation so that it develops along the lines designated by that person. The very essence of a peer group precludes such generalised status differences, though differences may appear (or be designed to appear, for example when a designated leader is selected) temporarily or partially. In situations where peers share roughly equal status and responsibility for the conversation, the talk which ensues can be freed from the limited type of question–answer series specified above. In an educational setting it also becomes the responsibility of the group to progress the discussion, but to do so in ways compatible with the educational requirements of the task. Thus, peer group classroom talk shares with everyday talk the feature of being collaboratively managed and shares with institutional talk the feature of having an institutional aim.

Who Holds the Power in Peer Groups?

The removal of the teacher does not remove inequalities of status and power and so 'asymmetry' in the talk. An asymmetry similar to that between a teacher and a pupil may also occur when a speaker uses technical vocabulary or expresses ideas which are normally the 'property' of the teacher and with which some participants are not wholly familiar. One area of concern in the Spoken Language and New Technology (SLANT) project was the confusion caused by mathematical terms in some computer software. For example, the command 'spot the difference' in the mathematics program 'Connections' was not understood as a subtraction task by some of the children. This led to a dichotomy in the performance of those that understood the command and those who did not, even though the sums themselves were not difficult. Pupils then showed signs of hesitancy and 'distancing' as if to acknowledge their own lack of credibility in the area.

Unfamiliarity with the type of language being used, what Halliday calls the 'register' (Halliday, 1978), may also lead to a lack of fluency in discussion. Yet participants may be unaware of the strategies for developing precise vocabulary definitions (Fisher, 1996). In addition, they may find it difficult to take on joint responsibility in a context in which they have a poor understanding of the content and are not sure how to go about developing and improving that understanding. Since their experience in everyday talk and in previous teacher–pupil talk, will be only partially relevant to the peer group seminar, they must select and develop new ways to facilitate the interaction.

Roles to Play and Goals to Aim At

This leads us to consider the participants' roles which may be particular to peer group educational talk. As suggested above, peer group talk requires that all group members contribute to the overall talk. In some groups, specific functions are explicitly allotted. In others they seem to emerge and be implicitly accepted. These functions are, however, important aspects of the participant roles (Levinson, 1992) and therefore to the talk which occurs.

The most obvious role which is sometimes adopted in classroom groups is that of group leader, or at least task manager, though this role is seldom explicitly allocated and may frequently 'change hands' within the course of a session. Keppler and Luckmann (1991), suggest that in everyday talk, where generally no one is authorised in advance to be a teacher, if a participant wishes to adopt a teaching role, however temporarily, they must establish their authority in some way. It seems likely that we might find a similar feature in peer group talk in educational settings (see Sequence 1.1 and subsequent discussion).

Participants' goals in class discussions may also be problematic. Apart from any social purposes (showing off to friends, maintaining allegiances and status), it may also be the case that the participants (or some of them) wish merely to complete the task as given to them by the teacher with the minimum effort. This minimal approach may 'hijack' the teacher's intentions and is likely to lead to talk which focuses mainly or exclusively on procedural or superficial aspects of the task and fails to explore issues of content and understanding (as demonstrated in Chapter 3).

In this chapter, two strategies for interactively developing ideas, questioning and challenging will be examined in order to explore the development of the talk over time. Four possible discursive events will be the focus of the analysis. When a statement is made it can either be challenged or accepted. Questions which are taken up and responded to are contrasted to questions which are ignored. The four events which will be the focus of the study are as follows:

(1) A question is asked which is responded to by other participants.

(2) A question is asked which is not responded to by other participants.

(3) A statement is made which is accepted, implicitly or explicitly, by other participants.

(4) A statement is made which is challenged by other participants.

Focus on these four discursive events is not intended to limit the analysis but is intended as a useful tool to support an exploration of more general issues.

Analysis of Discussions

Peer group discussions will be explored using the following transcript data:

(1) That collected from first-year undergraduate students of psychology, video-recorded during the course of their normal classes while they discussed tutor-designated topics in groups of three or four.

(2) Discussions among five colleagues, audio-recorded during their regular project progress meetings.

(3) The recordings and transcripts of children's talk around computers collected in the SLANT project will also be referred to as a contrast with the data from Higher Education.

The analysis will be concerned with the content of the talk and the 'work done' in terms of the relationship of one turn to the next. Consequently, the transcription used is sufficiently detailed to indicate pauses and overlaps, which are important aspects of the operation of 'turn-taking' in conversation (Sacks *et al.*, 1974) (See the Note on Transcriptions, page xi.)

Asking Questions

Sacks and his colleagues have shown that questions and answers are commonplace in everyday conversation. Questions were frequent in the SLANT and the student data. For example, in the group below three students were just beginning a session planning the outline for an essay on biological psychology:

Sequence 1.1: 'The mind–body debate' essay

1	**Alex**:	(...) Introduction
2		/
3	**Clara**:	Intro.
4		/
5	**Alex**:	Intro. Right so we wanna know, have we set the question?
6		(2)
7	**Clara**:	Huh =
8	**Alex**:	= Have we set the question like/ [different
9	**Clara**:	[yeah
10	**Alex**:	Words in other words
11	**Betsy**:	Mmm =
12	**Clara**:	= What is [the mind body debate?
13	**Alex**:	[(...)
14	**Clara**:	Yeah s- say what it is (writing) (3) what is it then?
15	**Alex**:	Erm (writing)
16	**Betsy**:	Is the mind and the brain two separate elements or one (1)
17		and then you've got about dualism and monism
18		(writing) (6)

Detailed analysis of Sequence 1.1

In this sequence, an initial procedural managing move was made by Alex (line 1). It seemed to be accepted by Clara's (line 3) repetition (see Schegloff, 1982) and implicitly by Betsy who said nothing even though there was a pause opportunity either side of Clara's turn. Alex repeated 'Intro.' and moved to a question on the task content (line 5) 'so we wanna know, have we set the question?'). After a two-second pause, Clara's 'Huh' was presumably a request for clarification and was taken as such by Alex who repeated his earlier utterance and went on to explain it. Betsy's 'Mmm' at 11 might be interpreted as an acceptance (Schegloff, 1982 suggests such 'backchannel responses' may serve as continuers), though the later discussion suggested she was not be wholly satisfied with this approach. Clara, however, responded to his question by stating the actual topic which they had to address (line 12) and calling Alex's bluff by agreeing that they say what it is, but after a three-second pause added an open question 'what is it then?'. Alex's 'Erm' (15) indicated uncertainty. The question was then answered by Betsy (line 16–17) and the subsequent six-second pause suggests this was accepted by the other two.

Discussion of analysis

In this and other classroom transcripts, questions were frequent, particularly at the beginning of sessions when participants were orienting to the task. The questions were not always answered and were often responded to by other questions or ignored. As would be predicted by Sacks *et al.*, (1974) for social conversation, this led to a lack of progress in the discussion, and could be the result of insufficient knowledge on which to base appropriate answers, or a lack of confidence in what is known.

Levinson (1992) says that the role of questions depends on the type of game being played. In peer groups questions sometimes serve to establish both an individual and a group identity in a situation of relative ignorance. In the sequence above there was a lack of support for an initial statement of how to proceed. Clara's subsequent question not only precisely sets out the nature of her own ignorance (and incidentally of Alex's) but also made it acceptable for Betsy to take the floor as teacher. Even though this teaching possibility was interactively produced, it is not necessarily the case that the role would be successfully adopted, but in this group Betsy seemed to have earned her teaching credibility, no doubt enhanced by her successful inclusion of the appropriate technical vocabulary 'monism' and 'dualism'. Betsy went on to display her superior knowledge in several places in the ensuing discussion, though Alex and Clara struggled for some time with how to get started and with their understanding of the task.

This discussion displayed not only the collaborative nature of knowledge building, but the shifts in role which occur. Alex's initial bid for managerial status did not give him any demonstrable elevated status with regard to content, though he maintained a managing role throughout the session. Indeed, Alex's willingness to expose his lack of understanding through questions (once his bluff was called in line 14), enabled Clara also to explore her own ideas and Betsy to use her knowledge to develop and progress the discussion. These questions served to clarify the content, since they were followed by relevant answers.

Challenges

Gricean rules suggest a 'co-operative principle' which is adhered to in everyday conversation (Grice, 1975). According to Lakoff (1981), persuasive discourse follows other Gricean norms (e.g. the truth principle), but breaks the co-operative principle in that speakers may ignore the rapport rules. Small-group discussion, in which ideas are argued and developed, might be expected to show similar characteristics to persuasive discourse, with some turns in which the speaker expounds views at length, thus breaking the usual conversational norms of short turns. Furthermore, it might be expected that other speakers, also developing their ideas, might challenge expositions with which they disagree, thus breaking the co-operative principle.

In the SLANT data and our student data, there are relatively few explicit challenges to the content of what is said. The challenges that occurred were usually either in the form of questions or were implicit in a lack of response. Statements which are ignored or minimally acknowledged, often by 'mmm', 'yeah' or 'uhuh' are common in social conversation (Schegloff, 1982) and were common in our data. Schegloff suggests that such minimal responses serve to indicate the listener's continued participation in the discourse, rather than denoting agreement or understanding. Where there is no explicit evidence of acceptance it remains unclear whether statements that are ignored or only minimally acknowledged are significant to other participants' learning. Where they were minimally accepted, it may be that the acceptance arose from politeness or perhaps an unreadiness at that point to challenge the speaker. Talk which contained unsupported or unclear statements where the opportunities for correcting or clarifying were not taken up, could have resulted from an adherence to the normal social rules of conversation rather than from a lack of knowledge. In the discussion which followed the sequence above, Alex was allowed to continue his pedantic repetition, though at least one of the other two participants had a clearer understanding of the issues.

Challenging ideas represents a break with Gricean norms, but it is an important part of academic debate. Tracy and her colleagues' work exploring the nature of 'intellectual talk' and also the beliefs held about it (Tracy & Baratz, 1993; Tracy & Carjuzaa, 1993; Tracy & Muller, 1994; Tracy &

Naughton, 1994) has been valuable in describing academics' beliefs about 'intellectual talk', the strategies they employ and the pervasiveness of status in affecting how faculty and research students challenge ideas in research colloquia. Of particular relevance here are two of their findings: firstly that faculty colleagues believed that intellectual discussion involves discussing ideas on their merit; and secondly that the degree to which 'barracuda attacks' are acceptable reflects the seniority and intellectual standing of the participants. Both senior and junior academics believed it desirable to challenge the ideas of senior faculty members, but felt graduate students should be dealt with more gently. There was also the view that 'good' questions would be more than simply asking for clarification. Graduate students reported that they avoided showing their ignorance by saying little in colloquia, and the discourse of some senior faculty members showed that they sometimes did a great deal of conversational work to avoid displaying theirs! Among professional academics, it would seem that there is a progression in the kinds of questioning which is expected, in the seriousness of challenges which are acceptable (and useful), and an increasing sophistication in knowing how these may be appropriately employed, while also protecting the 'face' of the challenger.

My own recordings of research colleagues discussing their research contained challenges, sometimes effected through the use of questions but more often by contradictory statements, albeit with a great deal of 'padding', which served both to save the 'face' of the first speaker and also that of the challenger if s/he later proved to be mistaken. In the sequence below, a group of researchers were discussing a research video recording of children talking around the computer in the classroom.

Sequence 2.1: The research team

1 **Grace:** And so she's got [that teacher authority vested in her =
2 **Jim:** [
3 = that's right but but I mean before one gets into sort detailed (1)
4 analysis
5 I mean this point has come up before looking at other video tapes
6 and that is how do you conceptualise (5) the total situation that
7 you are dealing with in the research now
8 there's been a tendency to look at it er pupil talk (2) in the
9 context of computer me mediated activities (1) erm
10 knowing that the teacher intervenes from time to time
11 but that's a subordinate element in the [situation
12 **Grace:** [Mmm

13 **Jim**:   but basically what you are looking at / is / computer talk
14   with the major variable if you like / is the Computers [/ Now

Detailed analysis

Jim's long exposition (2–11,13–4) was a serious challenge to the approach taken by the other researchers, and came after a first failed attempt to gain the floor while Grace was still speaking (2). When he actually began his turn (3), he did so by stating agreement with the previous speaker (That's right) before launching into a long turn in which he suggested that the team's focus was restricted to 'computer talk'. He attacked their approach in terms of its limited focus (5, 8–9 and 11) and suggested that his colleagues should take a broader view. He was allowed a long turn, despite several pauses and hesitations ('erm', etc.) No attempt to speak was made by the other participants (except for 'Mmm' – line 12) till line 15 when a series of short turns occurred, challenging and defending the issue based on procedural rather than academic content issues. The discussion continued in this vein for 60 lines, until Tony joined as follows in Sequence 2.2:

Sequence 2.2

80 **Jim**:   [Well let's
81 **Tony**:   [I mean I want to come in on what you said before and build on that
82   because the tapes I've watched and the situations I've seen
83   It seems to me that there is there is something very much more
84   powerfully there than either the teacher / at any moment we see
85   them or the children or the computer erm
86   ( ) shall I put / its the culture of the classroom
87 **Grace**: [mmm
88 **Ellie**: [mmm
89 **Tony**:   And in most classrooms that culture is about fairness /
90   and about social order and about social turn-taking
91   and its very very rarely about (1) er intellectual rigour
92   whatever that might be / its very rarely about cha[lenging ideas
93 **Grace**: [lenging ideas
94 **Tony**:   It's very rarely about saying to each other 'How do you know that?'
95   'Why do you think that?'
96   It's always about who has what turns and so on
97   / And so when the teacher comes in ( ) a teacher like this
98   And says something / however minimal it is about taking turns

99		It was so reinforcing what was taking up most of the kids' thinking
100		in the past that that's what they concentrate on/
101		Which would explain why Mary's things is ignored
102	**Grace:**	Mmm
103	**Tony:**	It's actually not about getting it right which Mary ( ) maybe
104		[thinking what happens
105	**Grace:**	[And
106		there's Mary thinking that she's got a problem to solve/[yeh

Detailed analysis

Tony's long turn went unchallenged in spite of his hesitations and self-corrections, and the only intermediate turns which occurred were very short and supportive. Tony achieved this by developing an exposition in which he began by suggesting that he wished to 'build on' what Jim (his boss) had said. In fact what he said was a direct challenge to Jim's view that the team were focusing merely on talk at the computer. Instead, he proposed a consideration of a much wider context. This was a skilful manoeuvre. Not only did it draw the team from a mundane discussion (not included here) of who knew or thought what, but it allowed Tony to challenge Jim without blatantly disagreeing with him. When Jim finally returned as speaker, it was to accept and extend Tony's comments, and to make a joke of the issue (perhaps to 'save face'?).

Discussion of analysis

This kind of challenge requires a sophisticated talk strategy which breaks the normal 'one utterance per turn' rules proposed by Sacks *et al.*, (1974) as well as the Gricean norms indicated above. Maybe it develops only after lengthy service in academic or other closely defined communities. It also requires confidence in the discipline's knowledge and familiarity with the appropriate register. Not surprisingly, these kinds of exchanges are not common among pupils or undergraduates, though we can sometimes see the beginning of them in pupils as young as six. For example in Chapter 3, Sequences 1 to 3, both Milly and Charles challenge one another. Although their turns are not as lengthy as the sequence above, nor as sophisticated as some in our Higher Education data, they do illustrate the emergence of challenges which serve as part of the knowledge building within the talk.

Conclusions

In this chapter, the nature of small-group talk and the effects of the strategies used on the progress of academic discussion have been examined by means of four possible discursive events; the response or otherwise to questions and the challenge or otherwise to statements.

The data I have presented suggest that there may be a developmental progression within groups as the task proceeds from the use of procedural questions, which may or may not elicit a response, towards questions which address the content of the task. I have also argued that there may be a developmental progression with academic experience towards fewer questions, longer expositions and more challenges. It is not surprising that questions are more common in novices still 'feeling their way', while a readiness to express opinions and provide arguments to support them are more developed in experienced researchers. However, it is also clear from our Higher Education data that some student groups engage effectively in the more sophisticated style of discourse. Where this does occur, students generally first spend time defining their terms (Fisher, 1996). It may be that this serves not only to facilitate a mutually agreed understanding of those terms, but it also allows participants to practise their use. More significantly perhaps, these ways of interacting encourage an exploration of the content issues rather than a focus on procedure, roles or status. But, as we have seen here and in Tracy *et al.'s* work, status issues may continue to interfere with the expression and challenging of ideas, even among senior academics.

Chapter 5

A Dialogical Framework for Researching Peer Talk

RUPERT WEGERIF AND NEIL MERCER

Section 1 began with a question about the relevance of neo-Vygotskian theory to the study of peer talk. In this, the final chapter of Section 1, Rupert Wegerif and Neil Mercer return to that theme and propose a framework for the study of peer talk which, they claim, goes beyond some of the limitations of neo-Vygotskian theory. This framework is called 'dialogical' because it is based on a characterisation of types of interactive dialogue. The schema of three types of talk introduced by Eunice Fisher in Chapter 3 is taken up and elaborated here, in order to argue that these three types of talk reflect basic possibilities in the ways in which speakers of similar social and educational status can relate to each other in dialogue. Finally Wegerif and Mercer offer an analysis of the types of talk, using four distinct levels of description running from the interpretation of the fundamental orientation of the talk through to the level of surface language features such as key words. In these ways, the chapter consolidates the theoretical content of Section 1 and links it with Section 2, where analyses of different types of talk are used to explain observational classroom data.

Introduction

In Chapter 2 questions were raised about the relevance of neo-Vygotskian theory for the study of peer learning. Concepts such as the Zone of Proximal Development (ZPD) and 'scaffolding' focus on the learning and development of individuals – it is difficult to see how they can usefully be applied to the study of pairs and groups of children working at computers. A new theoretical framework appears to be needed. In Chapter 3 Eunice Fisher discussed some progress which had been made in this direction by research which focused on the quality of children's talk while engaged in joint intellectual activity. She described a schema of three types of talk, each of which had, as she put it, 'significance for education'. This framework of types of talk can be used to analyse how language is used as a means for thinking together by children. But first we need to understand exactly what is meant by a 'type of talk' and consider more carefully what each of the proposed types of talk represents. This will be the main work of this chapter. We start by explaining where our theoretical framework comes from.

Going beyond Vygotsky

Whereas cognitive psychology has tended to view thought as an abstract reality independent of social contexts, the paradigm of sociocultural research which has emerged in recent years treats the process of thinking as one intimately related to processes of communication, and embedded in human social and cultural activity (Wertsch, 1985a,b). Vygotsky – whose pioneering work inspired the development of sociocultural research – argued that 'cognitive development' results from a process of linguistic socialisation, or what he called 'internalisation', and is an important source for the contemporary sociocultural paradigm in education. As he put it:

> We might formulate the general genetic law of cultural development as follows: any function in the child's cultural development appears on the stage twice, on two planes, first on the social plane and then on the psychological, first among people as an intermental category and then within the child as an intramental category. (Vygotsky 1991: 40)

Descriptions of the emergence of sociocultural research commonly place great emphasis on a theoretical confrontation between Vygotsky and Piaget (see Mercer, 1994 for an elaboration of this). However, Vygotsky's overall theory of development was not as different from that of Piaget as some commentators, notably Bruner (1962) have implied. While Vygotsky claimed that thought, at least 'the higher mental functions' such as logic, originated in social practices, he certainly did not claim that thought was fully embedded in language use and in social interaction. Despite some ambivalence in his writing, it seems that, for him, the process of thinking remained essentially something that only individuals do. This is implied in his concept of 'internalisation'. While he described language as a 'tool', or 'mediating means', he appears to have meant by this that it had a function for facilitating cognitive development of individual children in the direction of a purely logical thought (which he associated with 'scientific concepts'). As Wertsch (1996) points out, Vygotsky shared with Piaget an 'Enlightenment rationalism' which included the assumption that abstract rationality is the goal of development. This is apparent in his model of development in which thought passes from a stage where it is embedded in concrete contexts, towards what he called true conceptual thought (van der

Veer & Valsiner, 1991: 263; Vygotsky, 1986: chap. 6). He does not appear to have been concerned with the developing use of language as a culturally elaborated tool used by people for thinking together – i.e. as a means for joint intellectual activity. That is, his work was not directly concerned with the ways language can be used as a *social mode of thinking* (Mercer, 1995).

Vygotsky's commitment to an abstract view of rationality reflected the dominant scientific discourse of his time. Our concern here is not to criticise Vygotsky, but to point out the source of a certain ambivalence in contemporary sociocultural theory, especially as this has been applied to education (e.g. Newman *et al.*, 1989; Wood, 1992). On the one hand, it is argued that cognition is embedded in language use, and this is used to justify close attention to social, collaborative processes of learning. On the other hand, language use is still treated as little more than a 'mediating means' for supporting individual cognitive development towards abstract rationality. One reason for this limited appreciation of the intellectual significance of language use is that the sociocultural research community is dominated by the influence of developmental psychology; although references to anthropological and linguistic studies are often made in such research, its focus is still essentially individualistic. But ways of thinking are embedded in ways of using language, and the development of culturally based 'educated' ways of thinking and communicating thought is an end in itself; language use should be researched in such terms, and not simply as a factor in individual learning or development. We believe, then, that the time has come to move sociocultural research beyond the limitations of Vygotsky's horizons, and allow the social perspectives of anthropology, linguistics, and certain kinds of educational research to have a more profound influence on theory and empirical analysis. Education could then be studied critically as a process for enabling children to use language more effectively as a means for carrying out joint, social intellectual activity.

The Dialogical Turn

The model of reason which Vygotsky shared with Piaget was essentially a 'monological' model. By this we mean that the idea behind it was of a self contained logical system, a system in which each element is perfectly defined by the other elements so that there is no ambiguity or conflicting interpretations. Vygotsky sums up this 'monological' vision in *Thought and Language* as 'the equivalence of concepts' whereby pure concepts can be perfectly substituted one for another in the same way that numbers can be defined in different but equivalent ways in mathematics (Vygotsky, 1986: 200). This mathematical model of reason was essentially the same as that which Piaget embodied in the 'formal operations' stage of his theory of development.

Curiously, a basis for our critique of monological views of reasoning (and of the creation of meaning in general) was laid by a Soviet contemporary of Vygotsky whom he never met, Bakhtin (who some claim also wrote under the name Volosinov). The term 'dialogical', taken from Bakhtin/Volosinov, has become widely used (Hermans *et al.*, 1992; Maybin, 1994; Sampson, 1993; Shotter, 1993; Wertsch 1991; Wold, 1992) perhaps because of the contemporary value of its central insight that understanding always requires more than one voice or perspective. As Volosinov/Bakhtin puts it:

> To understand another person's utterance means to orient oneself with respect to it, to find the proper place for it in the corresponding context. For each word of the utterance that we are in process of understanding, we, as it were, lay down a set of our own answering words. The greater their number and weight, the deeper and more substantial our understanding will be. (Volosinov, 1986: 102)

'Meaning', Volosinov/Bakhtin continues, 'is like an electric spark that occurs only when two different terminals are hooked together'. It follows from this that utterances have no meaning in themselves but only have meaning in the context of a dialogue which includes and interanimates different voices and different perspectives.

Some of the implications of this turn away from monological accounts and towards the dialogical have been explored in the new 'discursive psychology' which emphasises the dynamic construction of meaning and self-identity within dialogue (Edwards & Potter, 1992; Gergen, 1994; Harre & Gillet, 1994; Potter & Wetherell, 1994; Sampson, 1993; Shotter, 1993). Sampson, for example, argues against what he calls 'the container model' of the self, a model strongly implied by Vygotsky's concept of 'internalisation', in favour of a view of the self as inherently multiple:

> Even when we pause to think and reflect, we do not do so in one voice only but always in a dialogue containing many different voices. When we interact with another person, although one genre may be primary, other genres lie at the ready to help us reformulate, reframe and newly understand our experiences. (Sampson, 1993: 125)

This kind of dialogue-based formulation of the process of thinking requires the development of a new kind of theoretical framework to understand cognition and development – a theoretical framework predicated not on the principle of self-identity, as assumed in neo-Vygotskian theory, but on the principle of inter-subjectivity. By inter-subjectivity we mean what

Rommetveit calls the 'attunement to the attunement of the other', which is at the heart of dialogue (Rommetveit, 1992: 20, quoting Barwise & Perry, 1983). This 'dialogical' perspective is a deepening of the sociocultural paradigm which takes the emphasis on social context a little further through putting emphasis on the dynamic and interactive nature of the social construction of meaning within dialogues.

'Cognitive development' can be loosely translated into ordinary language as 'the process by which children learn to reason'. We have seen that Vygotsky assumed, as did Piaget, that the ultimate goal of 'cognitive development' was abstract rationality, based on the model of logic or mathematics. But when we describe someone as a 'logical', 'rational' or a 'reasonable' person we do not normally mean that they are good at abstract logic or at mathematics but that they can make appropriate, clear and useful contributions to discussions, in ways that enable solutions to shared problems to be achieved. In other words, when we talk about our 'reasoning' in an everyday, situated sense, we are describing how we engage in a social process of thinking – to use Rommetveit's favourite phrase again, how we 'attune ourselves to the attunement of others'. This is a point which the social philosopher Habermas makes strongly. He argues against a monological view of reason, based on a model of an isolated individual making sense of an objective world:

> By contrast, as soon as we conceive of knowledge as communicatively mediated, rationality is assessed in terms of the capacity of responsible partners in interaction to orient themselves in relation to validity claims geared to intersubjective recognition. (Habermas, 1991a: 314)

> This communicative rationality recalls older ideas of logos, inasmuch as it brings along with it connotations of a non-coercively unifying, consensus-building force of a discourse in which the participants overcome their at first subjectively biased views in favour of a rationally motivated agreement. (Habermas, 1991a: 315)

On the basis of a switch from what he calls 'the paradigm of consciousness' to 'the paradigm of mutual understanding' or 'intersubjectivity', Habermas (1991a) argues for a model of rationality that is defined not through logical rules but through social ground-rules or guidelines based on an appeal to an 'ideal speech situation' in which the best arguments win out over coercion or self-interest. While Habermas's model of reason has been criticised as too abstract and idealised, we none the less find his ideas a useful resource for exploring the relationship between cognition and language use. He offers the valuable insight that different types of communicative relationship embody different ways of thinking together.

This is where the 'types of talk' analysis put forward by Fisher in Chapter 3 becomes relevant. These types of talk represent ways in which pupils or students orient themselves towards each other in a dialogue. Each type of talk also represents a way in which participants in a dialogue can engage in the joint construction of knowledge. And the type of talk which we have called 'exploratory' appears to embody Habermas's concept of 'communicative rationality'.

Three 'Social Modes of Thinking'

The three educationally significant types of talk characterised by the SLANT (Spoken Language and New Technology) project team (Fisher, 1993; Mercer 1994, 1995) emerged from an analysis of data collected in several schools, with children from a range of age-groups working at a variety of computer-based educational tasks. Mercer (1995, Wegerif & Mercer, 1996) has since elaborated the definitions of the three types of talk, and discussed their nature as 'social modes of thinking':

- **Disputational talk**, which is characterised by disagreement and individualised decision making. There are few attempts to pool resources, or to offer constructive criticism of suggestions. Disputational talk also has some characteristic discourse features – short exchanges consisting of assertions and challenges or counter assertions.
- **Cumulative talk**, in which speakers build positively but uncritically on what the other has said. Partners use talk to construct a 'common knowledge' by accumulation. Cumulative discourse is characterised by repetitions, confirmations and elaborations.
- **Exploratory talk**, in which partners engage critically but constructively with each other's ideas. Statements and suggestions are offered for joint consideration. These may be challenged and counter-challenged, but challenges are justified and alternative hypotheses are offered (cf. Barnes & Todd, 1978). Compared with the other two types, in exploratory talk *knowledge is made more publicly accountable* and *reasoning is more visible in the talk*.

'"Disputational", "cumulative" and "exploratory" are not meant to be descriptive categories into which all observed speech can be neatly and separately coded. They are nevertheless analytic categories because they typify ways that children observed in the SLANT project talked together in collaborative activities. We suggest that the typology offers a useful frame of reference for understanding how talk (which is inevitably resistant to neat categorisation) is used by children to "think together" in class.' (Wegerif & Mercer, 1996: 51)

To understand what is meant by these 'typifications' it helps to have illustrations of types of talk felt to approximate to them.

Sequence 1: Disputational talk

In the first sequence, two boys are engaged with a piece of mathematics software. They are taking it in turns to try to find the co-ordinates of a lost object in a grid.

Stuart: I'm getting fed up with this. Where's mine, five.

Len: You have just done eight fives going away (*reads from screen*) 'you are getting close', 'getting close'. You have done it, you have just done it, dickhead, you have just done it – look!

Stuart: That's not my one.

Len: That was. That was mine, that was yours.

Stuart: Look I'll prove it.

Len: Look: I've done that one, you have done that one, I have done that one, you have done that one. No you have done that one.

Although in this exercise each boy learns from the other's mistakes they none the less each claim to have 'won' when they hit upon the object in their own turn.

Commentary

In disputational talk each speaker defines themselves through their difference with others. Participants treat interaction as a competitive game between individuals each having their own interests and which each try to win. What is said is motivated by the desire to defend or to promote the interests of the speaker, or the interests that the speaker represents, in opposition to the interests of others. We can see from the illustration that the 'winner' takes all the credit despite having been helped by the information he gained tacitly from his partner's choices.

Sequence 2: Cumulative talk

In this sequence two girls are involved in a joint writing task. Notice the repetitions and the confirmations.

Sally: Yeah. What if she says erm erm 'All right, yeah'. No, just put

'Yeah all right'. No, no.

Emma: *(laughs)* No. 'Well I suppose I could ... '

Sally: '... spare 15p.' Yeah?

Emma: Yeah.

Sally: 'I suppose ... '

Emma: 'I suppose I could spare 50p.'

Sally: '50?'

Emma: Yeah. 'Spare 50 pence.'

Sally: '50 pence.'

Emma: '50 pence.' And Angela says 'That isn't enough I want to buy something else.'

Sally: Yeah, no no; I want a drink as well you know I want some coke as well.'

Emma: 'That isn't enough for bubble gum and some coke.'

Sally: Yeah, yeah.

Commentary

In cumulative talk speakers define themselves through their identification with other participants. The ground rules of cumulative talk work to maintain the cohesion of the group. Cumulative talk is co-operative talk and can lead to knowledge construction through the sharing of perspectives. It is limited from an educational point of view in that it does not produce critically grounded knowledge. This is very evident in the illustration where Sally is misheard by Emma. Emma thinks she has heard '50p' and continues with this. Sally reacts to this because she in fact said '15p' but she does not challenge the mistake. The ground rules of cumulative talk give more value to group harmony than to the issue of personal ownership or to any idea of the 'truth'.

Sequence 3: Exploratory talk

In this sequence, two nine-year-old children discuss a moral issue presented by a hypertext narrative on a computer. Where we join them, the heroine of the computer story, Kate, has been told by her friend that he has stolen a box of chocolates to give to his mother for her birthday. The children now have to decide whether Kate should tell her parents or not.

Susan: So what do you think – 'cos is it bad, stealing? Do you think?

Adrian: No – 'cos he was doing it for his mum.

Susan: But I think that's stupid 'cos he could always get some money couldn't he?

Adrian: No.

Susan: Even off his grandparents or something?

Adrian: No but his grandparents might of died mightn't they?

Susan: Oh yeah.

Susan: So we go for yours yeah?

Adrian: Doesn't tell.

Susan: Doesn't tell.

Commentary

Exploratory talk appears to be more complex than either disputational or cumulative talk. In exploratory talk critical challenges are supported but are contained within a co-operative framework. This structure can lead to competition between ideas rather than between people, with the argument that is considered to be the best winning out over other arguments. This aspect of exploratory talk can be seen in the extract where critical challenges and debate lead to Susan changing her position with no apparent loss of face. A sense of shared co-operative identity is maintained as a framework within which different perspectives can be tested out.

The structure of the typology

Exploratory talk is a rational, communicative achievement. It is a situated and contextualised version of the kind of argumentation which, Habermas claims, occurs when communicative action becomes reflective. When the claims implicit in speech acts are not accepted instantly but are questioned then there are only two possible outcomes: the first is a retreat into strategic action where each side tries to coerce the other into agreement, and the second leads to explicit reasoning where the validity claims are suspended and debated with a view to restoring the broken consensus. In exploratory talk the instant 'yes' of acceptance and the instant 'no' of self-defence are both suspended and a dialogue between difference is inaugurated. The ground rules of this type of talk allow for challenges and disagreement, but these are contained within a co-operative social framework which is actively maintained. In other words, the ground rules define the paradoxical 'difference in identity' of dialogue in which participants are both brought together and separated at the same time.

We are probably all intuitively familiar, as participants, with the possibility of abrupt transitions in talk: for example, a shift from a co-operative enquiry into personal competition when something said suddenly pulls us back from open participation into an acute awareness of our own separate identity and interests and the need to defend them. This kind of discontinuity shows how the typology of talk does not just describe language variation, but also certain basic possibilities of human intellectual relationship.

The next sequence illustrates an abrupt transition of this kind: three nine-year-old pupils were working on a series of graphical puzzles taken from a reasoning test (Raven's progressive matrices, Raven *et al.*, 1993). They have been given only one answer sheet for these puzzles and asked to co-operate to reach agreement on each answer.

Sequence 4: A transition

Jane: Yeah but there's three of them and there's 3 of them and that and that makes that.

Natalie: No look you get three and 1 and 3 and 1 and …

Jane: Mr Wegerif does that and that make that?

(Jane appeals to the researcher who comes over but doesn't intervene.)

Natalie: I just disagree.

Researcher: You must give a reason. You must explain why Natalie.

Natalie: No, because look. (*Points to the page with the graphical puzzle but does not explain.*)

George: You have to have a reason Natalie.

(Natalie leaves the group table and goes over to another group.)

George: Natalie you're supposed to be working with us not with Sujatta.

Natalie: I'm thinking. (*Shouted from the other table.*)

Natalie: All right number 3. (*Natalie has come back to the table. She speaks aggressively.*)

Jane: Don't get in a strop I want to explain something.

Natalie: I agree, I agree.

Commentary

Up to this point the children have apparently reached a reasoned agreement on the right answer to each puzzle. Towards the end of the task, however, Natalie begins to propose answers more strongly than before, and shows exasperation with her partners through her raised voice and sharp manner. She makes it quite clear that she is simply bowing to group pressure in finally saying she agrees. She gives no reason for agreeing with the others that the answer is number 3 and refuses to listen to Jane's offered explanation. This sequence shows a fairly abrupt breakdown of the co-operative framework, as the talk moves from exploratory towards a more disputational style.

Exploratory Talk as a Situated Model of Reason

There are occasions on which both disputational and cumulative talk can be effective ways of communicating. Disputational talk may be used quite appropriately to represent irreconcilable differences between participants' personal beliefs or interests. The mutuality established by cumulative talk is useful for the sharing of uncontroversial knowledge, and for recording the joint product of earlier deliberations (such as when a written summary of conclusions must be provided by a group). But exploratory talk has a special status as a dialogical model of reasoning. Its 'ground rules' are those which allow different voices to inter-animate each other in a way which not only constructs shared knowledge but also critically assesses the quality of that knowledge. The 'yes' of cumulative talk and the 'no' of disputational talk move almost instantly, with only the briefest hesitation, to the construction of different kinds of self-identity. The first constructs and maintains self-identity as in solidarity with the physically present group, while the second constructs individual self-identity in opposition to others. Exploratory talk, on the other hand, does not appear to imply or require a specific form of identity commitment. By engaging in exploratory talk, participants maintain a psychological detachment both from themselves as individuals and from the group. This does not mean that what is heard is a decontextualised 'voice of reason' however, as it is necessary for participants to engage and share the perspectives of others in order to understand them. In exploratory talk 'rationality' is characterised by agility in moving between perspectives and, in particular, alternating between taking the perspective of another and standing back to critically assess that perspective. In exploratory talk, then, one ultimately identifies neither with one's own self nor with a group but rather with the dialogue. This makes it possible to try out many alternative perspectives and proposals. But of course a consistent state of detachment, in which we identify with the dialogue, is not entirely possible because in using language we necessarily construct identities: in arguing for proposals, and offering reasons in support, a speaker necessarily takes on an identity. So in exploratory talk identification with the dialogue must take the form not of avoiding perspectives, but of a kind of perpetual openness to alternative perspectives.

Levels of Analysis for Researching Types of Talk

In Chapter 3 Fisher characterised types of talk in terms of 'speech acts' such as initiations and challenges. This is obviously an important level of analysis but on its own it is not sufficient to describe the nature of such types of talk as social modes of thinking. A type of talk is defined by the way in which participants in dialogue orientate themselves towards each other. Participants act out this orientation pragmatically by following (usually implicitly) particular sets of 'ground rules' for selecting speech acts. In so doing, participants will be drawing on their learning of cultural norms and associated language practices. The acquisition of 'educated' ways of thinking is essentially a matter of children acquiring and appreciating certain ways of using language to construct knowledge – ways of thinking which are realised in the communal, cultural practices described as 'genres' and 'discourses' by systemic linguists (e.g. Bhatia, 1994; Fairclough, 1989; Martin *et al.*, 1987; Swales, 1990). Educated activities such as science involve the practised use of specific, culturally defined ways of using language as social modes of thought. We might therefore try to capture the nature of 'types of talk' in four levels of analysis:

Level 1:   At this level we are concerned with the type of talk as a 'social mode of thinking' (Mercer, 1995), meaning the fundamental way in which participants in dialogue orientate themselves towards each other when they engage in the joint construction of knowledge.

Level 2:   At this level, we are concerned with the ground rules which govern the production of appropriate utterances; for example, the sequences of speech acts that are allowed and those that are not.

Level 3:   At this level, we deal with specific 'speech acts', or utterances classified according to their apparent function in the immediate context.

Level 4:   At this level we consider the actual, particular words recorded and transcribed. We believe that explanatory accounts of the nature and function of talk observed in children's collaborative work in class benefits from an explicit reference to these four levels of analysis.

Summary and Conclusion

In this chapter, we have proposed a new kind of theoretical framework for the study of peer talk around computers. In doing so, we moved from the initial neo-Vygotskian perspective to an elaboration of a 'dialogical' theoretical framework which goes beyond Vygotsky while remaining within the broad sociocultural paradigm. This framework is based on an assumption of inter-subjectivity and moves away from the focus on individual cognitive development found in both Piaget and in Vygotsky. Our new perspective enables us to define the kinds of thinking that are embodied in different types of talk. We have defined our analytic categories of three types of talk in terms of fundamental orientations that are possible between participants in dialogue. Thus, 'cumulative talk' and 'disputational talk' seem to be very basic structural possibilities, while 'exploratory talk' is a hybrid form combining elements of both. Our set of three types of talk is expressly provisional, and almost certainly not exhaustive. However, the framework as a whole illustrates the kind of analytic approach which we believe is needed in research on how, in educational settings, people use language as a social mode of thinking. As other chapters in this book will demonstrate, this framework is a practical tool for the analysis of classroom discourse, and one which can be used to evaluate and improve educational practice.

This chapter ends the first section of the book, a section which is intended to provide a theoretical basis for the descriptive analyses of children's talk and joint activity which follow in Section 2, and also for those chapters of Section 3 which show how teachers can apply research findings to improve their own practice regarding children's joint activity and the use of computers in classrooms. Many of the chapters which follow refer to the three types of talk idea elaborated here and several use a version of it directly as an analytic tool.

Section 2

Computers and Children's Talk

Chapter 6
Talk Round Adventure Games

TERRY PHILLIPS AND PETER SCRIMSHAW

This chapter turns to a widely used but not very fully researched form of software – adventure games. In the chapter the authors identify the distinctive features of the kinds of adventure games found in class-rooms, and look at the talk that groups of children produced when using three different games, selected to illustrate something of the range available. They conclude that while there may well be generic features to such games they also vary considerably in their detailed design, and that these variations are likely to be of considerable significance for the kinds of talk that their use might generate. In particular they appear to vary in the extent to which they both allow and encourage holistic planning rather than instant decisions, and thus in the extent to which they support exploratory talk.

The Educational Potential of Adventure Games

Adventure games form a distinct sub-genre of simulation programs, the latter being programs designed to provide a simplified presentation of some aspect or kind of reality. While adventure games are quite varied in their structure they mostly share some common features. Each game presents the children with a closed (and very simple) world, into which they step as actors. What actions they can take, and their results, are all predefined within the game, unless a minor random element has been added for interest. Usually the world presented is a fantasy one, but there are games which simulate realistic (but still greatly simplified) worlds within which the children decide where to go and what to do. Within this world some overall task is set, to give direction to their choices, and the children then move through the imaginary world, looking for objects or information that will help them with the task.

In concrete terms, the games require the children to read a page of text on the computer screen (sometimes with accompanying pictures) and then decide what action to take, usually selecting from a limited range of options provided. They then enter their choice. This moves them on to the appropriate page, and the process is repeated.

This sort of computer program has obvious potential attractions for anyone favouring the perspectives represented in this book. As Sherwood (1991) observes, adventure games may offer a way of supporting curricula marked by enquiry, creative expression, social interaction and co-operative effort. The underlying educational point here was picked up very soon after the development of the microcomputer. In an important early paper Malone (1981) argued that intrinsically motivating instruction using computers requires activities with uncertain outcomes. He showed that fantasy elements can be important to motivation, and that the learner needs to see their present knowledge as incomplete, inconsistent and less simply and elegantly structured than it could be. Subsequently Underwood and Underwood (1990) and Wishart (1990) have extended this analysis, emphasising the educational importance of the program giving the learners choices, and thus some degree of control over their activities.

It is clear that adventure games show many of these motivational features, and so could in principle provide a problem-solving environment that would support collaborative work and the talk that goes with it. As Crook (1994) writes:

> As an exercise in building and reasoning from shared knowledge, the adventure game format has a lot to recommend it. The appeal and accessibility of the narrative structure effectively motivates mutual engagement in the task. Moreover, the pre-set nature of the underlying adventure provides an external authority for evaluating the decisions that collaborators make. Under these circumstances, it seems less likely that asymmetries in the working arrangements will arise. (Crook, 1994: 181)

This assumes, however, that all adventure games are similar in structure and in their effect upon a group's working and discussion. Our impression from observing a number of sessions using such games is that this is not entirely true. To explore this further, we will look at three representative sessions in which different adventure games were used, and at some examples of the talk that was generated around them.

In summary, although there were substantial similarities in the patterns of talk there were variations in the balance between different kinds of talk, and in particular in the amount of exploratory talk that took place. In none of the sessions was this a majority of the talk, but it ranged from being virtually absent to being a substantial proportion.

Concept Kate: Short Exchanges and Repeated Closure

In Concept Kate, one of the games in the Concept Kingdom series, the children playing the game have to assist the eponymous Kate to escape from the land in which she is trapped by helping her to travel over hazardous terrain collecting helpful items along the way. The fantasy land through which they take her makes no reference to the real world; that is, the things that happen in the Concept Kingdom are the things we accept as reasonable in a fairytale land but would reject as odd in our own world. The Kingdom has a walled courtyard within which there are several roads; if the road is firm or cold Kate is safe to travel along it, but if it is soft or hot then it is unsafe. The Concept Kingdom has doorways leading to a variety of rooms, some of which constitute hostile environments. Whether or not a road is safe or unsafe, or a room hospitable or not, is an arbitrary matter. To avoid sustained contact with a dangerous road Kate can jump, and to prepare herself for the unknown dangers that lurk behind some of the doors she can 'pick up' items she encounters along the way. This seems to be the full extent of the pre-planning possible, however, because much of the problem solving is in response to a sudden threat. When Kate successfully negotiates her way along a road or out of an enclosed space she is free to 'dance' because dancing – which involves both a dance-like movement by the character on the screen and an accompanying piece of music – is the reward for having completed a stage of the game. The two six-year-old children, Andrew and Bethan, who are playing Concept Kate in our example, have played it before and therefore have some notion of what is possible. They nevertheless treat the game overall as a series of discrete incidents which have to be responded to as if unrelated to the previous happenings, although at the same time they are clearly operating in terms of a set of procedures (jumping, walking, picking up, dancing) that persist from one situation to the next. The talk consists primarily of imperatives intended to lead to action that will solve the immediate problem. Where the solution is not achieved another imperative is provided and its resulting action tested. What happens, then, is that the problem is explored in terms of a series of short-term plans that are made and tested within a self-contained and apparently arbitrary situation. Having finally completed the action in this situation, the children then move on to deal with the next one.

What the data show is that the children we observed working together on Concept Kate constructed conversation in short, easily identifiable exchanges. By 'easily identifiable' we mean that the opening utterance of the exchange can be seen to require a next move, and the final utterance clearly does not. This differs from many other conversations in which moves often project both forwards and backwards (i.e. they are required in response to a previous utterance but they also require a response of their own). In such cases it is difficult to decide where an exchange begins or ends. The following exchange is typical of the adventure game discourse that took place:

Sequence 1.1

Andrew: Press 'dance' ... you gotta press 'dance'
Bethan: Huh
Andrew: Press 'dance'
Bethan: (*Presses 'dance' on concept keyboard*)
Andrew: See ... I told yuh

This pattern varies slightly where there is some form of dispute between the speakers, or between the speakers and the computer, or between all three. In such instances the pattern is extended, as in the following example:

Sequence 1.2

Andrew: Walk away (*i.e. walk character on screen away from danger*)
Bethan: (*Presses keyboard; nothing happens*)
Bethan: I can't walk away ... I can't
Andrew: You can ... look ... just go there (*pushes Bethan off keyboard and presses key for self*)
Bethan: Hooray it's walking

Sometimes an exchange appears at first sight to be more complex, but closer examination reveals it to have the same basic structure. For instance:

Sequence 1.3

Andrew: I want to get to the shed ... oh come on ... we don't want to get to that house ... all we do is go up there ... (*pointing to screen*) ... we don't. We don't want to get up there do we... I don't think we do. We want to get over there. We want to go over there. You do this bit
Bethan: (*Singing, but not pressing key*) do da
Andrew: Go on get in the shed. Press 'walk away' that'll make it get it the shed

Bethan: (*Presses key*) mm

Here the basis structure is preceded by a convoluted short-term plan statement (see below) but is nevertheless clear.

Sequence 1.4

Bethan: (*Reading*) 'Can you put them in their own boxes?' oh this is easy

Andrew: Press 'go on'... this is quite ...

Bethan: now we've got to press them now...   oh [inaudible)] 'one' (presses key)

Andrew: 'two'

Bethan: 'two'

Andrew: 'three'

Bethan: 'three'

Andrew: No that'll do for one

Here the basic exchange is preceded by a reading from the screen (which may be an exchange in itself – see below) and a task-evaluation comment.

Essentially, the structure is the same in all the instances quoted so far. In the Concept Kate tapes examined there are a substantial number of exchanges of this type; they follow one after the other with very little deviation from the pattern. At the macro-level, therefore, the discourse is primarily structured into a series of rapidly closing Instruction Exchanges.

Not all of the exchanges in the adventure game discussions are of the 'Child/Child' type so far mentioned, however. A second type of exchange happens in response to a 'Screen' instruction. The reading from the screen item in Example 4 can, on inspection, be seen to be an exchange in its own right. The computer invites/instructs the children to read its text, and one or more of them responds by doing so. The structure of the exchange is: implicit instruction, verbal response. There are several similar examples, e.g.:

Bethan: (*reading from screen*) 'Please take a number or press escape to / leave there / this'... um (points at screen)

Andrew: (*presses key*)

This type of exchange marks an even more rapid movement towards closure than the already brief Child/Child type. The new pattern confirms the discussion's overall macro-level pattern as an Instruction Exchange one, and provides additional evidence that closure is typically happening rapidly and often.

From this analysis it is possible to construct a tentative description of the type of discourse that this adventure game generates. Such discussion consists of numerous instructions (given either by one child to another, or by the screen to the children), and the spoken response(s) to what happens when the instructed action is carried out. It is interspersed with statements about immediate plans, usually an individual's plan, but just occasionally an individual's version of the 'group' plan. In its latter stages the discourse includes comments which demonstrate the children's move towards a focus on the narrative of the game rather than the procedures for going through it. It is possible to say, therefore, that the majority of the discourse is characterised by short exchanges, and repeated closure, although from time to time there are indications of movement beyond the immediate in the form of planning statements and (re)creative comments.

Observation in the classroom and interviews with the teacher make it clear that the classroom environment is one where children are encouraged to work independently of the teacher for much of the time. It is also one where they are encouraged to talk together quietly while they work. The children have a routine which provides a supportive framework for them to 'try things out'. The general context then is one in which children are secure, oriented towards discussion, and happy to experiment. In response to the adventure games the children do talk freely, and they do 'try things out' by employing a mixture of trial and error and deduction (although we have little access to their deductive thinking). However, the Instruction Exchanges and repeated closure much more closely resemble the discourse structure so typical of traditional classrooms than the sort of discussion which the class teacher normally promotes. This must, therefore, have something to do with the nature of the program, which encourages task completion within a time limit. In fact, the exchanges are coterminous with steps in the adventure, or with attempts to progress to the next step. For these children the main focus of the activity is on 'getting to the end' rather than on planned problem-solving. Where planning is involved it is constrained by the need to get on swiftly. And the programme positively discourages solution-finding by entry imaginatively into the experience of the characters, so such involvement only occurs at the point where the children have begun to 'thumb their noses' metaphorically at the authority of the screen.

In this session at least, then, exploratory talk is almost completely absent.

Wizard's Revenge: Missing the Wider Picture

As well as 'read only' adventure games teachers can obtain programs that allow children to design and write their own text adventures or real life simulations: an authoring environment for adventure games. We saw some of these in use, but as they raise quite different issues (see, for instance, Martin, 1988; Straker, 1989) they are not discussed further here. Our second example is a game called 'Wizard's Revenge', known to the children and teacher as 'Wiz'. This was an adventure game provided by the developers of one of these authoring packages, The Last Adventure, to illustrate what could be done with it. We, however, saw it being used in its own right, and it is this use that is discussed here.

Like Concept Kate, Wizard's Revenge is a magical adventure involving a quest and travel through a strange landscape of forests, magic wells and lakes, inhabited by gnomes and witches. The teacher or children can set the maximum time allowed on the adventure at the outset. Again like Concept Kate at each location there is a description (but no picture). When the space bar is pressed a challenge is set or the user is asked to solve a problem. The locations are linked to the function keys, so that to move to a new location the children just press another key (hence the references to 'F7' etc. in the extracts below). However not all locations are interconnected with every other; quite often the child is not allowed into a new location because they need to have been somewhere else first, or to have solved a specific problem earlier. On reaching the end of the adventure a conclusion is displayed which congratulates the children. If they attempt to leave before completing the game they (or the teacher) can obtain clues as to where they went wrong, comprising a list of places not visited, and a list of the problems or challenges not solved.

In this classroom the teacher ran her computer-using sessions alongside mathematics and language work, groups rotating through the activities over a period of time. During the project she tended to work mainly with other groups but was available on demand to the computer-using groups. In the session discussed, the children involved were Karen and Ruth, two eight-year-old friends used to working together and quite familiar with the computer. In this extract they are making the first of two attempts to find a way of getting to a cottage they are told is visible across a lake.

Sequence 2.1

Karen: Right. I think we ought to go to F7. We've solved F6.

Karen: Hooray.

Ruth: *(Reading the screen display)* You can see a lake ahead through the trees you can see through the trees so you walk along the path until you come to the lake. You continue on the path until you reach the (...). Across the other side you see an old cottage. The water is cold, deep and frightening.

R and K: There is a /(*R puts out hand to restrain K's hand. K begins taking over*) boat tied up

Karen: (*inaudible*) on the water's edge on the board it says 'Take notice. No swimming!' Press space bar to continue.

Karen: (*Reading faster*) Oh dear, there are no oars on the boat. How do we get to the other side? I think I / Now what have we got?

Ruth: Have we got sw-im?
(3)

Ruth: Does it say we are allowed to swim?

Karen: Oh no it doesn't.

Ruth: Does it?

Karen: No. It says …

Ruth: It says 'No swimming'.

Karen: Oh yeah Um now what have we got? We'll have to walk.
(3)

Karen: Oh walk round. Easier.

Ruth: Walk round?

Karen: Yes.
(*pause*)

Ruth: W-alk / It'll most probably say you can't do that. Ro-und. You can't do that.

Karen: What have we got?

Ruth: But / anyway we don't have to do that now. / I wouldn't try and solve this.

Karen: Shall we try F um 7 again (*inaudible*).

Ruth: Take notice 'No swimming'. We are going to have to walk.

Karen: Walk. I think I'll walk. (*inaudible*)

Ruth: I bet it'll say it takes too long. / *You can't do that!* We're going to have to swim.

Karen: Uho. We / Okay we'll swim (*pause*) You're not supposed to anyway. (*pause*).

Ruth: Is that how you spell it?

Karen: No S-W-I- M / M.

Ruth: You can't do that.

Karen: Oh yeah, you're not allowed.

Ruth:	There's nothing more we can do / really.
Karen:	You can er use the boat.
Ruth:	Katy there are no oars / oars!
Karen:	We'll have to use our arms.
Ruth:	Use arms *(laughs)*
Karen:	Yeah we'll have to do that.
Ruth:	What is it?
Karen:	Use arms.
Ruth:	Use arms with boat. / Use
Karen:	That's what we're supposed to be doing.
Ruth:	Arms
Karen:	With
	(2)
Ruth:	With
	(2)
Karen:	Boat./ Boat. Spelt b-o-a-t.
	(2)
Ruth:	You can't do that. It's like lost in the whirling fog. We can't do anything.

At first sight this extract looks very different to those given from the Concept Kate session above. However, on closer inspection this turns out to be largely because the children are unsuccessful in their attempts to complete the move at once, and the talk actually breaks down into a number of discrete sequences rather similar to the Concept Kate extracts. Closure sequences of the child–child and child–computer kind appear again, but these children do not refer explicitly to the physical mechanics of key pressing, perhaps because they are sufficiently confident with the program to not need to prompt each other in this way, or because their attention is focused more firmly upon the problem itself. They also appear at first sight to be working to a joint plan; Andrew and Bethan's mixture of 'I' 'you' and 'we' in the Concept Kate extract is replaced here exclusively by 'we'. However, closer inspection shows that the talk has an intertwined parallel pattern. Within this each child offers individual solutions to the shared problem, each of which is accepted without dissent by the other. Thus the basic structure of the sequence is:

- Ruth proposes the swim solution then voluntarily withdraws it without a trial.

- Karen proposes the walking solution, which fails.
- Ruth proposes the swim solution again, which fails.
- Karen proposes the paddling with arms solution, which fails.
- They both agree to go on to another problem.

However, they do move to a clearly exploratory mode, when they return to the lake problem later in the same session:

Sequence 2.2

Karen: We really need to solve to get across the lake don't we (...) to solve it.

Ruth: What do we solve?
(2)

Karen: Maybe we should have taken the potion.

Ruth: I know, let's go back to the <u>forest</u> (*Excited and hushed*)

Karen: Yeah and get ... get all the other things. Um where's the forest? (...)

Karen: Um.
(2)

Karen: No. Let's take the potion.

Ruth: No. If you take the right one we can go along the lake with the boat.

Karen: Yeah.

Ruth: Can't we?

Karen: There is just...

Ruth: No we could swing on a tree (let's get) over the other side of the lake.

Karen: Yeah, Okay (let's take that) then we could buy all the others.

Ruth: Yeah because we know that we've still got the ring (*inaudible*)

Karen: Oh

Ruth: It tells us (*inaudible*) heading more things. Yeah but how do we go north-east? Where do you want to go now?

Karen: I suggest we still solve ... I suggest we solve the lake thing before we go on.

The difference between these two sequences is that in the first they assume (wrongly) that they can work out how to cross the lake by considering only the immediate context. In the second sequence they have started to decentre and consider what they know as a whole, rather than focusing exclusively upon the lakeside situation. This in turn allows (and indeed requires) them to look for connections between the different things they have found out.

Unlike Concept Kate this adventure game invites (and indeed requires) some holistic planning, but in general this is not taken up in the session, perhaps because the internal logic is not consciously recognised by the children, who focus almost exclusively upon the screen they are discussing, generally not going outside it to find answers to the problem.

Viking England: Developing a Context for Informed Decision-Making

A rather different type of game is the one which attempts to create an imagined reality based on other times, places, or cultures. Viking England is such a game. Information about the culture and practices of the Viking era (*circa* 850 AD) is necessarily incomplete – it is based on those records and artefacts which have not perished and which were constructed by 'interested' parties who had their own reasons for presenting events in the way they did. the game capitalises on this fact, and sets out to demonstrate that it is possible to interpret evidence in more than one way, and that decisions about evidence have consequences for further action. at the outset, the program provides the children with a screen picture of an estuary and invites them either to choose a site for permanent or temporary settlement, or to explore the hinterland. the program is as open-ended as possible, given the constraint that all subsequent decisions are contingent upon this first one. the program offers the children an opportunity to explain why they make a particular choice (e.g. *Why did you decide to find a site first?*) and to key this into the machine.

This game invites holistic planning for two reasons. Firstly, because choices are contingent it becomes essential to consider before taking a decision what its outcome might be and how that might affect further action. Secondly, as the story develops it creates a more complex context for the events that take place in the latter stages of the narrative. This is very different from either Concept Kate or Wizard's Revenge where the context is almost an irrelevance in its effect upon choices. Children who play Viking England have to plan well ahead, and therefore they have a reason for explaining their choices to each other; there is something at stake in making a choice one way rather than another, and that something is more than whether it is possible to go on to the next move. The program 'scaffolds' this discussion by presenting the children with a visual version of 'the whole' (i.e. a map of the territory) so that they are able to move back and forth between the 'local' (the immediate situation) and the 'global' (the overall context). It also *requires* the players to consider alternatives before taking the action (the keying in of a C and pressing of return) that implements a decision and takes them on to the next stage. After a player has considered a particular course of action, the program raises questions which may have to be taken into account if that option is proceeded with, and allows them to reconsider if they wish. And it uses language that constructs the world as 'arguable', that is, as something that need not be taken-for-granted but can be considered in terms of alternatives. The screen text employs words and phrases such as 'possible courses of action' and 'preference', uses modalities such as 'might' and 'seem', and asks for 'reasons'.

In the example we draw on here, three 10-year-olds Cathy, Ronnie, and Ciara, begin by opting for simple solutions; the virtue of forward planning is not yet evident to them.

Sequence 3.1

Ronnie: (*Reading from screen*) Why did you decide to find a site first? – umm

Cathy: Wel-l-l

Ronnie: So we can *see* our site (*laughs*)

Cathy: So we can see our land?

Ronnie: Yeah

Cathy: Yeah

Ciara: Yeah

Ronnie: All right (*types in the reason*)

The structure of their talk is here very like that of Andrew's and Bethan's as they work their way through Concept Kate. The thinking about their choice seems to have come after the choice has been 'plumped for', the move towards closure is rapid.

As they move on, though, they are presented with increasing amounts of information about the territory in which they are located, and thus about the context for their choices.

Sequence 3.2

Ronnie: (*Reading from screen*) This is the coastline, it shows the estuary

Cathy: Press 'C'

(Ronnie presses key for Continue; more visual data appears on screen)

Ronnie: Where's that? (pointing) that's the estuary, that's island, that's Stone Island

Ciara: *(as a screen gives more data)* huh … oh

Ronnie: Marshy area

Ciara: Low hills

Cathy: Trees.

As the picture becomes more detailed the nature of the problem to be solved automatically becomes more complex. There is no longer any advantage in rapid closure; movement for movement's sake is shown to be both unhelpful and unrewarding. At some points of choice the children begin to collaborate to discuss alternatives.

Sequence 3.3

Ciara: OK. Press 'C'

Cathy: That's it *(map displayed on screen again)* … where shall we have it. I think we should have it by there *(points to low hills at top right corner of screen)*

Ronnie: Yeah

Ciara: Yeah but the umm estuary – whatever it's called – right, is –

Ronnie: Mm

Ciara: You have to come all down there (to reach the site) so

Cathy: Why don't we build it just outside the trees, there *(pointing)*

Ciara: Well

Ronnie: In the trees there, or there *(points to wooded spots either side of estuary)*

Cathy: Yeah

Ciara: Well actually, because like, you know, the um … the other ships, they come along here *(points)* don't they

Ronnie: Yah

Cathy: Um when me and Ronnie and Karen done it

Ciara: If you're in the trees they don't see you

Ronnie: If they come there.

In this particular instance the focus on alternatives is encouraged by the fact that this game is the third in a series, and by the fact that two of the children have played part of it before, so precedents have been set.

The action in Viking England, then, takes place within a 'world' which is fully contextualised both visually and textually; it invites strategic planning; it foregrounds decision-making rather than decision-taking processes; it provides a motivation for collaborative discourse because what is at stake is 'real' insofar as it will have real consequences within the game; and it constructs the world as 'arguable'. This has consequences for the way in which the children use their own language. Their talk is exploratory, with the emphasis on planning, and reflection upon the possible outcome of the strategic choices they might make as part of the planning process. As such, it avoids closure until the moment that reflection has been carried out to the satisfaction of both the children and the program. This game does not encourage 'what if' speculative talk, another form of exploratory talk, but it does facilitate a 'what implications' type of exploration. Just as importantly, perhaps, it presents the world of the game as one which is open to argumentation (or interrogation), and in that way too encourages the delay of closure.

Discussion

So what might be the important differences between different adventure packages and their context of use, as far as effects upon the ensuing discourse structure (and thus upon learning) are concerned?

Firstly, adventure games offer a range of approaches to 'textualisation' and, through it, to contextualisation. Where a game includes a series of more or less discrete episodes linked by a 'journey' from one episode site to another there is little necessity for the players to look at the text as a whole. Where problems are embedded in incidents that are constructed as context-free, perhaps the only way of explaining it as a coherent text is by imagining the incidents linked in terms of the procedures to be adopted.

Secondly, because of the technological and conceptual limitations currently characteristic of computer software, computer simulations (of which adventure games are a sub-genre) necessarily simplify reality. Some programs offer 'more complicated simplifications of reality,' than others, however. Problems are 'solved' in 'the real world' in one of two ways. Where problems are 'simple', that is, involve only a small number of variables and require a solution to be found from within a limited number of options, the problem is 'solved' by applying a procedure developed for dealing with the archetypal version of the problem. Where problems are 'complicated', in other words, where they involve variables that cannot be abstracted from the situation and where consequently choices are context-dependent, the problem is 'resolved' by careful analysis of the features which make the situation of which it is a part a unique one. Complex problems are made *simpler*, in one sense, by conceptualising them with reference to the indicative features of a previous analogous 'case', but they are not solved by the uncritical application of a procedure from that earlier experience. Even when reference is being made to another case, the present contextualised problem can only be solved by exploring it in terms of its own peculiar features and relationships.

Adventure games such as Concept Kate, encourage the simplification of problems and the seeking of procedural solutions. Other game-like programs, of which Viking England is a good example, invite players to treat problems as complex and, taking a holistic perspective, to examine a range of possible solutions and their medium-term implications before making a decision. Both types of game encourage problem solving, but the nature of the problem, the type of strategy needed to find a solution, and the talk which therefore tends to accompany the activity, are quite different in each case.

But program structures do not determine the ensuing talk, for the context of use is highly variable too, with the teacher, the general curricular context and the overall classroom ethos important factors. To take just one aspect by way of illustration, the group of children themselves, and the match between their current competencies and those required by the game, can vary greatly.

To start with, even if the game world has a coherent logic this will not always be visible to the children. The pair working with Wizard's Revenge, for instance, could only intermittently grasp the importance of the wider framework to the solution of their immediate problem. More generally, a group may misinterpret features of the adventure game genre, perhaps conflating it, as the Concept Kate group may have done, with video games, where problems are solved by personal intuition and individual and rapid action, rather than reflection and discussion. Another example of this is the difficulty that the children using Wizard's Revenge had in establishing what sort of real life knowledge was applicable in the adventure game world. In real life, walking round the lake and paddling a (very small) boat with your hands are entirely sensible options to consider; here they are ruled out by the game designer. Similarly, for a good swimmer the option of swimming across is sensible; the children fail to pick up the cue that the water is described as cold and deep, which within the genre is coded advice to forget the possibility of swimming or wading.

More prosaically, a group may simply find the language used too difficult to understand, in a way that makes it impossible for them to complete the task. Similarly, if there are embedded problems involving, say, mathematics, they may find these too easy or too hard. In particular, it is a weakness of some adventure games that the children, if they make an error, are returned to the start of the game. This means that they have to retrace steps they have already taken, perhaps further encouraging the sort of short exchanges we have found.

Can these mismatches between the requirements built into the program and the children's expectations and capabilities be reduced by groups working together? This too is likely to be highly variable from case to case. At the very least, it presumably depends upon the different members' relative levels of capability and confidence, as far as each aspect of the activity is concerned, namely reading, discussing, handling any embedded tasks and, indeed, basic computer-using capabilities. What constitutes the best way of organising the groups and the activity will therefore vary from case to case. But this means that the children (or the teacher) also have to identify the optimum approach for the group. This is not likely to be easy.

On the basis of these three cases alone we cannot draw firm conclusions about the relationship between program structure and the talk that their use generates, for other contextual factors will always be involved. Nevertheless these three cases do at least suggest that program structure may well be one important determinant of the nature of the ensuing talk. This is a possibility that is explored in more detail in the chapters that follow.

Chapter 7

Children's Talk and Computer Software

EUNICE FISHER

In this chapter Eunice Fisher describes the spoken language which occurs when primary school children work in groups at the computer and explores the influence on that talk of contrasting types of software. For example, talk which accompanies highly structured programs such as adventure games is compared to that accompanying more 'open-ended' software such as an art package, or a story writing package. She argues that discourse accompanying highly structured programs conforms well to the IRF (Initiation, Response, Follow-up) structure identified by Sinclair and Coulthard in teacher-centred classrooms, with the computer often taking the initiating role. The more open-ended software, on the other hand, was, she argues, accompanied by more varied and wider ranging talk which did not fit the traditional IRF model, and in which pupils rather than computer took the initiating role. Reasons for these differences are discussed and the implications for children's language and learning considered.

This paper was written in 1992 in the first stage of the Spoken Language and New Technology project. Influenced by some of the findings, Eunice Fisher reports here she worked with Lyn Dawes to explore ways of coaching children in effective communication strategies before giving them computer work (see Chapter 14). This work produced different types of interaction around computers reported on in the next chapter by Rupert Wegerif. These new possibilities of group interaction with and around the computer led Wegerif to question and develop the provisional conclusions reached here by Fisher.

Introduction

Many researchers have reported that co-operative group learning at the computer is effective and valuable for children (e.g. Johnson *et al.*, 1986; King, 1989; Webb *et al.*, 1986), although some researchers have also suggested that there is a need for specific instruction in working strategies to get the best results (e.g. Farish, 1989; Hill & Browne, 1988; Rysavy & Sales, 1991). There have also been reports from across a range of activities and age groups both here and in the United States, suggesting that group learning with computers encourages and supports children's use of spoken language (for example, Cummings, 1985; Dudley-Marling & Searle, 1989).

The recognition of the potential importance of computers for enhancing learning through talk led us in the Spoken Language and New Technology (SLANT) project research team to begin a study which aims to identify those factors which lead to 'exploratory talk' in the primary classroom (the nature of exploratory talk is described and explored in Chapters 3, 4 and 5). Our findings so far indicate that a range of factors influence the quality of children's talk at computers including factors to do with the classroom methods, factors to do with the pupils' expectations and factors to do with the software. In this chapter I will focus on the influence of the software.

Setting

In the SLANT project we have been observing a wide variety of computer activities in 10 schools (first school and middle school). We have recorded the work of approximately 50 children, aged between 5 and 13 years, by means of video recording, researcher observation, interviews with teachers and with pupils. Choice of software was the teacher's, and the researchers asked to record activities which form part of the normal classroom life. A wide range of software, including adventure games, art programs, word processing and other writing packages and maths programs were used. Although much of the data has still to be analysed in detail, it is already possible to describe some of the talk and to attribute provisionally some of the differences that we find.

From our data examined so far, it would seem that we were right in our initial assumption that the way in which computers are used in primary schools, generally with more than one pupil working at the computer at a time, does indeed provide a context for a lot of talk. As one might expect, the type of talk varies considerably, and my intention in this paper is to describe relationship between those characteristics and the software with which it was associated.

It is possible to categorise crudely the program used according to the degrees of freedom that they allow the user, so that adventure games can be seen as 'closed' and at one end of the spectrum, with the more 'open-ended' programs such as word processing at the other. However, the way in which a program is used is also likely to affect the perceived freedom to the user, so that the child's perception of the task and their facility/familiarity with the processes involved in executing it interact with the restrictions or the freedoms arising from the program. This perception and the child's ability to deal with the task demands will themselves be influenced by characteristics of each child and the classroom situation within which she or he is placed.

This multiplicity of factors almost certainly means that it will be impossible to tease out the precise contribution of each one. However, one way towards developing a clearer understanding of their relationship to the discourse we have recorded would be to begin with examples from the range of software, and to describe and contrast those examples, to try to establish whether certain discourse features commonly occur in conjunction with certain software features. In selecting examples, I have chosen software across the open/closed 'range' suggested above, and shall use discourse extracts which seem to me 'interesting', but also typical of at least 20% of the total session. (In most cases a 'session' represents the complete activity at the computer. This is usually longer than 30 minutes and may be of up to one hour.)

The Software

Adventure games

In our data, adventure game talk is characterised by easily defined *transactions* and *exchanges* (as described by Sinclair & Coulthard, 1975). Their model for classroom talk proposed a hierarchical structure in which an *exchange* represented the minimal interactive unit, and in which *transactions* were made up to *exchanges*, and would normally be either a complete topic within a lesson, or an obviously marked section of a lesson. *Exchanges*, they claimed, are characterised by a two- or three-stage interaction as follows:

Initiation: the introduction of a topic by the teacher

Response: by the pupil(s)

Feedback: (later termed *follow-up*, a broader and less restrictive concept) by the teacher

Although there has been criticism of this rather restrictive model (for example, Stubbs, 1983) which in any case was mainly used by the authors for describing discourse in 'traditional' classrooms, (Sinclair & Coulthard, 1975) nonetheless our data suggests that this model may be a very useful one to describe the talk which occurs at the computer with 'closed' programs such as adventure games. In these cases the initiating move is often made by a computer instruction, rather than by the teacher as in the original Sinclair and Coulthard research. The response which follows may then be any of the following:

- a key press;
- a key press accompanied by an oral description of what is being done by the operator;
- some discussion of what should be done, followed by a key press.

Below are sequences taken from adventure game talk, illustrating these alternatives. In fact it very seldom seems to happen that a key press occurs with no talk at all. At the very least, the children (or one of them, sometimes a 'reader' who has been nominated by the teacher) reads aloud the instruction or comments on the screen, and this is invariably followed by a comment on the screen event by another member of the group.

In the following five sequences (Nos. 1–5), the groups are all drawn from the same class who are using this particular program for the first time (though they are familiar with other adventure programs). The teacher uses group and pair working for a variety of classroom activities, and commonly assigns specific roles or functions to the group members. In Sequences 1 and 2 below, the groups have worked together several times before on a variety of activities. However, the teacher does not explicitly teach strategies for group interaction, though she does make suggestions for coping when the children are in difficulty (for example 'Read it again, Harriet', at a point where it is clear that none of the group has properly read the question).

Sequence 1: (8 year olds using Nature Park Adventure)

	T:	(reads from screen)
1		You are looking at the blue butterflies that have been taken
2		from the nature park. Remember you are still only 10
3		inches tall
	M:	(leans towards screen)
4		What?
5	T:	(correcting) centimetres
6		Its your turn
7	M:	At the end of part 1 of this adventure you were crossing the
8		stream (presses space bar)
9		As you went across you fell into the stream.

(Computer screen shows person falling in water)

| 10 | T: | You fell into the ... Wuh. (hand over mouth – smiles and mock horror) |
| 11 | M: | (reading) you fell into the water |

12	**T:**	*(reading)* Press space button *(M presses).*
13		Help.
14		Go on then.
15		Oh you pressed it.

As the instruction to press bar is generally printed on the screen, we could interpret both the information which is read out and the space bar pressing as responses to the computer's input to the discourse. In the extract above, we then have the following:

Initiation (by computer):   Inform (lines 1–3)
                                                      (lines 7–8)

Response (by **M**), pressing space bar: Action response
                                                                           (line 8)

Follow-up (by computer) giving new further information
                                                      (line 9)

Response (by **T**):   'Wuh' and action of holding her hand to mouth
                                                      (line 10)
(by **M**): presses space bar   (line 12)

Sequence 2

In the same game, another group of children have reached an impasse. They have misread the computer's instruction and are puzzled that their simple addition (pressing 2p and 10p in response to a request which they interpreted as a need for 12p) produces a negative response.

1	**H:**	It's ten and two
2		The computer's wrong
3		It's ten and two but we've pressed another two
4		And it's only ten and two
5	**T:**	Yeh
6	**H:**	I'll just press *(she presses)*
7		*(reads)* You have used too many coins
8		Try again.
9		Right
10	**T:**	Yeh yeh
11	**H:**	Count this first
12		Five and five and two
13		Yeh?

14	**T:**	Yeh yeh
15		Well go on
16		Better
17		Enter
18		All right now you've got to press two

(H presses but they still have the wrong answer)

19	**T:**	Now what?
20	**H:**	Now what are we going to do?
21		We've done it

In the first move (lines 1–4) **H** reads the screen instruction, and verbalises her response (the press, line 6). The computer then provides feedback, indicating that they have gone wrong again (lines 7–8). This is then followed by some discussion in which they make explicit which keys they will press, though since they are still seeking the same total they find they are still wrong (lines 9 ff.)

In fact the children are unable to solve their problem and call the teacher who asks them to read out the question. They then realise their error (they should have been selecting *twice* twelve pence) and quickly do the correct calculations.

These sequences illustrate the type of discourse which occurs much of the time, with the computer playing an integral role in the discourse and constraining the users within a narrow band of options. When difficulties occur, children very often try 'more of the same' or carry the options by guesswork. It is not often that they review what they have done, nor do they seem to draw much on their more general 'world knowledge'. In fact, most games do not encourage them to do so, often being soluble without any reference to wider knowledge and with the possibility of a quicker solution by random key pressing than by logical deduction, though there are exceptions to this. (See Chapter 7, for a more detailed discussion of talk around adventure games.) Some games are designed with the stated intention that they will develop the children's thinking in a variety of curricular areas. *Nature Park Adventure* makes such a claim, and has within it a variety of puzzles which are constructed to draw on the mathematical, geographical and biological knowledge of the users. Indeed, almost all of the extended discussion of the four groups of eight year-olds observed using the software took place around these types of 'typical school' problems. For example, the group in Sequence 2 above, later in the same session:

Sequence 3

1	**T:**	*(reads)* Little owl tells you to find tracks left by the rabbit
2		and follow them
3	**B:**	We got (...) tracks (...) footprints
4	**H:**	*(reads)* in the dark forest you can find the trog's secret
5		hiding place
6	**T:**	Oh on
7		Just keep going along there
8	**B:**	No
9		We're going to that thing now
10		So I know which animal we're getting
11		Rabbit
12	**T:**	Oh yeh
13	**B:**	My go?
14	**H:**	No
15		One down and one more down
16		Now your go Bobby
17	**T:**	(...) Harriet
18		Right
19		Blah Blah Blah *(as she looks at screen)*
20		We've heard all that
21	**H:**	Which animal tracks must you find
22		(...)
23	**B:**	Rabbit *(points to one of found paw prints marked A–D on*
24		*screen)*
25	**H:**	But is that a rabbit feet?
26	**B:**	Yes *(with stress)*
27		I've been looking for rabbit tracks all my life
28		Now I've found some

Although this extract is again represented by a tight IRF structure, **B** (a quiet boy in the group with two girls) twice goes outside the immediate information to draw on other knowledge. Firstly, in line 11, he correctly deduces from information earlier in the game that they will be looking for rabbit tracks. He then correctly identifies the rabbit prints (line 23) from a selection of four pictures of prints on the screen, and is uncharacteristically confident about his choice (lines 24–6). Even though he subsequently bows to **H's** decision to try something else, this series of exchanges concludes with **B's** assertion:

> I've been looking for rabbit tracks all my life.
> Now I've found some.

This is not an isolated example of the occurrence of problem solving through inductive thought and through drawing on wider knowledge, but there is no doubt that there are also many instances where the children fail to use these strategies, even though they would be appropriate, and in spite of the programmer's stated intentions and the teachers' claims that problem solving occurs. Consequently, there is little deviation from a rigid IRF structure, with the computer generally playing the initiating and the feedback/follow-up roles.

I will go on to examine sequences of discourse which, in contrast to the above, occurred while the pupils were using more 'open-ended' software.

Art Packages: *Paintspa*

The next sequence comes from the same classroom (and with one of the same pupils, **H** above) using an art package, *Paintspa*. The task required the pupils to draw on the screen a two-dimensional cardboard model of their ideal village (already planned and built by the whole class). The model was hung up on the wall in front of the computer. They worked for about an hour on this task. Their main difficulties are with manipulating the mouse and understanding the range of possibilities which the program offers (it is **H's** second time and **L's** first time of using this software, and they are unused to the mouse. They do not usually work together.)

Sequence 4

The girls have drawn the 'backbone' of their map – the roads and the river – but are now experiencing difficulties finding enough space to fit everything else in. **L** is currently working the mouse:

1	**H:**	Stop
2		We've made the river too big
3		It's not (…)
4		It's not that we don't have (…)
5	**L:**	We're not doing the er
6		We're not doing the river again
7	**H:**	Yes we are

8	**L:**	Oh no we aren't
9	**H:**	Yeah well it's still wrong
10		Looks it's too big
11		We'll have to do it again won't we
12	**L:**	No (…)
13	**H:**	Yeah Well we've got to really
14		Because look it's too big and we're going to have the
15		school there and the church and the church hall and
16		the block of flats
17		It's … too big
18		Yeah
19	**L:**	So we want undo do we
20	**H:**	No we want rubber

Here we have an extract which is typical of this session in so far as the computer has only a minimal (implicit) role in the discourse. The exchange is initiated by **H** (lines 1–4) who thinks she has found the source of the problems they are having in fitting in the buildings on their map. (In fact, the real source of their difficulty is that they have drawn the roads far too wide.) There follows an argument or dispute (lines 5–18), in which **L** first of all refuses **H's** proposal, and only accepts (line 19) after **H** has justified her suggestions. We have characterised this type of talk, in which challenges are proposed and may be justified, and in which the final solution does not represent a collaborative extension of the initiation, but merely the acceptance (or rejection) of one person's ideas, as disputational talk (see Chapters 3 and 5 for a more extended account).

Like the adventure game talk, almost all (approximately 95%) of the talk is 'on task', the difference here being that the nature of the talk encourages both topic-content-related and practical (computer control) talk of a wider variety, which is not constrained to an 'IRF' format.

The girls find using the program quite difficult and they make mistakes because of their poor understanding of the options available as well as some difficulty with the manual guiding of the mouse. But their talk is not initiated by the computer, at least not explicitly. Where the computer does play some role is where the child switches to a different program function. For example:

Sequence 5

1	H:	Wait wait wait
2		I'll put it to 'fill' and then I can see it
3		Fill *(clicks mouse)*
4		Now give it grey … grey … grey
5		Then just check there's no holes *(clicks mouse)*
6	L:	No
7		Come on let's go

What is different in these sequences is that the computer now plays the role of respondent, with the children initiating and providing any follow-up. The complications of the activity are under the children's control and rest entirely on their skills and their ability to resolve their conflicts and develop a shared understanding. These in turn will be in part influenced by the children's awareness of the appropriateness of particular discursive strategies, an awareness which can be increased by the explicit teaching aimed at developing 'talk skills' (for example see Chapter 14 and Fisher *et al.*, 1992). In this case, no such explicit teaching had taken place. The computer has only a minimal role in transforming what they do (for example, producing a colour change when they select it), and they must rely on their own representational and communicating skills to progress. In the adventure games, on the other hand, the children select from a limited range of options and generally have to press only one key (often the space bar). Not only is their decision making severely restrained, but also their manual input. The computer, in the games software, is generally the participant taking all the 'complicated' decisions, transforming the children's minimal input (generally a single key press) into attractive, dynamic and complex representations which are of a completely different nature from the original input.

Word Processing/Story Writing Programs

Also very open-ended, these programs share with the *Paintspa* program a need for some degree of expertise at keying in information. We have recorded them being used with children of a variety of ages, and the sequences I shall give come from two 12-year-old boys.

Mystery Island: This is a program which aims to provide a structure for children's story writing by offering a series of 10 picture outlines, to which the children can add their own selection of characters and objects. For each scene that they produce, the children are then required to write a text in story form.

Sequence 6

In the following extract, the two boys are writing a story which, without any explicit pre-planning, is becoming an adventure story. The picture they have composed is of a beach with a boat, two persons and some sharks in the water, but when composing their story they did not make explicit the role that any of these components would take. In this class the pupils often work in pairs or small groups, but the teacher had not, at this point, given any explicit instructions in strategies for discussion. However, the boys are friends and have often worked together. Neither of them has used this program before, though they have both previously used computers at home and in school, mostly for playing computer games, though one of the boys is a skilled 'typist'.

We join them as they begin to write the text to accompany their second picture scene.

1	S:	All right
2		What are we gonna say (…)?
3		How about
4		'When you manage
5		When you fi
6		When you manage to get back
7		When you mange to get back on the boat
8		You notice that you are surrounded by sharks'
9		What do you think?
10	M:	Yep OK
		(S types this in)
11	M:	(…) surround
12	S:	*(still typing)* by
13		by … sharks]
14	M:	sharks]
15	M:	And the sea (...)
16		What shall we put
17	S:	A sea serpent is across your leg
18	M:	Yeh … but you don't notice
19	S:	Well how can you tell them if you don't notice it is
20		(…) whether you saw it or not?
21		What do you think?

22	**S:**	(…) Yeh
23		(*typing*) A sea serpent <u>crawls</u> across your leg
24	**M:**	Mmm it sounds a bit better
25	**S:**	You knock it over the edge
26		Yeh?
27	**M:**	You <u>throw</u> it
28		That sounds better

In so doing, they are using what the SLANT team have characterised as *Cumulative talk* (see Chapters 3 and 6 for a description), which is talk in which an initiating hypothesis/proposition may be taken up and superficially restructured or added to (lines 16–8). They also challenge one another's ideas and discuss the justification (or otherwise) of some inclusions (lines 19–14), and in SLANT we have called this type of talk *Exploratory talk*, (Chapter 3, 4, and 5). They do spend some time refining their writing by changing the vocabulary (lines 24 and 30), but this does not dominate their talk in a way that has been reported elsewhere (Daiute, 1986) and as we ourselves have sometimes found with some younger children.

This sequence is typical of the whole of the one-hour session as either one of the boys will put forward an idea, the other may modify or refine it and they then quickly 'add on' that bit to their story. They do not at any time make an advance plan for the whole story – a fact which leads them into trouble because of the complicated nature of what they attempt to do.

I shall now examine a later part of this session in some detail because I feel it offers some interesting insights into one way in which the children's perceptions of the computer and its software may affect their views of narrative and their preferred ways of representing space and time. As they go along, one of the boys raises the issue of whether or not it is possible to write alternative story endings. He is familiar with 'optional endings' in computer games, and he enquires of the researcher whether the program will allow them to do this. However, the idea seems to arise originally from a *pictorial* aspect of their story (i.e. which way to move the boat, which is placed so that it is entering the picture from the bottom), rather than from any *verbal narrative* aspect (either oral or written) so far expressed.

Sequence 7

1	**S:**	*(typing)* which way will
2		you go]
3	**M:**	you go]

(This is the first mention of direction. Heroine in trouble; boat surrounded by sharks)

4	**S:**	Full stop
5	**M:**	That'll do
6		Forwards
7	**S:**	No (types in ,)
8		Right
9		How do you go up?
10		Oh there (types in ^)

(First indication that S has something other than verbal representation of movement in mind)

11	**M:**	Yeh
12	**S:**	Or up *(searches keys)*
13	**M:**	Or down
14	**S:**	Yeh but down is just going back to where you were
15		*(i.e. in the <u>picture</u> down is the direction from whence the boat came)*
16	**M:**	(...)
	S:	*(deletes ^, puts up hand and turns round to researcher behind)*
17		Excuse me
18		Do you know how to get it to ask which way you're going?
19		Then when you press the key it will go that way
20		
21	**R:**	Sorry
22		What do you want to do?
23	**S:**	Like if you put in the arrows *(types < >)*
24		You can choose out of those two
25		You can press either of them and then it will go
26		that way
27	**R:**	Are you trying to choose your own adventure?
28	**M:**	Yeh

29	**R:**	So you can have alternative endings?
30	**S:**	Sort of like a game
		(first mention of a game)
31	**R:**	Ah right
32	**S:**	So that you can either get killed by sharks or
33	**R:**	Yeh I know what you are wanting to do
34		That you have to do with a special program like
35		<u>Story tree</u>
36		This one doesn't really do that
37	**S:**	Oh
38	**R:**	Um
39		Unless you want to say well all right (points to
40		screen) make this one go to
41		Is this your second ()?
42	**S:**	Yeh
43	**R:**	Right
44		You could have three or four
45	**S:**	Right
46	**R:**	OK (2) and then you'd have to do page three being one
47		alternative and page four the other
48	**S:**	Right
49	**R:**	Do you see what I mean?
50	**S:**	Yeh
51	**R:**	But it won't just press on automatically
52		You have to put the numbers in yourself

[R = Researcher]

The boys then go on to write their story and to provide three alternative endings. They do not take up the researcher's suggestion of numbering the endings, not do they take up her later suggestion that they note down the 'page' numbers on a piece of paper. Once they have killed off their heroine for ending 1, they then have problems accepting that she can reappear for endings 2 and 3. One possible interpretation of this is that, while they are very familiar with the spatial displays which the computer offers, and in which time and alternatives can be spatially represented, they have greater difficulties with conceptualising alternatives which can only be produced sequentially (though had they made a paper record of their endings,

relating these to alternative options, perhaps they would have had less difficulty. They could also have drawn a branching plan showing their
alternatives). Yet these boys had no difficulty in reviewing what they had
done, and from discussing this with them afterwards, I could only interpret
their belief that they had 'naffed it' as being due to their inability/unwill-
ingness to accept the alternatives offered by the pencil and paper scheme.
This is not because they have never used the two methods together in an activity – in an earlier session they had been collecting data on paper to enter
into the computer database.

This seems to be an attempt of the computer's influence on what they
chose to write. I doubt they would have *chosen* to write three different endings on paper. However, it is the children's *perception* of the computer
activity in which they are engaged, rather than the limitation of the software *per se* which influences their talk and what they do. As with *Paintspa*,
the computer only constrains their talk indirectly, and its transformation of
what they input is minimal (far more so than they had wished!).

One further effect of their perception of the computer activity is their use
of the second person and the present tense throughout most of these transcripts. The use of the second person and present is common practice in
adventure game software, where frequent repetition of 'you are now …'
followed by direct instruction such as 'Go to…' seems to be aimed at
encouraging close engagement with the computer and a heightened sense
of immediacy. In fact the boys began their story using the first and third
persons, and even at the beginning of the extracts here when they are some
way into their story **S** asks 'What are we gonna say' (Sequence 6, line 2).
However, when he refers to the character in the story, although it is a girl
and his colleague is a boy, he uses the second person consistently from then
on (see Sequence 6, lines 2 ff.). In the same extract, line 16, **M** asks 'What
shall we put?' but uses the second person in line 18. However, **S** remains
consistently in the second person, and **M** too follows this in lines 23–4. This
use of the second person, initiated by **S** precedes his attempts in Sequence 7
(beginning at line 6) when he first shows signs that he is attempting to
transform his narrative version of what is going on into a *spatial* representation on the computer games.

One interesting question is also the extent to which these effects might be
gender related. Although we have data of girl-girl, other boy-boy and girl-
boy pairs, there are no other examples of a choice of 'branching endings'.
Indeed, when these boys are split and each paired with a girl, they then produce stories which are less dramatic (no one dies, for example) and are set
in a gentler and less fantastic setting with more traditional storybook language (e.g. the use of the second person singular, reported above, does not

occur in the girls' talk). In the case of both pairs, the girls' ideas tend to dominate and these girl partners are, at 12 years, bigger and seem both socially and physically more sophisticated than the boys, becoming quickly irritated by the boys' witticisms (this view contrasts with those expressed in Chapter 11)

Discussion

In these last two sequences we see the computer being confined much more to the role of a tool, albeit an influential one. We find discourse in which problems are explored, ideas are challenged and alternative solutions proposed, which go beyond the minimal 'next move' decisions characteristic of the talk which accompanies much adventure game activity. Even where the boys try to convert *Mystery Island* to a game format, the requirements of the software task are such that they must invent and structure their input rather than simply respond. As a result, there is no rigid IRF structure, but rather a series of exchanges in which it is often difficult to know who is initiating and who responding. What is more, where feedback/follow-up occurs, this may be from the initiator of the topic or from their partner and often extends or even transforms the initiation. The computer's role is confined to a direct, non-transformational response to the children's input, and it is suggested that it is this more restricted role which provides the context within which exploratory talk can occur.

The data from talk around other software so far examined supports this argument. We have recorded talk with pupils using other rigidly structured software (for example with 11-year-olds using the *Smile* program, which poses mathematical problems within a game format), whose talk is also characterised by responses to the computer's initiation and feedback in similar ways to that in adventure games, illustrated above. We also have data from younger children than those cited above using writing programs; for example, six-year-old pairs working with *Folio* and a concept keyboard to produce their own version of the Nativity story. Though, as suggested by Daiute (1986) these children spend much of their time focusing on relatively superficial aspects of what they write (the spelling, punctuation, etc.), they do make oral plans for their story at the outset (though they sometimes fail to keep to them!), and as they write they discuss possible content and appropriate vocabulary. Even younger children, still struggling with basic spelling and reading, can discuss the options available in an exploratory way, so that the computer is relegated to a responsive rather than an initiating role, at least until they run into difficulty. However, we have also found that the extent to which the potential for exploratory talk is taken up by children depends not only on their previous experience of discursive strategies, but also on how the teacher structures the computer task.

The data presented above suggests that the nature of the computer program will affect the talk which goes on among the children using it. What seems to occur is that the tightly structured programs significantly constrain much of the discourse which occurs. However, it should be pointed out that:

- not all adventure games lead to talk which is rigidly structured all of the time;
- open-ended software can lead to equally formalised talk, depending on how it is used and how children perceive the aims of the task;
- neither the programmer nor the teacher may see 'talk' as a primary objective of the program, though both programmers and teachers often seem to envisage shared use of the computer and so implicitly accept a need for some talk;
- children's previous experience of group work and the extent to which they have been made aware of discussion strategies will also affect how they talk together.

This research is still in progress, and we have yet to analyse other programs in detail. However, from our initial viewing of tapes, it seems likely that we shall find a definite pattern of talk, with the computer playing a participant role in the discourse where highly structured programs are used. Extensive discussions of an issue, initiated by the pupils, may be more common in 'open' programs, though it seems likely that the nature of the task for which the software is being used will also play a crucial role (Fisher *et al.*, 1992).

These results are compatible with the findings of Hoyles and her colleagues (1991), who found differences in the types of talk between pairs of children working on mathematical problems with two different types of software (*Logo* and *Spreadsheets*) and with pencil and paper. Although the Hoyles *et al.* (1991) tasks were all mathematical problem-solving, the nature of the medium affected the nature of an appropriate task, as well as the talk which ensued, so once again different strategies and talk might be expected.

The differences are not trivial, however. If computers, or other technology (including paper and pencil) are to be used to optimise learning, it is important that we gain an understanding of how they might influence tasks, not only in so far as they constrain but more importantly that we see which technology best serves which purpose. Vygotsky (1978) suggested that learning takes place first on an inter-psychological plane. The quality of discourse which occurs in the classroom is therefore crucial to children's development, particularly to the degree that it fosters the development and reformation of ideas. Where computers continue to be used by more than one pupil at a time, and where the software offers the potential for joint activities which will encourage a true sharing of ideas, they may provide a valuable medium for collaborative learning. However, as has been shown here, the talk which occurs at the computer may be of limited educational value. To facilitate talk which leads to exploration of ideas, teachers need to be aware of the importance of their own role in choosing appropriate software and in providing their pupils with a learning context which encourages and supports exploration. This includes providing suitable activities to accompany the software, as well as developing pupils' group working skills through explicit teaching.

Chapter 8

Children's Talk and Computer Software: A Response to Fisher

RUPERT WEGERIF

In this chapter Rupert Wegerif uses a mixture of quantitative and qualitative methods to reinterpret the Spoken Language and New Technology project data. He argues that the hypothesis advanced by many authors, including Fisher in the previous chapter, that there is a close link between the openness of software and its propensity to generate exploratory talk does not stand up to detailed analysis. This leads him to question and develop Fisher's application of the IRF (Initiation, Response, Follow-up) exchange model to the interaction between children and highly structured software. Wegerif argues that highly structured software can sometimes support children's exploratory talk and that when this occurs it leads to the educationally valuable combination of directive teaching software with children's active peer learning. As well as being a response to the previous chapter, this chapter can also be read as an introduction to the intervention study reported in Chapter 17 where the approach to using computers which emerges here as a possibility is consciously implemented in an educational program incorporating specially designed software.

Introduction

It is common to classify software, as Eunice Fisher did, on an open–closed continuum depending upon how much it constrains user freedom of choice (e.g. Newman *et al.*, 1989; Sewell, 1990; Underwood & Underwood, 1990). Having made this move, it perhaps seems reasonable to suggest, as Fisher does, that the tighter the control the software exercises the less active and exploratory the learning of the student. After all, there is plenty of evidence that when teachers use directive questioning pupil discussion is prevented or reduced (e.g. Dillon, 1990). Fisher is not alone in making this case, Anderson *et al.* (1993) present the results of a sophisticated statistical analysis of peer talk at different kinds of software to support the hypothesis that closed software prevents or reduces the possibility of valuable discussion occurring. In this chapter I use a less sophisticated quantitative analysis of a large part of the data collected by the Spoken Language and New Technology (SLANT) project to explore this claim further. The results lead me to question the transfer of assumptions that originate in teacher–pupil interactions to the area of computer–pupil interaction. Children do not relate to computers in the same way that they relate to teachers. This distinctive difference can allow computers to take on a new role in educational interactions – a role which combines structuring and directing children's learning with being used as a passive, and infinitely patient, resource for children's active exploration and discovery. Taking up Fisher's use of Sinclair and Coulthard's IRF (Initiation, Response, Follow-up) coding of the computer-user interaction I put forward a new possibility, the IDRF (Initiation, *Discussion*, Response, Follow-up) coding where an element of pupil-to-pupil talk is inserted into what would otherwise be simply a directive teaching exchange.

The Data

This study is based entirely on data collected for the SLANT project (this project is described in Chapter 1 and more details of the data I used are given in an appendix at the end of this chapter). The analysis in this chapter used video-tapes and transcripts of the interactions of small groups of children aged between 10 and 13 years over 25 sessions each lasting from 30 minutes to one hour. Details of the size and gender composition of the groups, the number of sessions for each item of software and the length of the transcripts are given in the appendix to this chapter.

In total, 13 different software packages were used:

SMILE: a mathematics package containing highly structured problem solving exercises.

Concept Kate, Nature Park, Hazard Rescue and Wizard's Revenge: all educational adventure games with problem-solving tasks embedded in a narrative framework and limited options given to the user.

Viking England: a historical simulation in which children role-play Vikings. In the most successful sessions, from the point of view of producing exploratory talk, they were role-playing Vikings raiding the coast of England. In a further session they explored Viking agriculture.

LOGO: a programming language used for teaching mathematical relationships.

Lost Frog: an authoring environment through which pupils can create adventure games according to a formula.

Bubble Dialogue: this uses a comic strip format and speech bubbles to promote discussion and to support role-play (see O'Neill & McMahon, 1991).

GRASS: a data-base system for schools.

Mystery Island: a simplified word-processing system with built-in support for pupils writing illustrated adventure stories.

Front Page: a desktop publishing system for schools.

PenDown and Caxton: both word-processing systems for schools.

The Key Usage Method

The SLANT project produced a large amount of data in the form of transcripts and audio-visual tapes. The task of exploring patterns in this data relating software features and features of children's talk, especially the incidence of exploratory talk, could clearly be made easier by the use of some quantitative measures. On the other hand, the understanding of exploratory talk, developed in Chapter 5, as talk that promotes the shared construction of knowledge, means that no coding scheme could be adequate to the task of capturing it. To assess the orientation of participants and the development of knowledge over time there can be no substitute for a proper reading of the transcripts and viewing of the tapes.

In Chapter 5 four levels of analysis were put forward as needed in order to apply the concept 'exploratory talk' to the analysis of transcripts. According to the third level of definition, the level of speech acts, 'exploratory talk' involves putting forward hypotheses, defending hypotheses with reasons and challenging hypotheses with reasons. In principle a coding scheme could be applied to the transcripts to count the number of times utterances served these functions. The ambiguous and multifunctional nature of many utterances (Draper & Anderson, 1991) and the large quantity of data involved would make applying such a coding scheme very difficult and time consuming. Given that a fuller interpretation would be required anyway because the functions named did not adequately define exploratory talk, this expenditure of time and trouble does not seem justified. On the other hand, a method based on the fourth level of definition alone, the surface features of the transcript, would not discriminate sufficiently between different ways of using words and punctuation. For example, a count of key words alone would not discriminate between words read from the screen, sometimes a high proportion of words in a transcript of talk around a computer, and words that were part of exploratory speech acts. It is necessary to look at the immediate context of each 'key word' to see if it is a 'key usage', that is to say, if it serves one of the functions given in the level three definition of exploratory talk: request for justification, giving of justifying reasons, putting forward a hypothesis. In this way what looks like a word-counting method is really a partial application of a coding scheme. Focusing on key usages made this partial coding much quicker, easier and perhaps less subjective than it would have been otherwise.

In English the hypothetical mode essential to exploratory talk is usually served by conditional tenses introduced by a limited set of words: 'if', 'might', 'would', 'could', 'should' and 'may'. Requests for reasons can be put forward in many ways but one common way is through the use of the question form 'why'. A limited number of words are used to link assertions with justifying reasons: 'because', 'as', 'for', 'since', 'if', 'so', 'therefore' (Thomson & Martinet, 1980: 285). Not all of these words were relevant for the given data. 'Therefore', for example, was not found in the children's active vocabulary. Sampling of the data led to the following short-list of usages being adopted:

- 'why' used as a request for justification;
- 'because'/'cos', 'if' and 'so' used to link justifications to assertions;
- 'if', 'might', 'could', 'would', 'should' and 'think' used to put forward a hypothesis.

One advantage of this method is that where, as in the case of the SLANT project data, transcripts are available in electronic form, searching for key words in their immediate contexts is simple, fast and accurate. In this case, search functions built into Microsoft Word were used. There is, however, specialist software available for searching for 'key words in context' (KWIC) and one of these software packages was used in the research described in Chapter 17.

Where there was a flurry of key usages, focusing in to interpret the talk almost always confirmed that exploratory talk was taking place. Exploratory talk not using these key usages is certainly possible but was rarely encountered in the SLANT project data. This meant that the method provided in practice a good indicator of the presence of exploratory talk and so a rough measure of the quantity of 'exploratory talk'. But it failed to say anything about the content of the exploratory talk and its educational value. Evidently this simple quantitative method has to be balanced by a qualitative analysis looking in detail at the content of the 'exploratory talk' detected.

Only pupil-to-pupil talk was analysed using this method. Teacher talk, which was found to include a high proportion of key usages, was excluded as were pupil responses to teacher talk. This condition led to a number of transcripts being excluded from quantitative analysis, particularly those with the younger age group. The set of transcripts available and suitable for analysis is not a complete set of the SLANT transcripts. The children recorded are all aged between 10 years and 13 years. (More details are given in the appendix to this chapter)

Results of the Quantitative Analysis

Figure 8.1 shows the results of the quantitative analysis of the available and usable transcripts of the SLANT project. The software is ordered along the X-axis according to the degree of user-freedom it allows. The broad distinction between directive software and open-ended software made by Fisher in Chapter 7 is relatively straightforward to apply. Directive software constrains users to a limited number of choices and often has a specific teaching aim within the curriculum. Tutorial teaching programs are directive in this sense as are educational adventure games. The most open-ended software, generic tools such as word processors or programming languages such as LOGO, allow the user considerable freedom in defining the paths taken and the curriculum ends pursued. However rank ordering within each group is much harder to establish. While a word processing package such as PenDown offers a greater degree of user-freedom

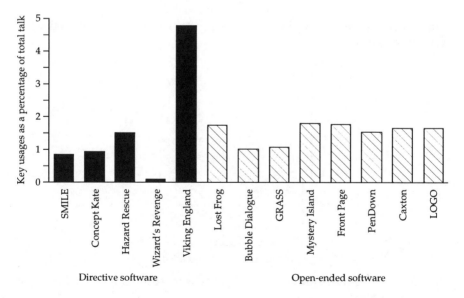

Figure 8.1. Results of the quantitative analysis of the SLANT data

than simplified word-processing software designed to support only a certain kind of story writing such as Mystery Island, it is not so evident that one can compare the degree of freedom offered users by a word-processing package with that potentially offered by a programming language.

The vertical axis shows the occurrence of the key word usages indicative of exploratory talk as a proportion of total word use. Even in the most exploratory talk this proportion would not be large. Continuous exploratory talk with 11-year-old children produced around 5% of key usages.

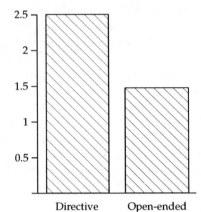

Figure 8.2.   Directive and open-ended software results compared with Viking England

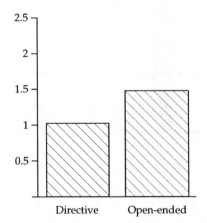

Figure 8.3.   Directive and open-ended software results compared without Viking England

Discussion of the quantitative results

The results presented in Figure 8.1 appear to contradict the widely held view that more directive software limits discussion. Software labelled more directive actually supported a higher proportion of key word usages indicative of exploratory talk than software labelled 'open-ended'. This is confirmed by Figure 8.2 which contrasts the number of key word usages as a percentage of the total talk produced in collaborative work at directive or 'closed' software with that at more open-ended software. The high degree of exploratory talk occurring around Viking England contributes significantly to this imbalance. In Figure 8.3 the results for Viking England are removed to show that without Viking England the percentage of key usages in the more directive software goes down below that of the more open-ended software.

It turns out that there are pedagogic reasons which might explain the anomalously high result obtained for Viking England. Viking England was used after the teacher concerned had taught oracy skills to her class (see Chapter 14), a decision taken after she had seen the first video-tapes of children failing to collaborate effectively at computers. The hypothesis that directive software limited discussion was put forward by Eunice Fisher before the experience with Viking England which shifted attention from the role of the software to the role of the pedagogy. Without the effects of this intervention the hypothesis that more directive software limits discussion would not be very seriously challenged by the quantitative analysis. With the addition of the data from the use of Viking England it is challenged and requires qualification. These quantitative results indicate that exploratory talk can take place in groups of users working with more directive software where some have predicted it should not. These results are not meant to be interpreted on their own. The method used is intended to help focus a more holistic interpretation. None the less the results do suggest that it might be worth looking in more detail at the distinctive features of the exploratory talk that can be supported by directive software.

The Structure of Group Work with Directive Software

Exploratory talk at more directive software occurs in the midst of 'closed' computer–pupil interactions where it could not occur in the midst of similarly 'closed' teacher–pupil interactions. Exploring further the reasons for these results sheds light on a distinct potential role for the computer in the teaching and learning process.

In Chapter 7 Eunice Fisher relates the structure of the interaction with directive software – particularly citing computer-based adventure games –

to the Initiation, Response, Follow-up (IRF) pattern used by discourse analysts Sinclair and Coulthard (1975) to describe interactions between teachers and pupils in classrooms. Although Sinclair and Coulthard's IRF coding of classroom exchanges has been criticised as an analytic tool, it is generally accepted as a description of a structure fundamental to classroom discourse (Edwards & Mercer, 1987: 9; Edwards & Westgate, 1994: 125; Elbers *et al.*, 1995; Mehan, 1979) and is a structure which has been transferred to a great deal of computer-aided instruction (Solomon, 1987).

In the following illustration from the transcript of a session with Concept Kate – an adventure game – two boys, Roger and Simon, have found an obstacle to their progress and decide to try to dig their way through. This passage was high-lighted for further analysis by the occurrence, in rapid succession, of several 'ifs' to put forward hypotheses, a key usage selected as indicative of exploratory talk:

Simon: Dig.

Roger: What can we do? What can we do?

Simon: To see if the grass is not that again *(pointing)*.

Roger: What can we do?

Simon: Just then we can see um um dig to see how if the grass is that hard.

Roger: No that's too hard remember.

Simon: Yeah but I know but that path is hard but we are going to be on grass. I (2) look if we go on there we need to get on the grass. If we if we walk in there we'll be on the grass, right? So we'll press dig to see if the /

Roger: Dig.

Simon: And then we'll see if the ground (...) now press dig.

Roger: *(presses key)* No, it won't work.

If we apply Fisher's coding we find that the exploratory talk which occurs here, involving both a reasoned challenge:

Roger: No that's too hard remember.

and a justification of the initial suggestion

Simon: Yeah, but, I know but that path is hard but we are going to be on grass. I (2) look if we go on there we need to get on the grass. If we if we walk in there we'll be on the grass, right?

occurs between the visual 'initiation' from the screen indicating a blocked path ahead and Roger's eventual 'response'. This illustrates that the apparently limited structure of interface dialogue does not, in itself, prevent the production of exploratory talk.

In this session the two boys took an exploratory attitude towards the problems they encountered but these problems appeared to be of too limited a nature to support extended discussions. The same is true for another session in which a pair of children used Hazard Rescue which also produced a quite high proportion of key usages without producing any extended discussion. The vast majority of the key usages recorded around both these adventure-game type programs occurred either singly or in the context of short dialogues consisting of only two or three turns at talk.

In the case of Viking England exploratory talk occurred in the same structural position, within a similarly closed interface dialogue, but, as Phillips and Scrimshaw point out in Chapter 6, the problems posed were much more complex. Figure 8.1 shows that talk between children working at Viking England had a very high percentage of key usages indicative of exploratory talk. Qualitative analysis confirmed extended sessions of exploratory talk between interactions involving the computer.

The computer-user dialogue with Viking England fits Fisher's application of IRF coding well. The computer initiated with questions, the pupils responded by selecting from a small number of options and were then given feedback, sometimes in the form of an acknowledgement and sometimes in the form of an evaluation. Pupil–pupil discussion occurs consistently within this framework between the initiation and the response.

This possibility is allowed for in Fisher's conversion of Sinclair and Coulthard's IRF coding to the context of computer use. Fisher describes the 'response' as 'any of the following: (i) a key press; (ii) a key press accompanied by an oral description of what is being done by the operator; (iii) some discussion of what should be done, followed by a key press.' Option (iii) describes the bulk of that exploratory talk which occurs between children working with more directive software.

The following extract from the transcript of a session on Viking England illustrates discussion occurring within an IRF exchange. Diana, Peter and Adrian are sitting around a computer screen which is displaying a choice of four sites on the East coast of England. In their role as Vikings, they must select one of these to raid.

Diana: Let's discuss it.

Peter: Which one shall we go for?

Diana: We've got to discuss it.

Peter:	There is one for each ...
Adrian:	And there's a monastery.
Peter:	Three (...) are unopposed (...) left in the area. So if we took / 1 we have got more of a chance of getting more money because
Adrian:	Yeh 'cos (...) over here and there's a monastery
Diana:	And if we take number 2 there's that monastery over there and...
Peter:	Yeh but, yeh, because the huts will be guarded.
Diana:	Yeh.
Adrian:	Yeh.
Peter:	And that will probably be guarded (2) and it will (3) and there will be.
Diana:	And it's surrounded by trees.
Peter:	Yeh.
Adrian:	And there's a rock guarding us there.
Peter:	Yes there's some rocks there. So I think ...
Adrian:	I think we should do 1.
Adrian:	Cos the / 'cos the monastery might be unguarded.
Peter:	Yeh 1
Diana:	1 Yeh.
Adrian:	1 Yeh.
Peter:	Yeh but what about 2 that / it might be not guarded. Just because there's huts there it doesn't mean it's not guarded does it? (4) What do you think?
Diana:	Yes it doesn't mean it's not. It doesn't mean to say it's not guarded does it? It may well be guarded. I think we should go for number 1 because I'm pretty sure it's not guarded.
Adrian:	Yeh.
Peter:	OK. Number 1 then.
	(Adrian keys in number 1 and Peter presses the return key)
Adrian:	No. You have to use them numbers. *(Reads from screen)* 'You have chosen to raid area 1'.

It is a little difficult to make out the content of the conversation because there are frequent references to information available on the screen which shows the features of the sites they are discussing. None the less I think it is clear that reasons for and against different sites are being explored co-operatively in a way directed to a rational agreement.

Applying IRF coding to the quoted transcript according to the rules suggested by Fisher in Chapter 7, the screen that precedes this discussion is the 'initiation', the whole of the discussion quoted up to and including the point where Peter keys in number 1 is the 'response', and the comment on the screen at the end read by Adrian is the 'feedback' or 'follow-up'. But such a coding would seriously misrepresent the interaction taking place by subsuming the sustained 'exploratory talk' of the children under the category 'response' as if it was simply an extended form of a key press. A more accurate coding of the educational interaction observed would therefore be: Initiation, *Discussion*, Response, Feedback (IDRF).

The Significance of IDRF

Previous approaches to the issue of stimulating and supporting exploratory talk with computers have tended to assume that the user–computer interactions stimulating exploratory talk need to be similar to teacher–pupil interactions serving the same purpose (see for example Baker, 1992; Cavalli-Sforza *et al.*, 1993; Cavalli-Sforza *et al.*, 1995; Cumming, 1993). This is a similar assumption to that underlying the 'open–closed' continuum hypothesis. Teacher manuals on facilitating discussion rightly recommend open questions and warn against closed questions (e.g. Dillon, 1994; Murris, 1993). Analysis of the SLANT data strongly suggests that this transfer of interpretative frameworks from the context of teacher-led education to that of computer-mediated education is misleading and that, given the right pedagogic framework, relatively simple and even 'closed' IRF type exchanges with instructional software can support pupil–pupil 'exploratory talk'.

The reason for this presumably lies in the difference between teachers and computers. Barnes writes:

> ... the very presence of a teacher alters the way in which pupils use language, so that they are more likely to be aiming at 'answers' which will gain approval than using language to reshape knowledge. Only the most skilful teaching can avoid this. (Barnes, 1976: 78)

Young (1991) points out that teacher questioning styles that involve eliciting answers from children tend to force pupils into the rather demeaning game of guessing what is on the teacher's mind. Young proposes, as an alternative, that teacher and pupil should engage together in shared enquiry. This ideal of epistemological equality fostering genuine discussion also seems to lie behind the 'philosophy for children' movement (Lipman, 1991; Murris, 1993). While it might work for the open questions of philosophy, such an ideal would make life very difficult for teachers in most subject areas where there is a particular curriculum to communicate.

The suggested IDRF coding for some forms of computer supported discussion combines two very different kinds of interaction. The 'IRF' part refers to the user–computer interaction via keyboard presses or mouse-clicks and the 'D' to the spoken pupil–pupil discussion. Where, as in the cases quoted above, the discussion between pupils is exploratory, IDRF also combines two very different educational genres. Taking the IRF sequence alone, users are passive and the computer plays the role of a directive teacher. In exploratory discussion mode, on the other hand, users actively consider their options using the information offered by the computer in the knowledge that the conclusions of the discussion will later be tested out with the computer. In this way the computer acquires the role of a learning environment. IDRF therefore suggests a way of informing subject area knowledge with exploratory talk through which children construct and own their own understandings by combining, in one basic educational exchange structure, directed teaching and active learning.

Conclusion

In this chapter I have taken up and developed further Fisher's suggestion in Chapter 7 that more directive software forces an IRF (Initiation, Response, Follow-up) exchange structure on learners. However, I have challenged her extrapolation from this that directive software must limit the quality of the talk of groups of users. To do this I developed a quantitative method for exploring the incidence of exploratory talk in an electronic database of transcripts. This method is based on the four level description of types of talk outlined in Chapter 5. It is used to support a qualitative survey of all available SLANT project data in Chapter 13 and is taken up again and further developed in Chapter 17. In this case the method was used to suggest that in fact talk at more 'directive' kinds of software was not less exploratory than talk at 'open' kinds of software. Focusing in on the kinds of exploratory talk occurring at more directive software led to a new characterisation of this kind of talk as Initiation, *Discussion*, Response, Feedback (IDRF). The IDRF analysis shows how groups at computers have a different potential to both individuals at computers, who lack the discussion element, and to groups working with directive teachers where peer discussion is less likely to occur for social reasons to do with the teacher's classroom role. So while the IDRF characterisation of group work at computers is a kind of coding scheme, it is also, more importantly, an analysis which reveals the unique pedagogic potential of this kind of educational activity. That unique potential is the possibility of enabling learners to actively learn for themselves while being guided within a planned curriculum. This pedagogic potential was taken up and applied in a further study the results of which are reported on in the last chapter of this book, Chapter 17.

Appendix: Summary of the SLANT data used in this chapter

	Total no. of words	No. of key terms	Key terms as % of total	Pupil group composition*
Bubble Dialogue 1	540	3	0.56	bb
Bubble Dialogue 2	2,880	12	0.42	bg
Bubble Dialogue 3	2,514	10	0.4	gg
Bubble Dialogue 4	1,150	4	0.35	gg
Bubble Dialogue 5	5,400	17	0.31	ggg
Total	12,484	46	0.37	
LOGO 1	4,600	6	0.13	gg (turns)
LOGO 2	1,600	8	0.5	gg (no turns)
LOGO 3	3,250	11	0.34	gg
LOGO 4	1,900	8	0.42	gb
Total	11,350	33	0.29	
Viking England 1	5,125	122	2.38	ggb
Viking England 2	8,000	143	1.79	gbb
Viking England 3	3,000	58	1.93	ggb
Total	16,125	323	2.00	
PenDown 1	900	3	0.33	xx
PenDown 2	3,450	18	0.52	xx
PenDown 3	4,500	28	0.62	xx"
Total	8,850	49	0.55	
Concept Kate 1	2,550	32	1.25	bb
Concept Kate 2	1,650	7	0.42	bb"
Total	4,200	39	0.93	
Lost Frog 1	3,250	11	0.34	gg
Lost Frog 2	3,800	11	0.29	gg
Total	7,050	22	0.31	

Appendix   (continued)

	Total no. of words	No. of key terms	Key terms as % of total	Pupil group composition*
Mystery Island	2,400	13	0.54	bb
Wizard's Revenge	1,900	3	0.16	bb
GRASS	3,200	7	0.22	gggg
Hazard Adventure	4,500	32	0.71	gg
SMILE	5,400	7	0.13	bb
Front Page	7,740	47	0.61	gg
Nature Park	600	1	0.17	gg

* All pupils 10 to 13 years old: g = girl; b = boy; x = unknown; " = same pupils as row above.

Chapter 9

Tinker Town: Working Together

PETER SCRIMSHAW AND GARY PERKINS

Peter Scrimshaw and Gary Perkins provide a detailed analysis of a short classroom sequence where two children worked together at a word-processing task. In the analysis they identify two of the 'types of talk' described in Chapter 5 and a third type of talk which they call 'tutorial talk'. They then use this detailed focus to explore factors affecting the type of talk produced and the educational quality of the children's interaction looking particularly at the expectations that the children have in coming to the computer and at the role of the teacher in shaping those expectations and the activity as a whole. In the following chapter this same session of work at the computer will be taken up and re-analysed by Joan Swann who demonstrates that a different, 'gendered', interpretation of the session is also possible.

If individual writing is a personal struggle, then collaborative writing is an interpersonal contest. For two or more writers to make meaning which satisfies each of them the negotiation is complex and socially mediated. Writing is no longer a separate language entity, resulting from an isolated activity. It is part of a whole language process, oral communication, dramaturgical action and the relating of self to others. Each writer must draw the attention of her or his peers to the reasonings underpinning: the selection of a word or phrase; the juxtaposition of ideas and arguments; the raising and resolving of a particular conundrum; the rejection of alternative voices ... (Susan Groundwater-Smith, 1993: 10)

Introduction

The primary teacher cannot spend much time with an individual pupil, so classroom conversations tend to be between pupils, with the teacher as an important but occasional contributor. A study of the role of computers in pupil talk is thus very often a study of how computers contribute to semi-independent group learning.

The 12-minute sequence analysed in this chapter comes from a session of around an hour, that is in turn only one of several sessions that the pair of children involved spent working together. Although on first viewing it appears to be fairly representative of their talk, detailed analysis reveals a rather different picture from that gained by viewing the tape in the normal way. It may be therefore that closer analysis of other, apparently similar, extracts may uncover quite different patterns.

In this sequence two children (who we will call Craig and Emma) work unaided with a word processor (PenDown) at a task set for them by the teacher and presented through a worksheet. The task, called 'Pioneers' was to describe moving into a new town. The name 'Tinker Town' was chosen by the children for this new town (see Figure 10.1 in the next chapter). The teacher (Gary Perkins) and the observer (Peter Scrimshaw) were interested to find out what happened when the teacher withdrew from the situation and let the pupils (using the computer and worksheet provided) define how the writing task was conceptualised and carried out. This experiment was part of Gary's general search for ways of encouraging the greatest possible degree of teacher independence in his pupils. By seeing what happened when the children attempted to work together completely unaided, we hoped to identify what help they needed from teachers to sustain successful collaborative learning. In the event the analysis also raises a number of questions about how children interpret the notion of working together, and the role of the word processor in collaborative writing. It also unearthed a category of talk (which we call tutorial talk) additional to the three raised in earlier chapters. These issues are discussed later in the chapter.

The Context

Emma and Craig are both 12, in their last year at a middle school. They were put together for this series of sessions because Gary thought they would work well together, and because Craig was one of the few boys in the class whom he thought would be willing to work with a girl. They are in the fifth session of the series, and had not worked together before the series began.

In Gary's view Emma is a highly spontaneous girl, who is always willing to take the lead. She is impetuous, talkative and, while still cheerful when things go wrong, does not accept that she might avoid mistakes by taking things more slowly. At the end of a previous session, for instance, she accidentally deleted the entire text.

Gary sees Craig as much more reserved, and also very much more knowledgeable about the technicalities of computer use. However, he is unwilling to assert himself, and though sometimes visibly unhappy with what Emma does on their behalf is slow to complain, pulling back and letting her get on with it. He has been regularly writing a very long story at home for some months, into his computer.

The computer equipment was located in the school's 'Shared Area', a large communal space available to several classes, containing work benches, computers, bookcases and chairs. Four classrooms and a passage to the hall and school office open onto the Area. Gary thought that it unusual that during these sessions the children (especially Emma) did not come to see him very often, and believed that this was because they were physically separated from the rest of the class, which made them think twice before coming in.

The equipment was set up on a rectangular trolley placed just outside the double doors into Gary's classroom. This had a wooden top with a half-width shelf fitted above it. The camera (and Peter as observer) were positioned a metre away, placed to have a partial view of both the children's faces and the screen. The BBC computer system was in front of one of the two chairs provided, with the printer and disk drive in front of the other. It was quite difficult for the children physically to share the use of the keyboard, so if they wished to change roles they would have had to swap chairs. In this session they did not (see Figure 9.1).

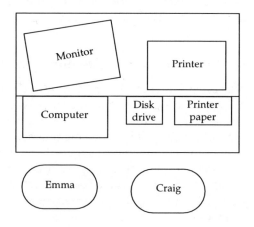

Figure 9.1 The layout of the workstation

This layout may encourage the children to feel that they 'own' one part of the equipment and thus have first refusal on the activities to go with it. It is after all very unusual for children to sit in front of anything in school that they are not encouraged to see as 'theirs' in some sense. In general the child sitting in front of the keyboard (Emma) did the typing, although the other occasionally leaned across to type something in. During the 12-minute period analysed below, Craig touched the keyboard only occasionally. Similarly, the worksheet which was kept on top of the disk drive in front of Craig was handled almost exclusively by him, and it was he who read out its contents.

On the other hand, the monitor screen was easily visible to both children, and was apparently considered a shared resource, each child referring to it as they wished. In that sense it appeared neutral in terms of ownership in a way that, say, one of their rough books (the other usual way of recording a joint text) would presumably not be; how often does a child pass their rough book to another to write in?

Although Gary deliberately did no more than set up the task initially, he potentially exercised an indirect influence over the session through the content and layout of the worksheet he had prepared. This had an introduction explaining the overall task, followed by a set of questions. In using the previous worksheet the children had taken a similar list and just worked through it, apparently assuming that following this sequence was essential. The result was that one major aspect of planning their text (deciding the order in which points should be introduced) was simply by-passed. It also meant that their using the word processor to re-sequence blocks of text around would be less likely. To try to prevent them simply 'working down the list' again, Gary this time laid out the questions in a circular fashion with no order of working indicated (see Figure 9.2).

Working together: Craig and Emma's interpretation

Earlier in the year one of us (Peter) had interviewed Craig and Emma about how they saw working together. The interview was written up from near-verbatim notes taken at the time. The notes reveal a complex view of what 'working together' involves. It was striking that neither child showed any hesitation in answering the questions, suggesting that they had either thought about the matter for themselves before, or that they had grasped and accepted the (considerable) importance Gary attaches to co-operation. They also had a definite (but only partially correct) picture of why they had been put together to work.

Question: Why does Mr Perkins want people to work together on the computer?

Emma: To see how well we work with people.

Craig: To see if we can get on well, so that if we don't work well he doesn't put us together for other things. Maybe to stop us getting bored and starting chatting and put each other off.

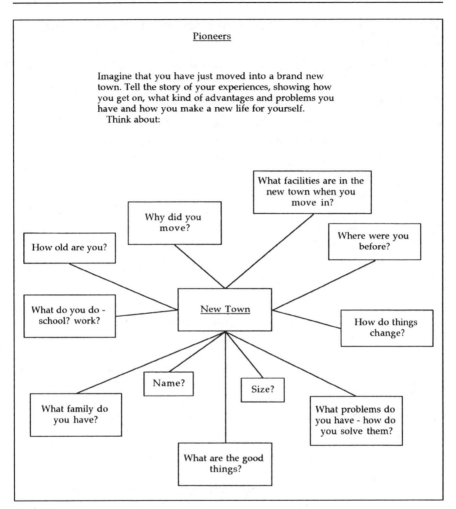

Figure 9.2 The worksheet for the activity

Emma: So we can put ideas together.

Craig: To help each other on the keyboard. You don't want one just on the keyboard.

Emma: Discuss each other's ideas. Showing 'how to teach' one might be good on the keyboard the other might not.

They themselves largely endorse the reasons for valuing working together that they ascribe to Gary:

Question: What are the good things about working together on the computer?

Craig: You can discuss what you are doing and get a better story out of it.

Emma: If one of us can't think of something.

Craig: Share ideas, make it into a new one.

Emma: When someone tells you fast and you're getting it down on the keys ... learning to use the computer.

Craig: Sometimes one does all the good things, like thinking of the ideas, and the other just sits there.

Question: But that could be a good way of getting the best story couldn't it, if one is good at things?

Craig: You're supposed to be working together, it's not both your stories if only one does it.

Craig is clear about what they are supposed to do: on the other hand, when using the word processor he tends to print out his and Emma's copies of the text with different fonts. He also often hand colours part of his copy thus distinguishing it from anybody else's. Perhaps he feels that this makes it more his own work? He has definite reservations about working together.

Question: What are the bad things about working together on the computer?

Craig: I like writing stories on my own, because I can get my ideas down quicker. I like to plan the ideas first. Sometimes I don't get on with the people I work with. I prefer to work with people with the same view.

Question: How the same view?

Craig: For instance they read the same type of books.

It is noticeable that in their joint writing Emma and Craig do not plan anything first, and during the composition at the computer they tend to move quickly to resolve any disagreements, rather than discussing them at length. Both of them are well aware of this, and have a clear rationale for it.

Question: What happens if you both have ideas at the same time?

Emma: We try to put them together.

Craig: We discuss the ideas. If one is rubbish we use the other.

Question: What if you disagree about which is rubbish?

Craig: Scrap both ideas, or try and discuss it. Scrap them to save argument.

The need to avoid argument, and the way in which this concern could inhibit Craig (the more advanced writer in the pair) came out when they were indirectly asked about the planning issue.

Question: Did you have an idea for the ending? When did you get that?

Emma: No.

Craig: I had a vague idea but I didn't think Emma would like it. We just do it as it comes one situation leads to another.

However, they are already at a stage of development where they sense that discussion is not argument, although they only characterise discussion negatively.

Question: Are discussion and argument different?

Craig: Arguing is mass rows and where you fall out with each other.

Emma: With discussing it you're sort of trying to get away from arguing.

Craig: Arguing is 'backing your own side and nobody else's' – like politics.

The pupils' view of the nature and importance of working together is, in this case at least, arguably the most important factor affecting the structure of the tasks and the talk that occurs around the computer in the section of the session analysed below. So how is their conception of co-operation instantiated in talk?

Two Old, One New: Three Kinds of Talk

As indicated earlier, the analysis that follows is based upon the transcript of an extract from a single session. Following this transcript is hampered by the fact that the children are dictating possible sentences for the text, reading similar sentences back from the screen and discussing the task, often all within the same extract. Clear cases of reading out from the screen are in quotation marks to aid intelligibility. Children and adults were often passing through the Shared Area, and sometimes their conversations were picked up by the microphone. For clarity these passages are deleted from the extracts below.

The extract analysed is taken from the start of the session. It contains a number of separable themes or topics of discussion. All the pair's talk is task-related, except for one external interruption and a short initial discussion on schools dinners. Some of the task-related talk is simple dictation of text by Craig, repetition of words by Emma as she types them in, or the reading back of the text from the screen by either child.

The text created during this 12-minute period is read out at the end by Emma:

Emma: 'Thank God we moved into this flat. Milton Keynes was such a dump I mean it still is. Tinker Town is a bit smaller than Milton Keynes but it doesn't bother us because this place is more neighbourly.'

While this may seem a rather modest product for 12 minutes' work, its creation actually generates a substantial amount of reasoned talk of varying degrees of complexity.

This falls into three categories that in part merge into each other:

- cumulative text talk;
- tutorial talk;
- exploratory talk.

Of these the first and last have already appeared in earlier chapters; tutorial talk has not, and its relationship to the others is something we return to at the end of this chapter. All three categories of talk are distinguished by linguistic features, by the conception of working together they appear to embody, by the different roles the two children take in each case, and finally by the nature of the reasoning that is present or implied in the discussion.

Cumulative Talk

By definition cumulative talk by-passes disagreement (and thus discussion or explicit reasoning) as there are no conflicting alternatives generated about which to reason. It is, nevertheless, clearly supportive of one way of working together, and meets the children's own specification that working together should avoid 'mass rows' and allow them to put their ideas together. However, the putting together here is very simple, involving no reworking of earlier material. It could be argued that this talk, because no reasons for proposed words are stated or asked for, is not 'reasoned' at all. On the other hand, it may be that the reasons for suggesting particular extensions are self-evident to both children, so are never stated. Only one example of cumulative talk (interrupted by a procedural digression which is omitted here) appears in the extract:

Emma: A bit ...

Craig: ... smaller

Craig: Milton Keynes ...

Craig: ... bit smaller than Milton Keynes

Emma: But it doesn't matter because ...

Craig: ... it's more neighbourly

Emma: Because this place yeah

Tutorial Talk

The second form that working together took was what we might call a tutorial mode. Here one child takes the role of the tutor and directs or corrects the work of the other. Unlike both cumulative and exploratory talk, the relationship between the children is not seen as an equal one, but one of them is mutually accepted as an expert relative to the other. Three substantial examples occurred in the extract, together with a number of much shorter ones usually involving Craig telling Emma how to change the screen layout of the text. Only the longer examples are discussed below.

In the first, Craig is reading out the worksheet to Emma. He stumbles over one part and Emma steps in quickly to interpret it:

Craig: Shall I read it out to you?

Emma: Yeah go on I'm listening

Craig: 'Imagine you've just moved into a brand new town. Tell the story of your experiences showing how you get on what kind of advantages and problems you make/meet how you make a new life for yourself. Think about why did you move what facilities are there in the new town when you move in where were you before how do things change what problems do you have how to/do you solve them what are good/the good things what family do you have what school do/you work no what do (*stumbles*) you what school work' (*Read in even monotone*)

Emma: Where's that '*what do you do school work*' on what do you go to school
(*leans across*)

Craig: I want to go/go to work

Emma: Oh that's all right

Here the tutoring is minimal, but it indicates some of the distinguishing features of tutoring. Both tacitly agree that there is a problem, and the tutee accepts and allows the tutor to propose a solution. The tutor has a solution and believes it to be objectively better than any the tutee may produce.

The second case of tutoring is similar, but the problem involves two spellings and a mistyping:

Emma: yeah oh yeah it doesn't bother because (*pause*) Em because it it is more neighbourly

Craig: Because neighbourly whatever

Craig: 'a', 'u', 's', 'e'. Because it's more neighbourly really
         (*provides spelling*)

Craig: 'i', is, 'i' is
         (*indicates typo*)

Emma: because it is

Emma: Now I've got that neighbour bit (1) neigh

Craig: How do you spell neighbour (1) How do you spell neighbour?

Emma: Neighbourly

Craig: 'n', 'e', 'i'

Emma: Oh no it's 'n', 'e', 'i' – yeah

This example shows that either Craig or Emma can initiate tuition. Emma understands at once what is needed and does not query what she is told. There is therefore no need for extensive discussion of each point.

By contrast, in the next case Emma has some problem understanding the grammatical difficulty that Craig sees, and he takes some time to formulate it clearly. The sequence opens with Craig dictating a sentence that Emma then attempts to extend (i.e. she goes into cumulative mode). However, Craig does not accept her extension. They discuss it and finally Emma sees what Craig is proposing and accepts it. As in several other cases, she signals acceptance (and thus closure of the exchange) by repeating the agreed formulation:

Craig: Milton Keynes was such a dump

Emma: Milton Keynes

Craig: It still is a dump (*Sotto voce*)

Emma: Was such a dump I mean well it still is yeah

Craig:	All right then (pause) I mean well (*Tacit query*)
Emma:	Yeah I mean well it still is well it still is
Craig:	A comma then (pause) otherwise it will sound like I mean well it is it still is (*Case for change*)
Emma:	still is comma / Right so I've got to put a comma up there then by mean (*Accepts problem*)
Craig:	You can miss out the well. Well I mean well it still is
Emma:	I mean well
Craig:	No you don't need to put that
Emma:	Well I mean well it still is. What so you want the comma there by well? (*Still confused*)
Craig:	It still is yeah (*Sees difficulty*)
Craig:	… it still is
Emma:	It still is

Here Craig needs to tutor quite carefully. Emma almost at once accepts that there is a problem but cannot grasp what it is. This implies that she accepts Craig's expert role; if he thinks there is a problem, then there is, even if the entry looks acceptable to her. However, both recognise that it is not quite good enough for Craig just to dictate the change and for Emma to type it in without any understanding. Craig therefore gives a reason ('Otherwise it will sound like, I mean well it is') but otherwise sticks to careful and emphatic repetition of the relevant phrase. Initially his approach is impersonal, pointing out facts rather than asserting his authority ('otherwise it will sound like') but he moves to a steadily more directive approach as Emma fails to grasp the point:

- you can miss out the well

- you don't need to put that

- No take the well off right

The final example of tutoring is difficult to interpret as it is not possible to tell from the observation notes or the video precisely what problem is being discussed, although it appears to be the way in which a misplaced phrase can be moved to the correct position on the screen. It is worth including because it demonstrates the existence of reasoned discussion that is intermediate between the tutorial and the exploratory modes.

Emma signals that she has finished the first part of the sentence, but in finishing it she has altered a phrase in what Craig considers to be an inefficient way.

Emma: I've dealt with that so that's done

Craig: You could have just moved 'this place' up *(inaudible)*

Emma: I suppose

Craig: 'When I moved into this place'
              (Reads from screen)

Emma: Ah

Craig: Just leave it

Emma: You should have told me

In this exchange Craig directs Emma's attention towards the problem ('You could have just'), but does not order her directly to make any changes. She accepts the implied criticism half-heartedly ('I suppose'), reserving the right to decide for herself whether to make any changes. She then attempts to make a change, possibly designed to meet Craig's criticism, and gets into a muddle. Craig immediately takes control ('Just leave it'). She then blames him for the problem.

Here although the dominant mode is tutorial, it is one in which the tutee is left in control until a serious error is made. Craig is here (as in the previous example) mirroring a teaching style in which the tutor is ultimately in control but chooses to conceal that fact for as long as possible, only becoming directive when there is no apparent prospect of the tutee grasping the point independently. Interestingly in this case when control is exerted, the tutee resists the implication that it was her fault (although not the tutor's claim that an error has been made).

Exploratory Mode

As we have seen in earlier chapters, this mode is one in which Craig and Emma propose ideas that are in some way not compatible enough to aggregate (cumulative mode), but are yet both sufficiently valued to make it seem inappropriate to just take one idea or the other. There is here then a disagreement of some sort for which they need to find a resolution. Four examples of this occur in the extract.

The first is fairly simple. They are trying to decide where their imaginary pioneer may have come from before:

Craig: Em what/something was so horrible what town can we use
             Oxford Cambridge

Emma: ... a totally useless/Milton Keynes *(laugh)*

Craig: Milton Keynes *(laugh)*

Emma: OK

This is on the borderline between the simply cumulative and the
exploratory mode. Because the question of the identity of the town only
finally allows a single answer, a purely cumulative response is not possible.
Instead Craig proposes a criterion for choice ('somewhere ...   horrible')
and offers two candidates. Emma ignores both, reformulates the criterion
and immediately she and Craig simultaneously think of a suitable choice
(Milton Keynes). This resolves the potential disagreement almost before it
has emerged as an issue. Here while there is no explicit stating of reasons
for the choice, these reasons can be inferred; they both think (or pretend to
think for the purpose of the story) that Milton Keynes is 'horrible' and/or
'totally useless'.

The second example occurs rather earlier in the extract, and illustrates
how an apparently very similar problem takes much longer to resolve.
They are trying to decide what to call the imaginary new town to which
their pioneer is to go.

Emma: Well what are we going to call it then Put it along to here so it's
             ready

             (moves cursor)

Emma: I dunno what the new town is going to be called

Emma: *(Giggles)* Perkins Town I'm only joking

Craig: What type of name would there be for a new town?

Emma: Newton Meads *(laughs)*

Craig: What's special about last year that could give us names?

Emma: Shall I get a brochure that we can we can

Craig: Oh don't bother let's just what could it be called?

Emma: Em the Realistic Town I dunno Em

Craig: What's a new town what type of things would they call them
             now then?

Emma: I dunno Oh they'd probably call it some dumb name like Tinkers
             Bridge.

             (a local estate)

Craig: Tinker Town

Emma: Yeah

Craig: Come on then

Emma: All right *(pause)* Tinker Town *(squeaks/laughs)*

Emma: Oh em yes

Craig: *(very quietly)* Tinker Town oh

Emma: Evil innit

One reason why this discussion takes longer is that initially they are conducting two monologues rather than a discussion. Craig is trying to identify a satisfactory criterion against which possible names might be tested, while Emma seems to be brainstorming to provide names to find one which feels right to her. When Craig does not initially respond to this approach she suggests getting a brochure to provide other ideas. (This may link back to the previous week's session, in which they had to write a guide to Milton Keynes for visitors, using a Development Corporation information sheet as a source of ideas.) This being rejected, she returns to the brainstorming mode. Craig meanwhile plods solidly through possible criteria, presented in the form of questions that may be directed as much to himself as to Emma. Eventually she responds and tries to link in one of her concrete suggestions to his criteria. On her second attempt ('some dumb name like Tinkers Bridge') she comes up with a suggestion that Craig then modifies into Tinker Town. They then both signal agreement with this, and the problem is resolved.

The third example arises from a more radical disagreement. Craig reads out what he sees as the next question from the worksheet, but Emma proposes that they deal with another question instead. (Interestingly the question she suggests was the only one that Craig omitted when he first read out the worksheet; possibly because it is placed rather differently on the sheet from the others.) The problem they have is how to resolve this conflict of agendas.

Craig: 'How do things change'/'describe how things changed'
              (Reading worksheet)

Emma: Look at the size though we've got to write about size We've got
              the name so we're

Craig: This is a bit smaller and a bit more neighbourly but you still have
              all the modern facilities

Emma: It is a bit/its a bit smaller yeah

Emma: I've got to make sure you agree with this because I can't write
              what you don't

Craig: It's a bit smaller than it's a bit smaller than

Craig's solution to the disagreement, here as elsewhere in this extract, is to look for a creative compromise. In this case he thinks up a sentence that actually answers both questions at once ('This is a bit smaller and a bit more neighbourly but you still have all the modern facilities'.) Emma signals agreement, by repeating the first part of his suggestion and adding 'yeah'. ('It's a bit smaller yeah'.) Perhaps because the point about it being smaller was her contribution to the compromise, she then emphasises that she is only writing what they both agree. Craig reassures her by also repeating her contribution only.

In the fourth example too they offer incompatible proposals and Craig finds a way of combining both:

Emma: Hello I'm here to tell you about Tinker Town
 (*Proposed sentence*)

Craig: No: God knows why I moved into this place
 (*Alternative*)

Emma: Or: No thank God I moved into this place it's better than the other place

Craig: Oh what and then it moves on so that they despise it and

Emma: … saying how they hate it

Craig: Yeah all right and how they despise the town after a while because they are going to have problems and that

In this case the disagreement is resolved by getting the character to have one feeling initially and then to change after a while. This is made retrospectively non-arbitrary by Craig offering an explanation for this change ('because they are going to have problems and that'.) Notice too that Craig's acceptance of Emma's idea as a starting point ('Oh what and then') is immediately followed by her endorsement, in a slightly modified form, of his basic idea too ('saying how they hate it'.)

Incidentally, this short outline by Craig of how the story might be developed is the only place in the extract where there is any direct reference to the story as a whole, or an explicit recognition of the need for some level of planning above that of the single sentence. This supports Craig's observation in the interview (see above) that 'I just do it as it comes – one situation leads to another'.

The final example is of a problem that has its roots earlier in the session. There Emma asks:

Emma: How do I put my name's something or other

Craig: No, don't mention a name be a boy or a girl

Emma accepts this without comment, but it leaves the identity of the main character undiscussed. Later it emerges that they are actually working with quite different ideas on this:

Emma: But it doesn't bother us

              (*a suggested phrase*)

Emma: ... yeah you have to

Craig: It's one person

              (*rejecting 'us'*)

Emma: All right doesn't bother me

              (*accepting change*)

Craig: All right then we'll have two of them I'm not bothered whether it's a family or what

Emma: ... it doesn't bother well we have to agree on this

Craig: have a single parent

              (*compromise offer*)

Emma: All right it doesn't bother us yeah us

Craig: (...)

Emma: Yeah me and in brackets me and the kids

Craig: We're going on to them later aren't we

In this case the urge to agree goes into overdrive, and the two children actually swap positions. Emma then again points out that they have to agree, and Craig provides an elegant solution to the problem of whether they are talking about one person or a family by suggesting a single parent. Emma attempts to reinstate her original family idea without cutting across Craig's preference for 'me' rather than 'us' by introducing 'the kids' in brackets. This move Craig neutralises without an overt disagreement by postponing their appearance until later.

Discussion

The first positive point about this 12-minute sequence is that the activity set generated a great deal of talk. Furthermore, nearly all of it was task-related. Of this, a high proportion was, in one or other of the three senses discussed above, reasoned talk.

There is also evidence of a mutual concern to adjust to each other's ideas, and sometimes the children were able to find solutions together that were more than the sum of their individual ideas. Craig in particular was adept at finding these possibilities. Between them they demonstrated a range of strategies for handling writing tasks, and they were able to select and deploy them very sensitively to solve the problems they believed themselves to have.

Taken together these strengths suggest that the children were able to reason together very effectively, up to a certain level. On the other hand, there were limitations in their performance, if judged against adult standards. These can be seen as reflecting weaknesses in task conceptualisation, planning and the handling of divergence of views. Each of these factors limited reasoned talk.

The task set was to produce a good story, working within the procedural constraints that Gary had determined, in particular that they work together, and use the computer. In practice they appeared to view a good story as a series of good sentences, chronologically presented and with a minimal plot. This approach excluded several levels of sophistication in composition, and with them the problems and discussion that these would have generated.

One way in which this conceptualisation revealed itself was in their view of the role of the worksheet. Gary had intended that they used the questions to trigger off their own knowledge about Milton Keynes to write a story, but they appeared to him only to have changed the names from those in Milton Keynes, and then just written about what they knew already. Neither was the effect upon the structure of their story what he had intended. Although the replacement of the list structure with a more random one did appear to prevent strictly sequential working, the questions were still worked through as they stood, and as individual items, rather than being a starting point for their own ideas.

This unquestioning use of the worksheet was part of a wider pattern, for their work was not pre-planned in any way. As a number of researchers have reported (see, for instance Daiute, 1985, and Bereiter & Scardemalia, 1987), the capacity for planning writing develops through the period of formal schooling, and one of the greatest differences between expert adult writers and others is their skill in and experience of, such planning.

In the case of Emma and Craig, their lack of pre-planning perhaps both arose from and created the view of writing a story that they appeared to work with. The obvious explanation for this absence is that they were unaware of the need for planning, but this was clearly not the case, at least as far as Craig was concerned. He was perfectly well aware of the value of prior planning, and in the interview with Peter he reported using it in his own stories at home, where he was engaged in producing a long animal saga on his computer, using ideas he had gained from reading *Watership Down*. The reason he did not use his capacity for planning in the classroom sessions we video-taped seems to have been a concern to avoid potential conflicts, and where a divergence of views occurred to resolve it as quickly as possible. This affected the story in a variety of ways. In particular, for both children it appeared to be the need to find a consensus rather than the demands of plot or character that led story development. Although both children were actively negotiating the text, when one of them had a dominant idea the other didn't challenge it sufficiently. The result was that there was little reasoned argument in the strongest sense, and the actual text was not shaped and revised as thoroughly as it might have been. This meant that Craig was working below his potential, and that Emma was at the very least denied the chance to learn more about planning writing from him; although in other more concrete contexts it was clear that both of them were willing and able to handle the sort of tutoring relationship that this would have required.

Tutorial Talk: Where Does it Fit?

Tutorial talk does not at first sight fit easily into the same framework as cumulative, exploratory and disputational talk. This is because all these three kinds of talk presuppose a perceived degree both of equality of status between the participants and of assumed knowledge. Taken together, these two conditions allow dissent and/or agreement about the problem under discussion but rule out deferring by one participant to the other. Tutorial talk, by contrast, assumes that, on the particular matter under discussion, one child is mutually agreed to be more expert than the other. In these circumstances what we get is a pupil variant upon kinds of teacher talk that might range from the purely directive and expository through to the provision of scaffolding closely attuned to the understanding of the learner. This suggests that one way to investigate this form of talk more fully would be to compare and contrast its use by children with its use by teachers, but in the event this was not an avenue the project team explored further, possibly because we were by then getting more preoccupied with exploratory talk in particular.

The Computer's Role

One striking thing that emerges in looking at this short sequence of activities is the difficulty one has in identifying any really distinctive contribution by the computer. If it had been replaced by pencil and paper what difference would it have made to the talk that took place? In this particular case arguably very little. Unlike (say) adventure games, word-processing packages are non-directive programs: unless children enter something nothing at all happens, and even when they do so, all that usually happens is that what they type in appears in print on the screen. In this respect, word processors act very much as a pencil and paper would do, for these are equally passive media. For example, like pencil and paper, PenDown does not signal mistakes as they are made (e.g. in spelling or style). The children therefore have to decide their own purposes rather than looking to the program to set these. Similarly, it is left to the children to solve any problems that arise as they attempt to realise their intentions, or to refer them to the teacher.

Of course PenDown, like all word-processing packages, can be used at different levels; as a simple electronic typewriter or as a more complex tool for altering the structure, sequence and style of a text. Used in the latter mode it is indeed a powerful tool for changing and developing writing capabilities. But the level at which the package is used rests with the children and/or the teacher. In this particular case the features that made the word processor much more than an electronic pencil and paper were never used. The reason has already been indicated; these higher level facilities are there to help writers plan, reorganise and improve the text, not simply to enter it and carry out surface editing. Because the children hardly ever moved beyond surface editing these facilities were never required.

The Teacher's Role

By deliberately withdrawing from the learning situation Gary made visible for analysis what the teacher's contribution might actually be. In this case, with the usual benefit of hindsight, this potential contribution appears to have three or four elements:

- to help the children modify their conception of working together to include a greater tolerance of disagreement;
- to enable them to develop strategies for handling that higher level of disagreement more productively;
- to endorse pre-planning as an important activity, even when using the computer;
- possibly to ensure that they were technically able to use the computer's more advanced editing facilities easily.

However, this leaves a number of questions unanswered. The first concerns the typicality of this situation. If working situations vary greatly from group to group, teachers cannot assume that their own contribution will need to be identical in each case. Observations of word processor use by a two-boy pair from the same class and of two other pairs of younger children in a second project school revealed four very different patterns of talk and activity that appeared to be related in part to the personalities of, and the relationships between, the pairs of children involved in each case. Furthermore, teachers' aims and assumptions when using word processors are very different, as work in the USA has demonstrated (Cochran-Smith *et al.*, 1991).

The second unanswered question concerns the practicability of providing these sorts of observations of classroom activities as part of the regular process of teaching. It is certainly possible for a teacher to set up and video such a session without an external observer, assuming the equipment were available; but the time required to view and transcribe the session would be considerable. If most of the practically useful information about talk round the computer can only be revealed through the analysis of detailed and very accurate transcripts, then the approach may actually be of little practical value to teachers researching their own practice in normal contexts. One possible way forward would be to look for easily identifiable indicators of the need for intervention that teachers can quickly pick up while monitoring a class in the usual way. Unfortunately the cruder signals (e.g. children visibly not engaged, or a lack of talk and keyboard activity) distinguish active from inactive groups, but are not sufficient to discriminate between active groups engaged in productive and unproductive talk. Nor (given the relative infrequency of exploratory talk, even in the sessions where it occurs most) will a short period of 'listening in' on a group's conversation necessarily reveal the real position either.

So how might teachers proceed? One way round the dilemma might be to take note of the conclusion drawn in several of the earlier chapters, that reasoned talk in general (and exploratory talk in particular) is probably far less frequent in most classrooms that might be wished. Given that, a reasonable assumption, in the absence of evidence to the contrary, would be that it was less frequent than desired in any given teacher's classroom. If so, the most productive approach might not be to work out very time-consuming ways of establishing its current frequency, but instead to look for teacher strategies that would be likely to increase it, whatever the current level. Section 3 considers this problem in greater depth.

Chapter 10

Tinker Town: Reading and Re-reading Children's Talk Around the Computer

JOAN SWANN

Here Joan Swann provides a substantial re-analysis of the session upon which Chapter 9 was based. When the first analysis was originally presented to the team two of the teacher members argued that it missed out a crucial element, namely the gender effects created within the boy/girl pair. Swann takes this divergence of interpretation as a starting point and, using a mixture of quantitative and qualitative methods, analyses the whole session to see whether there is any evidence of dominance in the data, how – if at all – such dominance is realised (i.e. what constitutes dominance in that context), and finally whether a dominance reading is compatible with alternative readings.

Introduction

In this chapter I want to present an analysis of a video-recorded interaction between two middle-school pupils working together at a computer. I became interested in the recording because there were two competing readings of the pupils' interaction. The recording had been made by a researcher and the children's teacher, Peter Scrimshaw and Gary Perkins, as part of their work on the Spoken Language and New Technology (SLANT) project. Scrimshaw and Perkins had used the recording to exemplify different kinds of collaborative talk. Their analysis is included in Chapter 9 of this volume. But other project members who discussed the interaction had focused on the issue of 'male dominance'. My own analysis below is designed to explore these potentially conflicting interpretations.

The 'dominance' interpretation can be located within a substantial body of work on language and gender. Interest in this topic has increased dramatically over the past couple of decades or so, with many empirical studies demonstrating systematic differences between the language used by women and men, and girls and boys. Gendered language use has sometimes been interpreted in terms of cultural differences between female and male speakers. Other researchers, however, have emphasised ways in which male speakers dominate in mixed sex interactions, relating their interpretations to power differences between females and males as social groups. (For general reviews of this work see Coates, 1993; Crawford, 1995; and Graddol & Swann, 1989. Maltz & Borker, 1982 provide an early statement of the 'cultural difference' position. For debates about 'difference' and 'dominance' positions, see e.g. Cameron, 1995; Tannen, 1996; and Uchida, 1992.)

There has been a parallel concern among many teachers and educationalists about the extent to which boys dominate various aspects of school and classroom life. In relation to classroom interaction, there is evidence that boys take up more physical and verbal space, take up more of the teacher's time and attention, make more contributions to classroom discussion, have more opportunity to develop their ideas and viewpoints, and generally have more say in what is going on. Such dominance may be achieved with the tacit support of the teacher and female pupils. (See Clarricoates, 1983; Delamont, 1990; Sadker & Sadker, 1985; Spender, 1982; Spender & Sarah, 1988; Stanworth, 1983 for general accounts of gender and classroom life; and Swann, 1992, for a review of studies of gender and classroom talk.)

Concerns about gender imbalances in classroom interaction have been social, to do with the use of language in the classroom, as elsewhere, to differentiate between girls and boys and to sustain asymmetrical relations between them. There have also been concerns in relation to the role of talk in learning: with the increased recognition of the importance of, particularly, exploratory talk for developing pupils' understanding it has been argued (e.g. Spender, 1982) that girls need greater access to classroom talk. There has been some discussion about male dominance in certain subject areas – in particular those areas in which girls are seen to have less confidence, such as science, technology and information technology. This forms part of a more general concern about girls' (relative) lack of participation in these areas, and a fear that certain aspects of classroom practice (including interaction patterns, the range of topics and activities selected and the content and presentation of textbooks, computer software, etc.) may contribute to girls' 'under-achievement' (Culley, 1988; Hoyles & Sutherland, 1989; Whyte, 1986). Given the SLANT project's interest both in talk for learning and in information technology, it is hardly surprising that, while the project itself did not have a focus on gender many project members were interested in this issue.

Much research on interactional dominance in the classroom has involved whole class talk in which pupils have to speak out in public, often competing to be selected to speak by the teacher. Male dominance in this context seems consistent with a (widely held) view of male talk as relatively competitive. Talk between female speakers, by contrast, is often seen as mutually supportive and collaborative; furthermore, small group and/or collaborative talk has been proposed as a strategy to counteract the dominance of one or two speakers and encourage more equal participation in the classroom and in other contexts (e.g. Claire, 1986; Holmes, 1992). This association between female speakers and collaborative talk has led me (along with a colleague, David Graddol) to speculate about whether the focus in many classrooms on small group/collaborative talk could be considered a process of 'feminisation' (Swann & Graddol, 1995). Such a process might be thought to favour girls, but we shared a concern with other researchers (e.g. Barnes, 1988; Fairclough, 1992) that the trend towards informal collaboratively organised talk in several public contexts (including the classroom and the workplace) may in fact depend upon and serve to uphold existing power relations. In one case, for instance, a re-analysis of a (highly collaborative) interaction between a young girl and boy who were building a crane together showed that the effectiveness of the collaboration depended upon the girl acting as an apprentice and acquiescing entirely in the boy's suggestions (Swann, 1992: 84–90).

When discussing the educational implications of gender differences and inequalities there is a danger in implying that gender is a binary distinction in which (for instance) dominant/competitive males and supportive/collaborative females appear as dichotomous categories. Empirical studies have always found a *tendency* for boys to behave in one way and girls in another. There are differences between girls and between boys, and the behaviour of individual pupils also varies considerably in different contexts. Furthermore, recent approaches to the study of gender, often influenced by post-structuralism, have emphasised the lack of fixity in girls' and boys' (and women's and men's) personal and social identities. Being a girl or a boy is seen not simply as a state but as something that has to be continuously achieved, often in interaction with others.' Gender, like other aspects of identity, is relatively unstable and often contradictory: there are different ways of being a girl or a boy; gender may be more or less salient on any occasion; and it may be played up, or down, at various points during an interaction. In line with such developments, research on the relationship between gender and spoken language has become less concerned with the itemisation of differences between groups of speakers and more with the question of how speakers 'do' gender (or power, or dominance, etc.) in different contexts. As well as acknowledging the complexity of gender, such approaches need to take account of the fluid and frequently ambiguous meanings of individual utterances. (These issues are discussed in, for instance, Cameron, 1992; and Crawford, 1995.)

My analysis of the SLANT video-recording is (necessarily) small-scale and broadly qualitative. I was not concerned with the establishment of definitive 'gender effects' (the data are, at any rate, not appropriate for this purpose). I was, however, interested in the detail of the pupils' collaboration: how they worked together to carry out the task they had been set, and in particular what aspects of their talk might have given rise to two arguably conflicting interpretations. In discussing the recording with the SLANT team, and in making my own analysis, I began to focus on three aspects of the talk:

- what evidence there might be of dominance of one speaker over another;
- how (if at all) dominance was realised (i.e. what would constitute dominance in this context);
- whether a 'dominance' reading was compatible with (an) alternative reading(s).

I shall discuss these points in more detail below.

Context for the Analysis

As Scrimshaw and Perkins explained in Chapter 9, the video shows one of a series of sessions in which two middle-school pupils, both aged 12, work together at a BBC computer using the 'PenDown' word-processing package. The pupils are writing a story about coming to live in a new town. Their teacher has given them a worksheet setting out the writing task and suggesting several questions to consider – e.g. 'what family do you have?'; 'where were you before?'; 'what problems do you have – how do you solve them?' (Figure 9.2). Within these constraints the children work independently – in fact one of the reasons for the activity was to see how they would work unaided by the teacher.

Scrimshaw and Perkins were particularly interested in the use of talk for collaborative learning. Their analysis seeks to identify different kinds of 'reasoned talk' and the relative value of these for collaborative work. They argue that the pupils do show a mutual concern to adjust to each other's ideas and are sometimes able to find solutions that are more than the sum of their original ideas; they suggest that the boy is particularly adept at finding such possibilities. A weakness in the talk is that, in this context, the children appear to view the activity of writing a story as producing a string of sentences; they are over-reliant on the worksheet, and they rarely plan large sequences of text. One reason why this happens, it is argued, is that the children wish to reach a consensus. When one of them has a dominant idea, therefore, the other does not challenge it sufficiently and there is 'little reasoned argument in the strongest sense'.

The children have been put together as a pair because it was thought they would work well together. The girl is seen as 'highly spontaneous' and 'always willing to take the lead'. The boy, on the other hand, is 'much more reserved'; although he has more experience of computer use he is 'unwilling to assert himself'; while sometimes unhappy with what the girl does he is 'slow to complain, pulling back and letting her get on with it'. There is some recognition of gender issues – the teacher believes the boy is one of the few in the class who would be willing to work with a girl. However, the talk is not seen as gendered, and there is no mention of gender in the analysis.

Two female teachers involved in the project, Lyn Dawes and Madeline Watson, interpreted the interaction rather differently. These teachers recognised that there were problems in identifying gender issues in a small sample of talk involving just two pupils, but felt nevertheless that differences between the girl's and boy's interaction styles were similar to gender differences that had been identified in other contexts: for instance, the boy was felt to take a dominant role, so that ideas dictated or sanctioned by him found their way into the written text. The girl played a much more supportive role and sought agreement from the boy for her suggestions. The boy therefore exercised greater control over the process of writing and also had a greater say in the outcome of the task. These teachers, then, saw the working relationship between the pupils somewhat differently from that outlined in the original analysis, and they related their interpretations to gender.

My initial reading of the interaction was similar in many respects, but as mentioned above I was also interested in the differences between the two readings. I therefore decided to look at the video more closely to see how the pupils worked together. I was interested to see what features of the interaction might have given rise to the two competing readings; how the production of the written text was jointly managed by the pupils (in particular, the extent to which one or other pupil had more 'say' in what was going on); and what each pupil contributed to the final text.

The complexity of the interaction meant that such issues were not straightforward. Identifying who had more say, for instance, was problematical. The pupils had to negotiate several different aspects of their writing task and one of them could, in principle, have a greater say in any one of these. They negotiated the content of their writing at the level of the topic they were addressing, and also at the level of which particular items of text they would use. They also discussed presentation (e.g. layout, spelling), and other operations they had to carry out on the computer (e.g. saving text). As they constructed their text they were also (re-)negotiating a working relationship with one another (which must have drawn on and had implications for their relationships in other contexts).

Because of constraints of space, I shall focus here on one aspect of the interaction: the pupils' negotiation of the content of their written text. Even here I shall be able to present only the beginnings of an analysis. I shall, however, draw attention to other aspects of interaction around the computer that merit further attention.

Negotiating Text Content

The video recording begins with the pupils coming to sit at the computer. This has been set up on a trolley in the shared area (a large area shared by four classrooms). There are two chairs in front of the trolley, one facing the computer keyboard and screen and the other to the right facing a printer and disc drive. The screen is angled so that it can be seen from both chairs (see Figure 9.1 in Chapter 9). Emma comes in first and stands by the chair facing the computer. Craig moves to the chair on the right and sits down. Emma then sits down facing the computer. The worksheet the pupils are to use is to the right of the keyboard and so nearer Craig. From where they are sitting Emma can easily reach the keyboard whereas Craig has to stretch to do so.

As they come into the shared area the pupils are chatting. Once they have taken their seats and picked up the worksheet they begin discussing the story they are to write. From this point there is very little talk that is not directly related to the writing task. For most of the interaction, Emma acts as typist, though Craig does occasionally reach across to type in some text or carry out some other operation on the computer. The interaction runs smoothly and the pupils seem to get on well together. They do occasionally challenge one another and there are one or two minor disputes over formatting, but these do not lead to serious breakdowns in the interaction. There is a more serious dispute towards the end of the interaction: it is break time, Craig wants to go but Emma wishes to finish typing in a final sentence. This culminates in Craig simply switching off the computer.

As the pupils discuss and write the text they frequently refer to the worksheet to see what questions have to be addressed. They identify and discuss a sequence of text, write this up and then move on to the next sequence. They rarely engage in long-term planning, nor do they return to discuss an earlier sequence of text in the light of what has been written subsequently – though they do, periodically, recap by reading out what is on the screen.

The pupils sometimes begin a new sequence of text by suggesting a topic they want to write about, e.g.:

Emma: What about the size though we've got to write about the size we've got the name

The topic may be accepted – in which case a pupil will suggest some form of wording; or it may be rejected, explicitly or implicitly.

The most usual way to begin a new sequence of text, however, is simply to suggest a phrase or clause for inclusion. Such phrases or clauses seem to function as prototypes: they may be accepted without modification; acted upon in some way (e.g. reformulated, perhaps after discussion); or rejected (again, explicitly or implicitly). The immediate acceptance of a prototype phrase or clause does not always mean it will appear (in some form) in the final version of the text – it may be superseded by a later suggestion. The reformulation of a prototype clearly gives rise to further suggestions which, in turn, may or may not be accepted. As an example of this process I shall look at two sequences, each running from the initial suggestion of a prototype to its final realisation on screen. The first sequence begins with a prototype suggested by Emma; the second with a prototype suggested by Craig.

Sequence 1: Development of a prototype suggested by Emma

(Note: The transcript follows the general conventions set out in the Note on Transcriptions at the beginning of the book. In addition, underlined text is commented on in the right margin and italics are used to indicate pupils' suggestions for their written text.)

Emma:	*and an extra large shopping centre to do all that shopping any day of the week* hmm <u>yeah</u>	*question*
Craig:	go on then	
Emma:	*(types)*	
Craig:	is it going to be a week in the life, or something	
Emma:	it's up to you	
Craig:	<u>no</u>	*quiet; (looks sideways)*
Craig:	[*to do all that shopping*	*(both read out text*
Emma:	[*to do all that shopping*	*as Emma types)*

Emma:	*whenever you feel*
Craig:	is it open 24 hours a day
Emma:	it's up to you you can
Craig:	oh come on then
Emma:	*(types)*
Craig:	*whenever you want*
Emma:	yeah *you want* sounds better don't know why

Here, the pupils have already agreed 'a big shopping centre' and this has been typed in. Emma recapitulates. She replaces 'big' by 'extra large' – this probably relates back to a previous suggestion, and is not followed up. Emma suggests a new prototype phrase: 'to do all that shopping any day of the week', with a question towards Craig. Craig accepts the suggestion: 'go on then'. Both pupils read out the first part of the text as Emma types, then Emma suggests an alternative ending: 'whenever you feel'. Craig queries this, accepts it then suggests an alternative final word ('whenever you want') which is, in turn, accepted by Emma.

Sequence 2: Development of a prototype suggested by Craig

Craig:	*the houses are nice* no *the houses aren't very attractive from the outside but they're lovely inside*
	(…)
Craig:	… *but lovely on the inside*
Emma:	*but once inside it's lovely* it's up to you yeah
Craig:	no
	(…)
Emma:	*once inside it is extremely* (…) *it's extremely nice extremely pleasant extremely attractive*
Craig:	*lovely*
Emma:	*extremely lovely* na *extremely nice* it's up to you (…)
Craig:	*extremely nice* that's a bit blunt really (…) it seems a bit blunt

Emma:	*extremely beautiful*
Craig:	why don't you just forget *extremely,* *it's lovely*
Emma:	*lovely beautiful nice*
Craig:	bye bye

(Craig puts index finger on delete button; Emma puts her finger over the top; Craig deletes 'extremely')

Emma:	*it is extremely*
Craig:	no we've just scrapped *extremely* just put *lovely*
Emma:	*it is a nice place to live*
Craig:	just put *lovely*
Emma:	*place to live* yeah do you agree or not *(types)*
Craig:	<u>yeah I agree</u>

slightly exasperated tone

Emma:	well I don't want to be writing things you don't agree with *place to* *live* full stop yeah

In Sequence 2 the pupils are discussing the second part of a prototype suggested by Craig, '… but they're lovely inside'. Emma offers an alternative formulation: 'but once inside it's lovely', which is rejected by Craig. Emma seems to interpret this as a rejection of 'lovely' and she makes several alternative suggestions ('extremely nice extremely pleasant', etc.). None of these is accepted, although Emma has typed up 'extremely'. Craig suggests she forget 'extremely', and he deletes the word. He then tells Emma 'just put "lovely"'. Emma offers a further alternative: 'it is a nice place to live'. Craig repeats, 'just put "lovely"'. Emma accepts 'lovely' as an alternative to 'nice', and checks that Craig accepts the remainder of the clause.

Sequences 1 and 2 illustrate a process of negotiation whereby initial prototypes are modified before being realised on screen. Sequences may be simpler (for instance when a prototype is written into the text without modification); they are sometimes more complex, running over several pages of transcript. In such circumstances, questions of ownership of the final text become problematical. What is clear is that both pupils take an active part in the interaction, contributing several suggestions for content. In Sequence 1, Emma seems to be making the running: her suggestions are accepted by Craig and Craig himself suggests only one modification (accepted by Emma). In Sequence 2, although Craig suggests the prototype, Emma makes several further suggestions. Most of these are rejected by Craig, however, and it is Craig who seems to have the last word on what gets into the text.

A preliminary analysis of the whole interaction confirms that both pupils play an active role. Table 10.1 below sets the number of proposals for text content made by each pupil, and whether these are accepted in some form or not. By 'proposals for text content' I am referring, in this instance, to specific items of text suggested by one pupil or another.

Table 10.1 shows that, in the text overall, a similar number of text items are proposed by Emma and Craig. There is a difference between the pupils, however, in that Craig's proposals are more frequently accepted by Emma than vice versa: 49 (59%) of Craig's proposals are accepted by Emma; 14 (17%) are not accepted; on the other hand, 36 (44%) of Emma's proposals are accepted by Craig whereas 25 (30%) are not accepted. There is a small

Table 10.1 Proposals for text content and how they are responded to

	Total text		*Page 1*		*Page 2*	
	Emma	*Craig*	*Emma*	*Craig*	*Emma*	*Craig*
No. of proposals	82	83	67	62	15	21
Responses:						
'accept'	36	49	29	36	7	13
'non-accept'	25	14	24	13	1	1
'ambivalent'	2	8	2	4	0	4
'no response'	16	11	9	8	7	3
other	3	1	3	1	0	0

Note: In this part of the analysis I have made no distinction between proposals for different types or levels of text item. A text item may be a clause, phrase or single word. It may be a prototype or a suggested rephrasing that falls within the framework set by the prototype. For instance, in the transcript in Sequence 1 above 'to do all that shopping any day of the week', 'whenever you feel' and 'whenever you want' would count as proposals for text items. Each of these is explicitly accepted by the other pupil. In the case of 'whenever you feel', acceptance comes after a very brief discussion. I could not observe any pattern in the way different types of text item are uttered, nor in how they are responded to.

number of 'ambivalent' responses – i.e. responses such as a comment on the proposal that constitute neither an acceptance nor a non-acceptance. Most of these are made by Craig. 'No responses', while not an unusual feature of the interaction, can normally be explained in some way. Emma frequently does not respond because she is busy typing; sometimes either Craig or Emma will propose a second text item, leaving no time for their first proposal to be responded to.

I have given a separate analysis for the discussion of Page 1 and Page 2 of the written text. The pupils save Page 1 before embarking on Page 2. There is, therefore, a break in text writing. Page 2 begins with a new topic – the problems of living in a new town – and it is marked by a change in the tenor of the interaction. Craig, in particular, makes a number of light-hearted proposals to do with things exploding, most of which are not realised in the final text. Craig then begins to look more tired and to switch off. He appears to have had enough – one of his proposals culminates in 'the end'. It also becomes clear that the session is almost over. In this context, proposals tend not to be explicitly challenged. Some prototypes are typed into the text with very little modification.

A closer examination of the types of text item proposed by Emma and Craig suggests that these differ in some respects. For instance, Craig proposes more 'novel' text items than Emma does: more prototypes and other items containing entirely new text. Craig does offer reformulations of text items, but these tend to be items that he originally suggested. Emma's proposals mostly involve rephrasings of earlier text – particularly text items suggested originally by Craig. While she contributes several proposals for text content, then, she tends, more than Craig, to operate within an existing framework. The fact that Emma accepts more of Craig's proposals than vice versa, and that Emma more frequently takes up and adapts earlier proposals, may contribute to the female teachers' perceptions of her as playing a supportive role in the interaction.

There are also differences in the manner in which Emma and Craig put forward proposals. For instance, Emma frequently seeks confirmation from Craig for the text items she suggests. In Sequence 2 she lists several alternative items: *extremely nice extremely pleasant extremely attractive*, which seem to require confirmation from Craig. One of her proposals in Sequence 1, *'to do all that shopping any day of the week* hmm yeah', uses 'yeah' with question intonation to seek confirmation. And in both Sequences 1 and 2 she actively solicits agreement from Craig 'it's up to you'; 'do you agree or not'). This is a common feature of Emma's proposals – throughout the interaction she frequently seeks agreement both verbally and non-verbally:

> *I mean well it still is* yeah   question intonation
>
> *because it is more neighbourly*   question intonation; (looks to C
>   and awaits confirmation)

> *I should do well* do you agree
>
> well if you don't agree tell
> me

Such confirmation-seeking is not a feature of Craig's speech.

While, for both pupils, the usual way of proposing a text item is simply to utter a phrase or clause, Emma sometimes suggests items that require completion in some way, e.g. the first constituent of a phrase, such as *including*, or the conjunction *and*. In this context such proposals result in Craig suggesting further text items.

Craig and Emma sometimes ask a direct question that seems designed to elicit further proposals from the other pupil:

Emma: Now what else?

Craig: What else could you have that was really expensive?

In the event this favours Craig: he answers Emma's questions but he also sometimes answers his own.

In Sequence 2 Craig formulates two proposals as directives: 'just put *lovely*'. This strategy occurs elsewhere in Craig's speech, but is not used by Emma:

> Miss out the *well*
>
> Write *in town*
>
> no make it three (big fields)
>
> just put *a vet* it's much simpler

Emma's use of questions and explicit soliciting of confirmation for her proposals, along with Craig's use of directives, provide support for the two female teachers' perceptions of Emma as frequently seeking agreement and Craig as directing ideas and exercising control over the process of writing. In this context they are probably also related to the pupils' seating position. As typist, Emma is not in a position to issue directives to Craig (or at least, not about typing in text). This is a possible option for Craig – although of course he is not required to issue explicit directives: there are many other ways of getting the other party in an interaction to carry out some activity. Also, as typist, Emma is checking what she wishes to type with Craig – which seems reasonable since the two pupils are meant to be working together. Again, though, such formulations are not requirements of the interaction.

Most of the negotiation over text items is verbal, but the non-verbal component is also important. In Sequence 2, for instance, Craig leans over and deletes *extremely*; Emma accepts 'just put *lovely*' simply by typing up the word. These are common features of the interaction, and again may be interpreted in the light of the pupils' seating position. As typist, Emma is in a position to accept a word or phrase simply by typing it. Craig cannot do this, so his acceptances tend to be verbal or to involve a non-verbal sign such as a nod. This difference no doubt contributes to the impression of Craig 'dictating' items that are incorporated into the text, and also 'sanctioning' Emma's suggestions.

When Craig does type (as in his deletion of *extremely*) he has to stretch across to reach the keyboard. This seems to constitute an incursion into Emma's space, and probably contributes to perceptions of Craig as dominant. Sometimes, as on this occasion, Emma accepts the incursion, but on other occasions she contests it:

Emma:	*the family of me and the two children* what are you doing	*(Craig formats)*
Craig:	you're going to get more on	
Emma:	no because when we do that it'll only just turn out one page and it'll keep printing what have you done oh what have you done wally	*(Emma places her hand over keyboard, and Craig removes his hand)*

In the analyses of Sequences 1 and 2 I've concentrated on the pupils' negotiation of the content of their text, but I mentioned that they also discuss other aspects such as spelling and presentation. Craig appears to be a more confident speller than Emma, and Emma also makes frequent typing errors. Craig corrects these – in fact Emma asks him to check her typing and complains when he does not do so:

Emma:	*Tinker Town is a bit smaller than* ah you should have told me	*(Emma types; discovers error)*
Craig:	go on I'll tell you	
Emma:	you'd better	
Craig:	carry on	

As mentioned earlier, Craig also seems to know more about using the computer, and gives frequent instructions on formatting, saving text, etc. (some of which Emma contests). These factors probably contribute towards the relatively dominant position Craig is able to adopt.

The pupils' different negotiating strategies affect not only the quality of the interaction. They also affect the outcome: the final content of the written text as this appears on screen. Figure 10.1 shows the written text, and also indicates which sequences derive from prototypes originally uttered by Emma or Craig. This information is summarised in Table 10.2.

Tinker Town

Thank God I moved into this place//*Milton Keynes was such a dump*//<u>I mean, it still is</u>//*Tinker Town is a bit smaller than Milton Keynes but it doesn't bother us because this place is more neighbourly and it's got all the range of modern facilities in town*//<u>including</u>//*an extra large leisure centre*//*twice the size of Bletchley Leisure Centre*//*three big fields for the whole of the town*//<u>and</u>//*a big shopping centre*//<u>to do all that shopping whenever you want</u>//*The houses aren't very attractive from the outside but once inside it's a lovely place to live*//*We have a load of extra conveniences*//*including*//*a garbage disposal unit*//*a fitted kitchen*//*a sunken bath*//*a den*//<u>with a smallish sofa</u>//*nailed to the floor*//<u>and</u>//*an extra large back garden*//*The overall size of Tinker Town is 27 miles by 21 miles*//*There are quite a few good schools in Tinker Town for Matthew and Rachel to go to*//*The job opportunities are really high*//*and as I have trained to be a vet*//<u>I should do well</u>//

Oh no, the garbage disposal has blown up//<u>Now what am I going to do</u>//<u>It's going to cost ever such a lot of money I can't afford to lose</u>//*Bzz Bzz oh damn, the electricity's gone*//<u>even more money I can't afford to lose</u>//*This flipping house is worse than the old place*//<u>I should never have moved</u>//<u>Mum told me this place was no good</u>//<u>I told her different</u>//*and now she can say I told you so*//

Figure 10.1 Final text keyed in by Emma

Notes: Prototypes are separated by double slashes //; italics denote prototypes suggested by Craig; underlining denotes prototypes suggested by Emma; the phrase 'an extra large back garden' is typed in without discussion.

Table 10.2 Number of successful prototypes contributed by Emma and Craig

	Emma	*Craig*	*Other*	*Total*
Page 1	7	19	1*	27
Page 2	6	4	0	10
Total	13	23	1	37

Note: * this is the phrase typed in without discussion

Of the 37 sequences identified in the text, 23 derive from prototypes originally uttered by Craig and 13 from prototypes uttered by Emma. The remaining sequence ('an extra large back garden') is typed in by Emma while Craig is looking for a pencil. These overall patterns of contribution mask a difference between pages 1 and 2 of the text. I mentioned earlier differences in the quality of the interactions concerned with pages 1 and 2 – that Craig, in particular, contributed several light-hearted proposals to the page 2 discussion then seemed to 'switch off' in anticipation of the end of the lesson. In this context Emma contributes a relatively high proportion of successful prototypes.

Negotiating a Working Relationship

The negotiation of the text of Emma's and Craig's story is inextricably linked with the negotiation of a working relationship between the two pupils. This latter negotiation is normally implicit in the interaction – it has to do with the ways in which suggestions for text content are made and responded to. I have already mentioned, for instance, Emma's use of question forms and question intonation to seek confirmation for her suggestions, and Craig's use of directives. Occasionally the working relationship itself is made more explicit. Emma, for instance, clearly sees the task as one in which they must agree about the text:

Emma: … I've got to make sure you agree with this 'cos I can't write (…)

Emma: … well we have to agree on (…)

Emma: well if you don't agree tell me

Emma: … well I don't want to be writing things you don't agree with

Emma: tell me if you don't agree

During the interaction Craig never mentions the need to agree, and occasionally seems slightly exasperated by Emma's insistence on this (I noted one example of this in Sequence 2). He makes only one comment on this aspect of the working relationship:

Craig: you can have ideas of your own

Craig is also keen to keep the interaction 'on task' and to complete the work. When the pupils stray slightly off task it is Craig who brings them back:

Craig: ha ha come on then we've got to get on with this

Craig: ... anyway let's get on with this

Emma and Craig seem to have different perceptions of how they should be working, or perhaps how they wish to work. In this context Emma's 'supportiveness', such as her use of question forms or intonation to solicit confirmation or agreement, could be reinterpreted. She could be viewed not simply as supporting Craig's ideas, but as attempting to impose her own definition of the working relationship as one in which pupils must reach agreement on the content of their text.

This interpretation is consistent with other aspects of Emma's behaviour. I mentioned above that she sometimes contested Craig's incursion into her physical space, and that Craig's correction of her spellings came at her insistence. On more than one occasion she refers to Craig as a 'wally'. And there are some examples of verbal banter during the interaction, in which Emma gives as good as she gets:

Emma: *fitted kitchen*   *(Emma reads out as she types)*

Craig: kiten   *(Craig reads, questioning spelling)*

Emma: I've been doing that all morning

Craig: You can't spell

Emma: I've just got an idiot next to me

These aspects of Emma's behaviour seem more compatible with the class teacher's perception of her as being spontaneous, and taking the lead than with the female teachers' perceptions of her as (in this context) dominated by Craig.

Discussion and Conclusion

The interaction between Emma and Craig shows the children engaged in a series of negotiations as they jointly construct a written text and also their own working relationship. Their negotiations involve the deployment of a combination of verbal and non-verbal strategies and, as such, illustrate the multimodal nature of talk. In any face-to-face interaction the interplay between verbal and non-verbal components will be important, but this may be of particular interest in the classroom when children are collaborating on some form of activity. In this case, for instance, the children contribute to the production of their text by suggesting phrases, by typing, by formatting, and by manipulating the equipment in some other way. Aspects of the physical context, such as seating arrangements and the placing of equipment, will affect what the children can do, or at least what they can most readily do.

I have tried to identify different aspects of the interaction and to show how these may give rise to apparently conflicting interpretations of the children's behaviour. Some elements of the interaction, in particular the negotiation of the content of the text, seem compatible with an interpretation that sees Craig as the dominant partner whose contributions are supported and sustained. I mentioned above that such ideas about male dominance of talk derive from an extensive literature on gender and spoken language use in classrooms and other contexts. It is perhaps not surprising that the two female teachers, who are familiar with these ideas, should foreground aspects of Emma and Craig's interaction that lend themselves to a 'dominance' interpretation, whereas the male researcher and teacher, who have different interests in the talk, should downplay or even fail to see such aspects.

There is, however, rather more going on in the interaction which makes a purely 'dominance' reading hard to sustain. The interaction exemplifies the by now well-established principle that indicators of dominance (or of anything else, for that matter) need to be interpreted in context. For instance, Craig may be seen as the dominant partner in the first part of the interaction in that more of his ideas are supported and eventually realised in the text, but it seems counter-intuitive to say that Emma becomes more dominant during the discussion of the second page simply by virtue of her increased number of successful contributions. The interaction also exemplifies the multifunctional nature of talk: it can be seen as a complex network of negotiations operating on several levels, which have to do with several different aspects of the writing task and, simultaneously, with the children's attempts to sustain different kinds of working relationship.

The two apparently conflicting interpretations of the children's behaviour, then, need not be incompatible: I have suggested that Emma can be seen as supporting Craig's construction of the text while simultaneously trying to impose her own definition of the working relationship. The collaborative and consensus-based relationship pursued by Emma does not, however, necessarily operate to her advantage precisely because in this context it depends upon supporting Craig's ideas, perhaps at the expense of her own. I mentioned earlier that collaboration between pupils in mixed-sex groups may be bound up with unequal power relations. This suggests that we need a more critical examination of the kinds of collaborative talk that are encouraged as children work together: it is important to consider more precisely the basis for collaboration around the computer, and what is being achieved as children talk.

Chapter 11

The Gender Issue: Is What You See What You Get?

MADELINE WATSON

In this chapter Madeline Watson continues to explore the gender issue raised by Joan Swann in the previous chapter. She first reviews research on the effects of gender upon computer-based activities to show that the gender composition of classroom groups has a significant influence upon group processes and sometimes upon outcomes as well. She then provides a detailed analysis of a single session in which a mixed group used a historical simulation program: 'Viking England'. This analysis demonstrates how gender effects can be investigated at the micro level of short sequences of group talk. Comparing the parts of the session in which the girl in the group was present and when she was absent Watson shows that the group processes altered. Sequences of talk from this same session were used by Eunice Fisher in Chapter 7 and by Rupert Wegerif in Chapter 8 to exemplify exploratory talk. In doing so they both made the implicit assumption that types of talk such as exploratory talk are gender neutral. Madeline Watson's detailed re-analysis of this same session from a gender perspective challenges that assumption. The question in the title, 'Is What You See What You Get?' raises the possibility that analysis in terms of types of talk can serve to hide important gender differences.

Introduction

Published research recognises the influence which differences related to gender can exert on the social and affective nature of interactions. Education is an area for concern about the effects of gender on learning expectations and outcomes. Sara Delamont highlighted the differences in educational experience for girls and boys in her book *Sex Roles and the School* (Delamont, 1990) and the work of Patricia Murphy highlights the importance of gender in performance and assessment (Murphy, 1991).

I became involved in the Spoken Language and New Technology (SLANT) project as a teacher/researcher with Neil Mercer. When I looked at the videos of girls and boys working together at computers I felt that what we *saw*, that is girls and boys working together to produce a piece of work or complete an adventure program, may not be what we were always *getting* in terms of an equal contribution by group members

I began to wonder if the girls were contributing as much to the outcome as the boys. Did the boys key-in more frequently than the girls, or were the turns equal? Was one member of the group having more say in what went onto the screen? Were the group supportive of each other's ideas and discussing them? Would a quantitative approach give the answer?

Deciding what will count as evidence of gender effects on group interactions is not easy. In classrooms a machine built for individual use may be shared by up to five children at once. This produces physical, practical difficulties to do with seating arrangements and screen and keyboard access. A group of children can be sitting in front of the computer seemingly fully participating in the collaborative activity, while one or more is so marginalised that they cannot see the screen or the other members of the group.

The seating and work area in front of the computer screen may be considered as part of the social structure of the group. How the children place themselves within the area may have an influence on the way in which they communicate and the work is carried out. If one member's position in relation to the keyboard prevents others from 'keying-in', this can influence what goes onto the screen, the educational experience of other members and the ownership of the finished product. Who will use the keyboard? Who will be able to see all the screen? How will it be decided what goes on to the screen and is 'saved'? All these matters have to be negotiated throughout the course of the work.

Gender Differences in Group Work at Computers

In *Girls, Boys and Language*, Joan Swann usefully summarises features of girls' and boys' talk (Swann, 1992). Some of the points are applicable to working in groups at a computer.

- Boys take up more 'verbal space' than girls, have more say in what goes on and receive more attention from teachers.
- Boys frequently maintain dominance by non-verbal means
- Girls are likely to talk less in mixed groups
- Boys usually make the most interruptions to speakers, and take longer speaking turns
- Girls in mixed-sex groups may miss out on their share of 'hands-on experience'.

Other research indicates that:

- Boys and girls have different interactional styles
- Mouse dominance plays an important part in group work at a computer (Barbieri & Light, 1992).
- Girls are more supportive and exploratory in the nature of their interaction within a group whereas boys tend to have a more competitive speaking style (Hoyles & Sutherland, 1989.)
- Gender may function as a status characteristic and exert an influence on the process of small group interaction.
- In mixed-gender groups males are more likely to be perceived as having a higher status socially and situationally than females.
- In mixed-gender, small collaborative working groups, males will be expected to be more competent and influential (Berger *et al.*, 1980).

Lee (1993) approached gender and group composition with the purpose of showing up broad patterns of interactions. The research produced numerical comparisons between different types of group interaction features. The children in the study were taken to a 'computer laboratory' and instructed to work co-operatively and make group decisions. One of the interaction features is 'task-related help', defined as a 'frequent exchange of and elaboration of task-related information'. This definition is an aspect of the SLANT category of 'exploratory talk'.

Lee found that when girls were in all-girl groups they:

- Were most likely to interact with other group members.
- Interacted more than twice as frequently as boys.
- Gave each other more task-related help.
- Made more frequent (1.356 interactions per minute) positive socio-emotional interactions compared to boys.

Whereas when boys were in all-boy groups they:

- Interacted less frequently (half as much) than girls did in same gender groups.
- Had lowered levels of 'total verbal activity' than when they were working in mixed groups.
- Received more task-related help than in mixed groups.
- Tended to ask questions and receive inadequate task-related help more frequently.
- Made less frequent positive socio-emotional interactions than girls (0.014 interactions per minute).

When girls were in mixed groups they:

- Were most likely to interact with group members in majority female and majority male groups but *not* in groups of equal numbers of boys and girls.
- Were more likely to ask questions and receive help from group members than were boys.

Whereas when boys worked in mixed groups they:

- Had a level of 'total verbal activity' which was much higher than when they were working in boy-only groups.
- Received less frequent task-related help.
- Asked questions and received inadequate task-related help less frequently.

These studies emphasise social aspects, including gender composition, as influencing the collaborative nature of work within a group. Whether ability and gender made a difference to a child's experience and the outcome of the group activity was investigated by Pozzi *et al.*, 1993. No significant differences were found and so style of organisation and pattern of interaction were scrutinised.

Three types of group organisation were identified:

- *fragmented* where there was usually a single-sex group, who had rivalry and competition with other groups and little co-ordination of group activity;
- *integrated* where targets were shared and considered by the whole group and one or two pupils dominated;
- *connected* where sub-groups collaborated and tasks were discussed.

Patterns of interaction were characterised as being:

- *'directed'* where one or two pupils dominated;
- *'mediated'* where pupils had equal influence;
- *'integrated'* where 'navigators' took control of 'global issues' and where one pupil – the driver – dominated local targets.

Girls were as likely to be directors, navigators or drivers or adopt co-ordinating roles, as the boys. Sub-groups in the least successful 'fragmented' style of working were all single-sex and antagonism with other sub-groups usually crossed gender lines. It is to the social system of a group that Pozzi *et al.* (1993) ascribe effective influences on the group organisation and thus, in turn, on the 'nature and extent of learning.'

The Viking England Session

A simulation program called Viking England was used by the class teacher Lyn Dawes after a series of lessons designed to encourage children to collaborate by thinking and talking together (see Chapter 14). Both teacher and researchers were pleased with the outcome, as were the children involved. This same session of work has been referred to already by Fisher in Chapter 7 and by Wegerif in Chapter 8. Through a re-analysis of part of the group interactions, I intend to illustrate gender aspects of group work around computers and show what these aspects may sound and look like when children work together.

The Viking England sequence of the SLANT data is interesting not only as it is held up by others as an example of good collaborative group work but also because the composition of the group is mixed-sex and therefore amenable to the question of 'who is doing what?' which I posed earlier. I have looked in detail at this sequence, because I felt that a program related to the humanities area of the curriculum might avoid any inherent gender bias which could be present in a mathematics or science program. Although of course the Vikings in question were men going on raiding parties!

Analysis of the Data

When analysing the SLANT data I first concentrate on the linguistic analysis of speaking turns, making a note of any characteristics of speaking style or contributions which have been associated with gender. This analysis can then be used to elaborate on working styles and organisation (as in Pozzi *et al.*'s study, 1993) or as indicators of group interactions in terms of Lee's (1993) measures.

A more complete picture of the background in which the Viking England program was used is given by Lyn Dawes in Chapter 14, so only a brief description of the classroom practice and the context is given here.

The Viking England sequence consists of three children working collaboratively in a group around a computer in the classroom. Particular emphasis was placed on making sure that all children contributed to final outcomes. The children were aware of the importance of sharing ideas and of taking collective responsibility for any decisions made when they were working together. All three children had worked before on the Viking program and two children, Peter and Diana, had worked together on other programs. Before the children started on the program, they had been given specific instructions, as follows:

Try and remember what you have learnt by doing it already … try and remember the best way and try to persuade the others that your way is the best way and give your reasons … and listen to their reasons and the whole group will decide … so whose fault will it be if something goes wrong?

The children replied 'Ours'.

The three children were of very differing personalities. These brief character sketches were given by the class teacher.

Diana: A good 'all rounder' who tries hard.

Peter: Very able. Rather isolated because of this.

Adrian: Pleasant, well-mannered. Could be aggressive and domineering with other children.

Diana was sitting to the right of the group as she knew that she had to leave for a music lesson.

I realised that it was not always the pupil who initially proposed an idea who had the final say in putting that proposal onto the screen and into the working of the program. In terms of keeping the talk going and working through the program it may not seem too important; however, one way of dominating or directing a group is to be the one whose proposals are taken up and keyed-in. It could be important to the collaborative nature of the group if each member felt that their contributions were acknowledged and discussed and accepted into the program. The acceptance of proposals could be an area of potential gender difference. If, as Berger *et al.* (1980) suggest, the males in a group seem to be more competent and influential within the group, one way this could be realised would be by having their proposals accepted or by taking other group members' proposals and offering them as their own and then having them accepted. A certain status could be afforded to the member of the group who always seems to make the 'right' proposals, i.e. proposals which successfully move the group onto the next stage of the program.

Note on the codes used in the analysis:

p: New proposals and ideas.

p*:   Proposals that are taken up.

s: Supportive, affirmative and confirmatory statements.

d: Directive statements.

dis: Where a differing opinion or disagreement is expressed.

w: Utterances (including mitigated directives) which employ the use of 'we' and 'let's'.

Sequence 1: From Viking England

(Diana leaves the group and returns with a worksheet related to the program.)

D:	Let's discuss it	**dw:**	*Looks at the boys*
P:	Which one shall we go for?	**dw:**	*Peter holds the paper*
D:	We've got to discuss it		
			Diana, Peter and Adrian read the sheet, Diana points to something. Peter reads out the information
P:	There's one for each		
A:	[And there's a monastery		
P:	Three () are unopposed () left in the area	**pw:**	*Peter points to a place on the map on the worksheet*
	So if we took / 1 we have got more of a chance of getting more money because		
A:	[Yeh cos () over here and there's a monastery	**s:**	
D:	And if we take number 2 there's that monastery over there and	**pw:**	*Diana leans over slightly and points to a place on the map*
P:	[Yeh but yeh because the huts will be guarded	**s:**	
D:	Yeh	**s:**	
A:	Yeh	**s:**	
P:	And that will probably be guarded … and it will … and there will be		*Peter points to map*
D:	and it's surrounded by trees		
P:	Yeh	**s:**	
A:	And there's a rock guarding us there	**w:**	
P:	Yes there's some rocks there so / I think	**s:**	

A:	I think we should do 1	**p*dw:**	
P:	Yeh	**s:**	
A:	Cos the / cos the monastery might be guarded		
P:	Yeh 1	**sd:**	
D:	1 yeh	**s:**	
A:	1 yeh	**s:**	
P:	Yeh / but	**dis:**	
A:	What about 2, that might be not guarded	**w:**	*Diana, Peter and Adrian all look at each other*
	Just cos there's huts there doesn't mean to say that it's guarded does it (…)		
	What do you think		
D:	Yes / but	**sdis:**	
	It doesn't mean it's not	**dpw:**	*Diana looks to the others – for support (?)*
	It doesn't mean to say / that it's / not /guarded does it It may well be guarded I think we should go for number 1 because I'm pretty sure it's not guarded		
A:	Yeh	**s:**	
P:	OK	**s:**	
	Number 1 then	**d:**	
			Adrian keys in
			Peter presses the RETURN key
A:	No	**dis:**	*Adrian points to far right*
	You have to use them numbers	**d:**	*of keyboard and reaches across and presses another key*
	You have chosen to raid area 1		
			Adrian reads from screen

P:	To alter this press number 3	*Peter reads from the*
	Which route	*screen*
	Diana	*Peter puts finger on key*
		pad ready to press for a
		choice

Diana makes a number of inclusive, mitigated directives (**w**) which direct the group into discussion. She makes the final, supportive directive 'I think we should go for number 1' which is keyed into the program. Although the initial suggestion comes from Adrian, as an inclusive, mitigated directive, 'I think we should do 1', it is Diana's suggestion which is supported by the two boys and Peter's directive 'OK, number one then' which ensures that decision is keyed in.

All three members of the group use the words 'we' and 'us', indicating that they see themselves working together. Adrian refers to '… a rock guarding us …'. Adrian makes the direct request for an opinion from the other two. 'What do you think?' but Diana uses the inclusive pronouns most often.

Although there is one occasion when all the children look towards each other, Diana twice not only looks at the boys but engages in eye-contact.

'Yeh' is used as a confirmatory expression, that is agreeing with what has been said or decided and as supporting an idea or proposal. Peter makes a supportive 'yeh' to Adrian's proposal and Diana makes a supportive 'yes' to Peter's proposal for '2', otherwise 'yeh' is used as confirmation.

Diana does not touch the keyboard during this sequence but both Peter and Adrian do. Peter reads from the worksheet and the screen and frequently points to places on the map on the worksheet.

The group go on to discuss which would be the most appropriate route to take, whether they would be attacked and whether they would run out of food. Diana asks the boys why they are choosing different routes. The boys justify their choices. All three members of the group are looking at the screen and pointing to the map on the screen. Peter suggests choice 'A' but Diana puts up good reasons why not, so then Peter changes the suggestion to choice 'B' and all agree, Diana having the final 'yeh'. Diana leans across to type in 'B' but Adrian puts his hand across and presses the letter.

This first sequence shows the group giving support for each other's ideas and Diana using mitigated directives to navigate the group. The pattern of interaction in the next sequence is different and no one makes any clear supportive statements.

Sequence 2: The number of horses taken on a Viking raid has to be decided

A:	Number of	**d:**	
	Horses now		
P:	No no	**dis:**	
A:	[and take		
P:	[camping equipment		*Peter reaches up and touches the screen – points to text*
A:	Take 17 yeh	**p:**	
P:	[cos horses		
A:	cos horses aren't very important	**sd:**	
	Yeh		
	but about 17 camping equipment. Yeh		
D:	Why		*Diana looks across at Adrian*
P:	Why	**p:**	*Peter looks across at Adrian*
	I'd say about 16		
D:	Why		*Peter and Adrian don't look at Diana when she speaks. Diana looks at Peter and Adrian*
P:	So you'll have a decent amount of horses		*Peter reaches up and points at the screen, then looks at Diana*
D:	You can have 4 horses	**d:**	*Looks at Peter. Peter looks down*
			Adrian looks at the screen
A:	Last time when our group took 17 equipment for camping		
	We / we um done well		

P:	Yes well to be on the safe side don't you think we should take more	**sp:**	*Looks at Adrian*
D:	18	**p:**	
A:	But then we only get 2 horses	**dis:**	
P:	14	**p:**	
A:	15	**p*:**	
P:	14	**p:**	*Stares hard at Adrian*
D:	Fif		
P:	Fifteen	**p:**	*Diana points at screen*
D:	[Fourteen cos its	**p:**	*Adrian keys in a number*
	[to be on the safe side.		
	Then we could have 5 units of horses		
A:	15	**p:**	
P:	Yeh but	**s dis:**	*Diana presses key*
	It says on the information Sheet		
	[3 units		
A:	[oh yeh		
	one horse takes 3 units of food		
	15		*Adrian puts his hand under Diana's and presses a key*
P:	It takes () units of space		*Diana presses 2 keys and looks at the screen*
			Adrian reaches across and presses RETURN
	So now all we've got		*Peter points to the screen*
	we'll only have one horse for each boat cos this says one horse		*Peter holds up worksheet and Diana looks at it*
A:	15 horses		*Adrian, Diana, Peter look at the screen*
			All three are silent as they look at the screen. Diana smiles

P:	It doesn't matter	**d:**	*Looks at Adrian who*
	So we take 5 units	**d:**	*laughs lightly*
			Looks at Diana
D:	That won't be enough		*Peter looks at Diana*
	Say we get attacked and we'd have to get another one wouldn't we		
A:	Oh no		*All look at the screen*
P:	Oh no	**d:**	*Peter points to the screen,*
A:	So / 3	**d:**	*then presses keys*
	15 horses	**dis:**	*Peter pressing keys*
	ENTER	**dis:**	*Adrian looks at screen*
	Oh no		*Leans back in his chair*
	Oh no		
D:	Stop because we got to finish loading	**d:**	*Diana reaches across and presses a key*
			All three look at the screen
			Peter presses a key
			Diana puts her hand to her mouth

The group go on looking at the screen to watch their progress. They wait to see how many days it will take them to cross the sea. Diana reads the worksheet and points to places on the screen. Peter points to landing areas on the screen and uses the phrase '… so I'd say' to make his point and propose action.

Detailed analysis

Peter and Adrian each individually speak more than Diana, and Peter is the most voluble of the group. Diana queries decisions ('Why?') and directs the group to carry out the teacher's instructions to 'discuss' it. (The number of times that she says 'Why?' becomes a joke between them).

Adrian makes the final decision on the number of horses by reaching across and keying in the number. It is Adrian's proposal which reaches the screen, but it is Diana who keeps the discussion going, exploring all the possibilities. By not accepting the first option voiced, Diana had approached the task in the way in which their teacher had asked the group to.

The word 'yeh' is used by Peter and Adrian to indicate confirmation or agreement with a previous statement made by themselves. When 'yeh' is used to support a suggestion, it is used by Peter in agreement prior to disagreeing with Adrian.

Instances of interruptions are by Peter to Diana and to Adrian and by Adrian to Peter.

Peter is very enthusiastic about the program and frequently points to or touches the screen and reads from the screen and worksheet.

Diana had been supportive not only of the teacher but of the situation. Through questioning decisions (she actually says 'discuss it, discuss it' at one point) and seeking agreement between the group, Diana tries to steer the group to come to collective decisions, as they had been requested to do. By engaging in 'cumulative talk', Diana played a leading role in keeping the discussions going and making sure that group decisions were made. Diana uses 'we' as a mitigative directive and she uses talk to hold or 'glue' the group together and thus keep the collaboration effective.

If the girl in the 'Viking' sequence had fulfilled the supportive role which research (cf. Swann, 1992 and Lee, 1993) has indicated, she would contribute more of the supportive statements than the boys. In the sequences chosen, Diana supports the group to carry out the teacher's instructions and encourages them to discuss decisions. Peter's confirmatory statements in conjunction with mitigated directives and the phrase '... well I think' seem to be used by him to direct the group decisions. .

Sequence 3: Diana has left the group

P:	We are going to have to do the discussing by ourselves	w:	*Peter moves his chair nearer to Adrian and leans towards the keyboard*
A:	Oops		*Adrian is pressing keys*
			Peter goes to press a key but Adrian's hand is there first. Peter's hand over Adrian's hand.
			Both boys look at the screen
			Adrian presses a key then Peter presses a key
P:	It takes 4 days to reach the target in battle		*Reading from the screen*
	30		*Leans forward and touches the screen*

	You lose 8 men		
	That's not bad.		*Peter presses a key*
	C		
	Your camp is attacked		
	Woe – look damaged!		*Peter touches the screen*
	No		
	Man killed – 5		*Both boys are leaning forward looking at the screen*
	Men injured – 5		*Peter removes hand from screen*
	Defence high priority		*Peter turns to speak to Adrian*
	Sacked property as well		
A:	Yeh	**s:**	*Peter presses a key and looks around over his shoulder*
	5 men killed so we still have 95 left on guard		*Adrian reading from screen*
P:	Yeh	**s:**	
A:	That's good		
P:	Yeh	**s:**	*Peter sits upright and touches*
	but we have injured 10		*screen then looks at Adrian*
	That's 85 left		*Peter sits back*
A:	Yeh	**s:**	
P:	So / let's see then/		*Adrian presses keys*
	Underestimated (...) 2 days		*Peter reading from screen*
A:	To s (...)		
P	I'd say we sail to another area		
A:	Yeh ()	**s:**	*Adrian looks at Peter*
P:	Wha ... What about scouting again?	**p:**	*Peter points to the screen and looks round over Adrian's shoulder*
A:	No	**dis:**	

	We might lose too many more men		
P:	Yeh so I'd say /	**s:**	
	Let's scout again yeh North	**p:**	*Peter leans forward and presses a key*
A:	No	**dis:**	
P:	M		*Peter starts to read from screen*
	You have decided to break camp		
	It takes three days to break camp		*Adrian presses key*
	You have 47 days left		
	Press C		
A:	I		*Adrian looks at Peter*
P:	Hang [on /nor		*then both boys look at the screen*
	[sail / Nor		*Peter nods his head*
P:	Just press once /	**d:**	
	And again	**d:**	
	Yeh!		*Peter sits up and touches the screen*
A:	Yes!		

The boys continue a similar pattern of interaction. Peter leans forward and touches the screen, following the route of their journey, Adrian says 'yeh' frequently and Peter uses the phrase 'so I'd say' when making a suggestion or decision for action.

Detailed analysis

In the third sequence, there is a striking difference between the quality of the interaction between the two boys without Diana. The boys don't discuss proposals in depth. When Adrian disagrees about scouting again and gives a single reason, Peter sticks to his own proposal and presses the key to 'scout again'. When Adrian suggests they 'hang on' because he wants to consider the consequences of 'I', Peter directs him to press a key. There is little reasoned discussion of the kind which took place when Diana was present. The difference in interactional style once the girl has left the group is difficult to explain solely in terms of numbers in the group, since Peter and Diana have quite long discussions over decisions on more than one occasion, as do Adrian and Diana. This evidence supports Lee's (1993) finding that boys in all-boy groups have a lowered level of 'total verbal activity' and positive socio-emotional interactions.

The boys look mainly at the screen and rarely look at each other. Peter is interacting more with the computer than with Adrian and looks directly at Adrian twice. Peter frequently points to or touches the screen and directs the activity. On three occasions Adrian presses keys on Peter's instruction. When reading from the screen, Peter leans forward and scrolls the screen to suit his reading pace and decisions. Adrian makes the most confirmatory utterances and frequently turns to Peter when speaking.

Discussion and Conclusion

In the Viking sequences, it is not always the *initial* proposer who finally makes the last proposal before acceptance. For example: Adrian in the third sequence says: 'Yeh. To ... What about scouting again?' Peter says 'No' but Adrian says: 'But we might lose too many more men'. Peter replies: 'Yeh so I'd say – let's scout again. Yeh. North'. Although this may be regarded as a confirmatory statement, the proposal is taken over and 'owned' by Peter: 'Yeh so *I'd* say ...' and so it seems to be his proposal. When Diana returns to the group, Adrian suggests they should hide the boats. 'After we set up defences ... hide our boats. Then after we have set up our defences, I think we should hide our boats.' Peter disagrees, but six speaking turns later says: 'I know, I know. Right, *I'd say* D. Hide the boats.' By using the words '*I'd say ...* ' Peter takes over the proposal as his own. Peter seems to use this 'taking over' strategy as a way of directing the group.

If one looks at the patterns of interaction used by Pozzi *et al.,* (1993) the role of Diana would seem to be that of navigator, influencing global issues by giving her support to proposals and ensuring that the group carries out the task set by the teacher. Peter either in the group or in the pair would seem to fit the description of a 'driver' i.e. he dominates local targets. The overall pattern of the group is 'integrated' in that Peter does not completely dominate the group and suppress alternative strategies and ideas but his contributions are more numerous and out of the many proposals made in the sequences, Peter has the most accepted. Diana contributes proposals when she is present but none of these are accepted.

Although there is evidence that girls can be disadvantaged in the organisation of some groups and that the program used may contribute to differing types of interaction, the 'Viking' sequence does show that with careful planning, collaborative 'training' and 'gender awareness' it is possible to eliminate cross-gender antagonism and promote gender integration. Nevertheless, it is the girl who makes most of the supportive contributions and has none of her own proposals taken up and contributed to the program. There are times when the girl is controlling and dominating the group through her use of questioning and insistence on discussing decisions. In both the 'Viking' sequences where she is present, Diana has the final confirmatory statement which decides that the proposal is accepted. Diana's support is not contradicted and may well have been perceived by both herself and the boys as being her proposal.

Diana interacts with boys in the majority-male group composition by asking them to consider and discuss decisions. The boys' level of 'total verbal activity' (Lee, 1993) was of a different character when the two of them were working alone and certainly has less exploration of the task. The interactions of Peter and Adrian were less frequent and mainly via the screen.

A point to consider in looking at group activity is whether the success of collaboration has come about because every member of the group has contributed not only to the discussion but to the outcome. Acceptance and keying-in are important points in simulation programs because each decision is made through a choice command which in turn determines what the following sequence will be. The short extracts of transcript presented in this chapter illustrate one way of analysing classroom computer-related interactions to investigate gender-related patterns in the talk and outcomes of group work around a computer.

Chapter 12

Children as Researchers Using CD-ROM Encyclopaedias

JANET COLLINS AND ALISON SYRED-PAUL

A single CD-ROM can store vastly more electronic data than the floppy disks previously used for educational software. This makes them ideal for software such as interactive encyclopaedias which stretch children's ability to handle information. Janet Collins and Alison Syred-Paul report on the value of cumulative talk for children finding information together from CD-ROM encyclopaedias. Their interpretation of their data leads them to criticise what they see as a hierarchical assumption in Wegerif and Mercer's account of the three types of talk given in Chapter 5. They also use their data to argue that the design of software can have an impact on the educational value of children's talk. Features such as a notebook facility can help to support and focus the shared construction of knowledge occurring through cumulative talk.

Introduction

Three types of children's talk are put forward by Eunice Fisher in Chapter 3 and elaborated upon by Rupert Wegerif and Neil Mercer in Chapter 5. Both accounts of these three kinds of talk imply a hierarchy in which exploratory talk is, implicitly or explicitly, viewed as the superior form of talk for educational purposes. In Chapter 5 Wegerif and Mercer recognise the social role of cumulative talk in maintaining group cohesion (an issue later developed by Madeline Watson in Chapter 11). Wegerif and Mercer also recognise that cumulative talk 'can lead to knowledge construction through the sharing of perspectives'. However, cumulative talk, which does not produce 'critically grounded knowledge' is seen as inherently inferior to exploratory talk in which 'critical challenges are supported within a co-operative framework'.

Rather than perpetuate this hierarchy we prefer to consider the appropriateness of different kinds of talk in different situations. Our observations suggest that the kind of talk produced is, to some extent, related to the situation in which it occurs. For example, establishing a consensus view and a strong sense of mutual support seems to be an important prerequisite for successful collaborative writing activities. As the following case study demonstrates, using factual data as the basis of collaborative writing is likely to be associated with cumulative rather than exploratory talk. On the other hand, debates about open-ended, potentially contentious issues, can only occur through exploratory talk (Wegerif & Mercer, 1996). The fact that cumulative talk is more common than exploratory talk in schools does not, of itself, invalidate it as a medium for learning.

Our observations of children carrying out information handling activities with CD-ROMs would lead us to argue that cumulative talk is extremely important in establishing and maintaining a sense of group cohesion and identity. It also provides children with an opportunity to establish common knowledge through an accumulation of ideas. However, an analysis of sequences of cumulative talk leads us to differentiate between cumulative talk which is task oriented, and is thus valued by teachers as likely to promote learning, and social chat which maintains group cohesion but does little to extend knowledge. Unfortunately, the discussion as to what constitutes being 'on task' and the extent to which this should be determined by teachers or children falls outside the scope of this chapter.

In examining the role of cumulative talk in learning this chapter will consider the role of the software in generating and supporting both task-related activities and cumulative talk. While all CD-ROM encyclopaedias provide huge databases, they differ considerably in the way in which they present information and the level of pupil interactivity they encourage. By comparing two CD-ROMs (*Information Finder* and *Creepy Crawlies*) this chapter will identify features of the software which support information handling and collaborative learning through cumulative talk. It will also critique software features which encourage random browsing rather than systematic study. In short, this chapter will develop the theoretical framework of this book through describing aspects of the three-way relationship between the features of the software, information handling and children's talk.

Features of the Software

In many respects, CD-ROMs can be regarded as merely another kind of software. In terms of classroom organisation CD-ROMs are being used to support small-group activities in much the same way as other forms of technology. A recent evaluation commissioned by National Council for Educational Technology (Collins *et al.*, 1996) found that 38% of the schools surveyed reported that children always worked with the CD-ROM system in groups of two or more, and another 48% of schools reported that this happened often. Only four out of over 1500 schools said that the system was used exclusively by individuals. Given these patterns of use, many of the issues raised by this book have clear relevance to the use of CD-ROMs. In particular, teachers should look very carefully at what is actually going on when children work together at the CD-ROM system, and what skills they may need to be taught in order to operate effectively as mutually supportive members of a 'problem-solving' group. As Madeline Watson has already identified (Chapter 11), cumulative talk has a social role to play in maintaining group cohesion which may be seen as an important precursor to many learning situations.

The fact that CDs can be used to store and play back vast amounts of information in a number of different media (text, diagrams, photographs, video and sound), creates new challenges to teachers and children. In order to get the most from these systems children will need help in developing higher order research and data handling skills (Collins *et al.*, 1996).

Information Handling Skills

CD-ROM or multi-media software are included in IT and English within the National Curriculum Orders for England and Wales (DfEE, 1995). There children are required to develop two major and related skills. First, to develop their skills in searching, selecting and retrieving information. Second, to be able to use the data constructively within the context of the curriculum.

The NCET evaluation (Collins *et al.*, 1996) identified the difficulties which teachers face in identifying appropriately structured but open-ended tasks:

> It is easy to set 'open-ended' tasks that leave even the most conscientious children marooned and frustrated in a tangle of information, with only a limited sense of how to navigate their way out, and such software does not always provide them with enough help in re-orientation. On the other hand, for children who are content simply to flick from one screen to the next without any particular search strategy, the same disk may offer no more than a stimulating but superficial pattern of novelty and movement. (Collins *et al.*, 1996: 16)

In developing research strategies with CD-ROMs it is important to distinguish between what Steadman *et al.*, (1992) have termed 'purposeful user' and 'serendipitous browser'. There is a similarity here to the use of books in that the purposeful user of CD-ROM (as opposed to the serendipitous browser) needs to have a clear research question in mind at the start, and bear in mind that no source can answer every question.

In the following case study, the children were given clear but open-ended research questions. Essentially they were asked to:

- choose an insect which they thought would be interesting;
- find out as much as they could about the insect;
- present their findings as part of a wall display.

The task was essentially the same whether the children were using *Information Finder* or *Creepy Crawlies*. However, the two pieces of software produced extremely different outcomes. When working with *Information Finder* the children remained 'on task' for the whole of the lesson. They searched the database for interesting facts which they copied or re-wrote into their notebook which formed the basis of their written presentation. The children also printed out pictures to illustrate their work. During this activity the children used task-related cumulative talk. By comparison, when using *Creepy Crawlies* the same children found it difficult to stay on task. They engaged in serendipitous browsing and produced little in the way of written work. Moreover, although their talk was essentially cumulative, they seemed to learn little from the experience.

Background to the Case Study

The five children (a group of three children and two 'child tutors') who feature in this case study were from a vertically grouped Year 3/4 class. They were all bright and articulate and all had a reading age above their chronological age. Their experiences of IT had involved the use of the library based CD-ROM for reference purposes and the use of a classroom based Archimedes and BBC master. They all had some experience of writing and redrafting work on a word processor. The activities discussed below were part of a topic on insects.

Before the children started work on the CD-ROM they took part in a class lesson on classification. The two episodes follow a similar pattern. Both sessions lasted about an hour. The children worked in the library with a 'more experienced' child providing technical support and information about search strategies.

Session 1: Using Creepy Crawlies

The children begin by identifying the alphabetical index as a useful starting point. As they flicked through the list they read out the names of the animals. They appeared to choose animals they had heard of or those with strange and/or exciting sounding names. They made no distinction between insects and higher order animals and they mis-pronounced several of the names. They were clearly anxious to choose an insect and, in their impatience, they did not allow themselves time to read the whole list. This made us wonder if we should have highlighted the benefits of browsing through the database before the children began work. Eventually the children seem to agree which insect they should select for further study.

Helen: *(reading the index)* Mosquito

David: Yeah, yeah, everyone said the picture was really nice

Helen: Mosquito

David: Can we do the mosquito then?

Helen: *(laughs)* We've got to see it first before we decide whether we want it *(clicks on mosquito to produce information and picture)*

David: We want it, we want it

Helen: We want it

Having been motivated by the idea of studying mosquitoes the children recognise the need to check that this is an insect. They do this by referring to the scientific classification tree which appears with every animal.

Susan: Yeah, but no, wait a minute, is it an insect?

(children check with the classification tree to see if it is an 'Insect')

All: Yes

The children were initially excited about their choice of insect and David had some prior knowledge of mosquitoes. Unfortunately, the other children are too preoccupied to hear his story.

(The two girls are reading the text and operating the computer)

David: *(in an exaggerated voice)* mosquito ... a mosquito

Susan: Oh Mosquitoes can kill

Helen: Shall I click on mosquito?

Susan: Yeah

David: On a children's wildlife programme once, I saw, mosquitoes have killed ... they are the most dangerous animals in the world. Mosquitoes have killed more people than any other ...

(The girls are not really listening to him. They are concentrating on operating the computer.)

David: What happened?

Susan: No, no ... what you do is ...

Helen: What have you done?

David: You've killed us!

I saw this wildlife programme once that mosquitoes killed more people than any other animal in the world.

David repeats his story in an attempt to interest the girls in the mosquito but they are unable or unwilling to hear or comment on what he has said. The extent to which this demonstrates their lack of interest in the subject or their refusal to 'give him the floor' is, of course, a matter of pure speculation. The group watched the mosquito video a few times and made half hearted attempts to sketch the mosquito from the picture. Despite their initial interest and David's prior knowledge their interest soon flags. They print out the page of information and without reading either the screen or the hard copy they resort to random browsing of the database. The children appear to be entertained by the software and, despite the fact that they are no longer 'on task' their talk remains cumulative. At no point do they regress into disputational talk.

David: I know what it is, I know what's happened ... We can see loads of pictures here ...

Helen: Ooh. That's a poisoned dart frog.

Sarah: Yeah

(Children become interested and animated in rather a flippant way)

David: Oh we can see loads of pictures. Isn't the one good?

Helen: I saw that on Blue Peter

David: Ooh that's nice. Thaaat's nice *(being silly)*

Helen: I love snakes. That's a spitting cobra I think ...

David: A huge snake

(A lot of laughing and giggling)

They were clearly fascinated by some of the higher order animals and were frustrated by the fact that they were compelled to restrict their search to insects. With the exception of David's account of the mosquito, the children do not actively engage with the information. On the contrary they appeared to be distracted by the wealth of information on offer.

Immediately after this episode David summarised his experience of using *Creepy Crawlies*:

Creepy Crawlies was fun but it wasn't interesting. If you had a long time for the *Creepy Crawlies* and you weren't looking for something in particular, you could have a lot of fun just sort of looking around and having a look at the pictures close up, seeing the films, reading bits of information here and there. We could have an awful lot of fun. But if you're looking for something particular and it's a particular topic like we're doing. It doesn't show that much information.

The fact that this software offers sound and video makes it a popular choice for many children as a piece of entertainment. However, as the episode above demonstrated, it may have limited value as a piece of educational software.

Session 2: Using *Information Finder*

The previous episode demonstrated the pupils' failure to engage with the software and their subsequent resorting to random and unstructured browsing. By comparison, the following episode demonstrates children engaging with text and consequently learning a lot about the insect of their choice. Given that this is the same group of children attempting to complete a similar task, we would suggest that the essential difference between the two episodes is the degree to which the software encourages pupil interactivity. More specifically, the existence of the notebook in *Information Finder* encourages the children to select information and through cumulative talk 'make the knowledge their own' (Collins, 1996).

Directed by the pupil tutor, the children began their search through an examination of the gallery which gives them easy access to all the pictures on the database. As with *Creepy Crawlies* they made their choice from the first half of the alphabetical list. Having found a picture they liked they then found the related article. They did this by going through the hierarchically structured 'info tree'. They had obviously not realised the direct link between the pictures in 'gallery' and the articles. Their approach seemed awkward and time consuming but, perhaps because they did not know a better way, they did not seem to mind.

David: That's interesting

Helen: I like that one *(referring to a picture of the life cycle of a bed bug)* they are all different

David: It's small, little

Richard: Is that why our parents say don't let the bed bugs bite, or something like that *(laughs – pointing at screen)*

David: Why?

David):

Helen): *(Muttering while reading the text)*

David: That sounds interesting

Helen: Yeah, it does

David: Yep, we'll do this

Helen: Wait

Richard: Wow, it feeds on blood

Helen: It pierces the skin of its victim and then it sucks up the blood. It bites. It's bites causes the skin of some people to swell and itch

Adam: So do you want to do that one?

All: Yeah *(all smiling and looking excited)*

Having decided that bed bugs looked interesting they began reading the text on the screen. The fact that they read this text but not the *Creepy Crawlies* text is interesting, especially as the text in *Information Finder* is both longer and in a smaller font. While they read they selected interesting information. Notice how the different contributions accumulate to produce a coherent whole.

David: That's an interesting bit. 'Bed bugs usually hide in the day and hunt for food at night.'

Helen: Yeah and look. 'They hide in mattresses and bedsprings, between floorboards, or in cracks in plaster.'

David: Yeah, let's put that down as a fact.

Adam: OK. so you want to highlight this …
(children reading silently David using the mouse)

Adam: '250 eggs … hatch in about one or two days …'

David: Now we want to put that down don't we … in our notepad?

Perhaps the existence of a cut and paste facility in this software helped children to focus on the available information and select that which seemed most interesting or relevant. The notebook or notepad certainly seemed to be a major factor in encouraging pupil involvement. The children accept and encourage contributions from everyone.

David: Hang on *(leaning towards screen)* Yeah that looks like a good beginning bit

Helen):

Richard): Yeah

Helen: Yes, we want to put all that *(indicating the text on the screen)*

David: OK, so lets

Adam: You want to click there go up there *(pause while David positions the cursor and clicks)* press the apple *(Helen presses the key)* and the C.

David: Apple and C at the same time

Helen):

Richard): *(look down at keyboard)*

Adam: Now press notepad – that's notepad

Through cumulative talk the children collaborate both in the selection of the material for their writing and in the handling of the technology.

Conclusion

This case study demonstrates a relationship between cumulative talk and group cohesion and support during collaborative research and writing activities using CD-ROM encyclopaedias. It also illustrates how features of the software and particularly the existence of a notepad facility have a role to play in encouraging children to stay 'on task'. This has clear implications for the choice and use of CD-ROM software in schools. The success of the *Information Finder* seemed to be related to the fact that children could inter- act with the software rather than passively watching the screen or listening to the sound track. The use of the notepad encouraged a close reading of the text and resulted in the children learning far more about the subject they are studying.

Teachers also have an important role to play in supporting children's learning with CD-ROMs. The benefits of collaboration through cumulative talk may need to be made explicit to children especially in social groups where disputational talk dominates. Our observations also suggest a need for teachers to provide children with some guidance in planning and carry- ing out independent research. Children are likely to benefit from advice on taking notes and reporting back to others. Without such support there is a danger that children will find it difficult to stay 'on task'.

Chapter 13

Factors Affecting the Quality of Children's Talk at Computers

RUPERT WEGERIF

In this chapter Rupert Wegerif returns to many of the issues raised in this central section of the book to survey the impact of different factors on the quality of the children working together around the computer. The factors considered include the type of software, interface design, the role of teachers, the composition of groups and the way children respond to working with the computer. Wegerif concludes with a list of guidelines for selecting or designing software to encourage exploratory talk as well as guidelines for teachers using computers as a support for exploratory talk in the classroom.

Introduction

All of the chapters in Section 2 explore the quality of children's talk around computers. In the course of these chapters the influences of different factors are raised and examined, including gender, student expectations, the type of software, the educational task and the teacher role. The chapters have been arranged to draw attention to the debates between authors. However through these debates there is some construction of what could be called a 'common knowledge'. In this chapter I will draw some of the insights and conclusions of this section of the book together in order to list factors that have emerged as important in influencing the quality of children's talk around computers. This summarising approach should not be read as an attempt to bring closure but rather as a recapitulation and reformulation intended to contribute to and encourage continuing debate.

As well as using the frameworks provided by the preceding chapters, to help focus my exploration of the data gathered by the Spoken Language and New Technology (SLANT) project I will also use the Key Word In Context (KWIC) method described in Chapter 9. This method uses a search of key terms to support a more qualitative exploration of the type of talk. The key terms I used in Chapter 8 – 'because' (or 'cos'), 'if', 'might', 'why' and 'think' – were intended to help focus in on the incidence of exploratory talk. Where a flurry of two or three of these key terms occurred within 10 or so utterances the type of talk was usually, but not always, found to be exploratory. In the first part of Chapter 8 I used this simple method in a deductive way to question a hypothesis about the relationship between exploratory talk and software. In this chapter the same method is used less prominently as a support for a more open-ended exploration of the available transcripts of children's talk around computers. Where I found exploratory talk in the data I looked for factors that appeared to support this and where exploratory talk did not occur I similarly looked for factors that possibly prevented it occurring. The arguments of the previous chapters in this section form a framework for my interpretation of what was found in the data.

Gender and Type of Talk

Both Joan Swann and Madeline Watson argued that the appearance of successful collaboration could hide gender-based differences in the way children were interacting. Turning back to the quantitative results of a KWIC survey of some of the transcript data presented in the appendix to Chapter 8 (page 111) it can be seen that male single-sex groups did not produce significantly different numbers of key terms indicative of exploratory talk than female single-sex groups. But the key words selected were intended to show only exploratory talk. If a similar study were done to explore the incidence of cumulative talk or disputational talk, then I think it is likely that gender differences would show up. Boy only pairs and groups appear to produce more examples of a disputational style than other types of groups, and girl only groups appear to produce more examples of cumulative talk. This would fit with findings on the effect of gender make-up on the style of interactions in groups reported by both Howe (1991) and by Underwood (1994). The gender differences suggested by both Swann and by Watson fit with this general analysis. In her chapter, Swann notes that the girl in the pair she considers, Emma, tends to seek confirmation, a key feature of cumulative talk (see Chapter 5), and a feature found less in her boy partner who uses many more directives. In her study, Watson explicitly brings out the cumulative talk dimension of the style of the one girl, Diana, who is working with two boys. Watson argues that this style helps bring about the cohesion of the group.

Swann and Watson should not be read as arguing that gender determines the type of interaction children adopt. In the next section Watson will describe how she used her awareness of the effect of gender on interaction to help create an intervention programme that improved the quality of the way children worked together. In other words she assumes that the effect of gender on talk is not a fixed variable but something that can be changed by teachers. This perspective stems from the sociocultural theoretical framework of this book outlined in the chapters of Section 1. Factors like gender do not only affect the quality of interaction, they are themselves reciprocally affected or even constructed by the ground rules of interaction, and these ground rules are open to change.

To explore the complexity of factors affecting talk, the next section will look in more detail at a sample of disputational talk which might be taken as in some way an extreme example of 'boys' talk.

Boys' Talk? Some Factors Leading to a Disputational Style

The transcript illustration offered of disputational talk (Chapter 5) took a brief extract from an exercise between two boys using a mathematics software package called SMILE. In this exercise two boys took turns to try to find an 'elephant' lost in New York, represented with a grid, by keying in co-ordinates. Each time the program told them how far away they were from the elephant.

There is something to be learnt from this game about adding and subtracting coordinates, but to learn it users would have to reflect on what they were doing and try to develop an optimum strategy together. It is probable that this is what the designers had in mind. Instead, what was observed was an enthusiastic competitive guessing game. Each boy keyed in co-ordinates learning from the extent of the other boy's error until one hit the elephant, in which case the boy who keyed in would yell 'I won!'. There were some apparently exploratory exchanges but within a disputational orientation which meant that they were isolated and did not lead to shared knowledge construction.

All the utterances of the two boys working at the computer are short. The action is fast and enthusiastic. Occasionally ejaculations such as 'wicked' are uttered or they swear at each other for being stupid. The style is very much that of interaction between children engaged in a competitive turn-taking commercial video-game. It is evident that this is how they see the activity. The design of the software does not impose this interpretation but it has done nothing to prevent it.

When the same users try a further SMILE exercise – a classic problem-solving puzzle involving transporting people over a river with only one boat – they find it resists this movement of genre assimilation. Their 'turns' have to be much longer, meaning that one of them is relatively idle and restless and they cannot manage without thinking about the strategy. More apparently exploratory challenges and justifications occur in this exercise than in the first exercise, but they still occur within a disputational orientation. The clash between the requirements of the software task and their expectations leads to frustration and they do not continue the exercise for long.

The video-game style is associated with boys rather than girls (Light & Littleton, in press). This style was mentioned in Chapter 6 which considered talk around adventure games. It is also a style in the culture which some users, perhaps those who have experience of arcade computer games, will associate with computers. The impact of gender here is not necessarily direct but rather mediated by the cultural context which may shape the expectations of children. The software interface is relevant in so far as it connects with these culturally influenced expectations. The design of the particular 'hunting the elephant' exercise supports competitive turn-taking through having a series of discrete tasks and only a single goal. By the word 'support' I simply mean that the software is sufficiently close to the competitive game model to be appropriated by the two boys into that model. The next exercise in the SMILE package is designed to promote collaborations and its design frustrates their attempts to compete. So here we see a complex of factors all interacting with each other to produce a particular type of talk.

The Impact of Taking Decisions in Turn

In the SMILE exercise referred to above, disputational talk occurred in the context of taking separate turns at a piece of software. In other contexts, turn-taking was associated with cumulative talk. For example, turn-taking was often adopted using Bubble Dialogue and this seemed to be related to the cumulative talk that was usually also adopted. Bubble Dialogue is a software package in which words and thoughts are put into the speech bubbles and thought bubbles of characters drawn on the screen to create a kind of cartoon story of a dialogue. The cartoons used all show two characters facing each other so, when used in pairs, it is not surprising that it led to role play. The illustration of cumulative talk given in Chapter 5 is taken from an exercise on Bubble Dialogue in which two girls, Emma and Sally, role-played a school bully and her victim. In the transcripts there was a lot of cumulative talk in which speakers take up a previous initiation without questioning it. The two girls seemed reluctant to challenge each other in a way required for critical discussion. It emerged that one reason for this was that each was taking the main responsibility for the utterances of one character and felt that it would not be right to criticise their partner's suggestions for the other character's speech.

Despite the co-operative attitude of these girls, very little exploratory talk emerged and so very little explicit reflection on the issues involved in their story. Other studies (Jones, 1996; O'Neill & McMahon, 1991) have shown the powerful potential of Bubble Dialogue to stimulate and support reflective thought, but in the studies which O'Neill, McMahon and Jones describe the children were working with an adult.

So far we have seen two instances of turn-taking, one with disputational talk and one with cumulative. Wherever turn-taking in decision making was encountered it seemed to prevent the occurrence of exploratory talk. One reason for this emerges from a comparison of exploratory talk in two different sessions using LOGO. In one session two girls, Linda and Janet, took roles as to who typed and who directed, swapping after each exercise. The video-tape and transcript show that this way of approaching the task was suggested by the teacher. This session produced no extended exploratory talk and 0.58% of key usages (LOGO 1 in the appendix to Chapter 8). An examination of the occurrence of these key usages found several occasions where exploratory talk might have broken out but was prevented by the procedure of turn-taking adopted. In LOGO numerical instructions are keyed-in to get geometric shapes drawn on the screen. An example follows in which Linda says they should use the command 'FRESH' to clear the screen and offers a reason. Instead of counter-claiming and engaging in exploratory talk Janet asserts her authority as the person whose turn it is to direct:

Linda: No, we need 'FRESH'

Janet: No, no, no, Linda

Linda: We'll need to because it's, otherwise it's gone too far and it won't rub out

Janet: No, Linda, I know what I'm doing. I don't want it. You were just told to *(inaudible)* it's me who makes the decisions, you are just typing.

Another session (LOGO 2 in the Appendix to Chapter 8) produced three times as many indicators of exploratory talk and, focusing in on these key usages, some modest sequences of exploratory talk could be observed. This session was also with two girls, Rachel and Karen. The significant difference seemed to be that they tackled problems together so that disagreements like the one above produced more discussion. In the following brief illustration they disagree about which command to give to make the shape they want:

Karen: … forward 25

Rachel: No, you see, it won't be big enough

Karen: It's a bit too big. Do 25, because that's too long

Rachel: Let's do 30

Karen: OK. Forwards 30

In the case of LOGO there was no imperative to turn-taking in the software design, but in some cases children adopted this strategy. The way the teacher sets up an exercise is an influence on the strategy that children adopt. The expectations of the children discussed in Chapter 9 are also clearly significant. In the data collected, engagement in the reasoned construction of each response seemed to be the only strategy that supported 'exploratory talk'. However, there is no reason to assume that shared reasoning could not be combined with taking turns to use the mouse or the keyboard in the case of SMILE or with taking ultimate responsibility for and identifying with a character in the case of Bubble Dialogue. Although teacher set-up and the style of software may encourage or discourage turn-taking, the most important factor encouraging shared thinking appears to be the expectations of the children that lead them to adopt a particular style of interaction. This factor has been explored in Chapters 6 and 9. It will also be the focus of the third section of the book where examples are given of teachers setting out to change the expectations that children have as they approach computer-based tasks. However, my retrospective survey of the available transcript data of children talking together around computers also revealed a number of blocks and supports for exploratory talk which are primarily issues of software design.

Does Typing Prevent Thinking?

Where the computer-based activity is dominated by the task of typing, the typing is likely to become the focus of the activity for the users. Mastering complex interfaces of all sorts was a common difficulty with open-ended software. Although struggling with the interface does not in itself prevent the discussion of other issues, it is likely to shift the task interpretation of users towards the procedural.

Bubble Dialogue, mentioned earlier, provides a good example of this problem. It was developed specifically to support reflective discussion-based learning (O'Neill & McMahon, 1991) and claims have been made for it in this regard. The software interface consists of a comic-strip format in which the users have to fill in the thoughts and utterances of the characters on the screen. In the sessions observed a small prologue was used to prepare the context of the dialogue. For four sessions this was about bullying at school and in the fifth it was a girl home late being confronted by her father.

The sessions with Bubble Dialogue had a similar pattern of activity over time. What to input was decided rapidly, by a variety of means, none of them involving extended discussion, then a much longer period was spent typing this input into the computer. This required repeating the sentence several times, saying each word and phrase while typing it and spelling out individual letters. Where discussion did occur it was as likely to be over spellings or how to manipulate the software as about the subject matter of the dialogue being created.

The fact that much more time and effort inevitably went into the typing than into the planning of the dialogue almost certainly influenced the children to interpret the task more in terms of producing a presentable output than in terms of thinking about the issues involved in the dialogues they were creating. On the other hand, this emphasis on producing a written output rather than on thinking and talking together was almost certainly also influenced by previous work in the classroom.

There was a tendency in all the sessions with Bubble Dialogue for ideas put forward to be accepted or rejected without reasons being given so that the dialogue between the pupils did not move into exploratory mode. A common form was 'Shall I put x?' followed by 'Yes' or, sometimes, 'No, put y', without any explicit discussion of reasons. This could be a result of the procedural emphasis on getting something down with less attention being paid to the quality of the thought behind what was put down.

The commonly held view (Laurillard, 1993; O'Malley 1992;) that interfaces should be as transparent as possible has recently been challenged by the work of Gilmour (1994). Gilmour quotes cases where difficulty in mastering the interface improves learning and encourages learners to think more about what they are doing. In the light of Gilmour's findings it might be considered feasible by some that having to stop and struggle to type a response can, in some circumstances be of educational value. However, if the main aim is to support discussion around the computer then the evidence of the SLANT data shows that typed input is a hindrance rather than a support.

The Depth and Nature of the Problems Set by the Software

Viking England has already been described in Chapters 6, 7 and 8. It shares some structural features with adventure games such as Wizard's Revenge, Concept Kate, Hazard Rescue and Nature Park but use of it produced much more exploratory talk (see Figure 1 in Chapter 8). As Phillips and Scrimshaw argue in Chapter 6 one significant factor accounting for the longer discussion found with using Viking England as opposed to other adventure games may have been a difference in the nature of the problems posed.

The challenges faced in Wizard's Revenge, Nature Park, Concept Kate and Hazard Rescue are local and extrinsic to the larger narrative. In one place in Nature Park, for example, the users have to solve mathematical sums in order to pass a barrier. In Viking England the puzzles or challenges concern decisions which have to be made in the course of a simulated Viking raid: what to put in the ships, which route to take, where to land. These challenges are intrinsic to the narrative plot. They do not have a discrete right answer independent of the exercise as a whole. Phillips and Scrimshaw refer to these problems as holistic. Their account suggests that it is necessary to make a distinction between simple problems, all the salient aspects of which can be grasped in a single act of comprehension, and complex problems or issues which benefit from being dealt with in a more 'distributed' manner through discussion.

Props to Support Debate

Most of the exploratory talk observed across the whole range of data involved used material ready to hand. Items were picked up from the context and used to support arguments or think about issues. Turning back to the transcript quoted in Chapter 8 of a session with Viking England we can see that the children refer to the information given pictorially on the screen when discussing which site to raid. The presence of key features on the screen is the visual equivalent to pre-packaging the main arguments to be used in the debate. A similar use of symbols on the screen was found in other cases where exploratory talk occurred. In using Front Page the position of text on the screen was pointed to. In using LOGO the key issue was the position of lines on the screen.

In Chapter 12 Janet Collins described the difference that having a notebook facility on one piece of CD-ROM software appeared to make. This facility allowed the children to objectify their search and have ideas in front of them. The notebook facility became a shared object to focus the task and discussion about the task. This finding is similar to that given by Crook (1994: 184–6). Crook describes a piece of primary mathematics software where children have to solve a spatial problem. He conducted an experiment by adding a notebook facility to the software where children could store patterns while they worked on the problem. Like Collins, he found that this simple addition greatly helped support discussion through serving as a shared focus.

Summary: Principles for Encouraging Exploratory Talk

This survey of the transcripts gathered by the SLANT project has produced several clear principles for both teachers and software designers who want to encourage exploratory talk around computers.

Discourage taking decisions in turn

One way of doing this in software design is to avoid any series of discrete actions, problems or exercises which users can divide up between them. Teachers should be careful how they set up problems. Physical turn-taking might be a way of making sure that everyone in the group is involved but it must not be conflated with the mental turn-taking where users do not discuss what they are doing together but each acts separately. One way to counteract this kind of turn-taking is to try to influence the expectations users have of how to work together when they find themselves in front of the computer; but software interface design also plays a part.

Minimise typed input

Typing appears to be such a daunting task for most children that engaging in it takes over the direction of the whole exercise. Teaching children keyboard skills at an early age might be another approach to overcoming this problem.

Make sure problems are sufficiently complex and 'holistic'

Only some kinds of problems are good for supporting discussion. Problems posed have to be sufficiently complex to benefit from the multiple perspectives brought to bear in discussion. They should also have significant consequences for the users perhaps through the way in which they are embedded in a developing narrative.

Provide supports for reasoning

Props should be provided in the form of supporting information or ready-made arguments for and against different positions. A 'notebook' for recording results so far can also serve as a shared focus for debate. These props might be provided by the software program itself or through materials made to be used with the program.

Plan for the expectations of users

Users always come to work together with expectations of how to proceed. These might have been shaped by many influences including gender roles, previous experience with competitive video-games and the climate of the classroom. It might be wise to design software in a way which resists rather than encourages competitive game-playing type of use. Time measures should be avoided for this reason as having small discrete tasks towards a single goal which the users could transform into a competitive turn-taking game. However, perhaps the most effective way that teachers can plan for the expectations of users is to shape those expectations by coaching them in co-operative and exploratory styles of working before they come to use the computer.

Conclusion

This, the concluding chapter of this section of the book, has combined a summary of some of the key themes that have emerged in Section 2 with a survey of the data gathered by the SLANT project. The focus has been on factors that support or hinder the occurrence of exploratory talk. Practical guidelines for teachers and software designers have been drawn out. The orientation towards improving educational practice will be continued in the next and final section of the book which will present accounts of teacher practice and of teacher-led intervention programmes designed to improve classroom practice. The final chapter of the book, Chapter 17, for example, will describe how the principles for software design outlined in this chapter were applied in creating two items of software to support exploratory talk within the curriculum.

Section 3

Teachers Make a Difference

Chapter 14
Teaching Talking

LYN DAWES

> *Lyn Dawes is a teacher-researcher who worked with the Spoken Language and New Technology project. Here she describes how she used the project to improve the way that computers were used in her classroom. Video-recording of children using the computer together showed that there was little useful discussion taking place. This led her to develop a series of lessons on talk for the children to increase their awareness of how they talked together. A set of ground rules for effective discussion was developed with the children and in the next computer-based activity a marked improvement in the quality of their work took place.*

Introduction

The National Curriculum for England and Wales (DfEE, 1995) specifies programmes of study for Speaking and Listening. At about the time that we began to implement the National Curriculum, and discuss its requirements in meetings, I became involved with the Spoken Language and New Technology (SLANT) project. At this time also my school had just accumulated enough computers for each class to have access to one for a block of time in each week. The effect of this practical point is not to be underestimated. The class of 27 children could use the computer for a morning, for example. A school morning is about three hours, that is, six minutes computer time per child. Putting children in groups of three would allow each group about 20 minutes to work together, which was a reasonable amount of time. The necessity for groups meant that the children would naturally be talking and listening to one another while they worked.

There was nothing unusual in putting groups to work together at the computer. Computers, though relatively new, had been available in schools for long enough for people to become familiar with the sorts of things they could be used for. Children talking together was not a novelty either. But involvement in the SLANT project strongly encouraged me to relate these three things, that had, up until then, been fairly separate:

(1) Grouping children for work together.

(2) Using computers to reinforce learning.

(3) Getting children to talk, and listen, in educationally effective ways.

Grouping Children

Grouping children to work together at the computer is not simple. Variables to consider include the time available, the general knowledge and ability of the children, their gender, sociability or otherwise, computer literacy, and imaginative powers, as well as their friendship groups, personalities, and listening and talking skills. There are other practical considerations, such as who is present or absent on a particular day, who is least behind with their 'real' classwork, and the exacting demands of the class themselves for 'fairness'. Almost everyone always wants a go on the computer.

Hardware and Software

I had found that organising computer-based work on the one machine available, while mainly occupied with looking after the rest of the class, presented me with problems. First, there was the problem of siting the computer somewhere sensible. If it was in the classroom, it was crowded, and nearby children would find it hard to keep their eyes off the screen. If the screen faced the wall, lots of dangerous wires were left exposed. If it faced the window, no one could read what it said. If the computer was sited outside the classroom, passers-by would stop, advise, and even take over. Any hitches would mean that I would have to leave the classroom to help, and that meant everybody immediately downed tools.

The choice of software depends on what is available to fit in with the current topic, or to match an educational need. The program I chose to use for the first SLANT videos was BRANCH. This provides a framework for classifying objects on the basis of their observable features. The class were using it to construct a key, which could then be used by other children to identify the given articles. The children were familiar with the program, and had used it successfully to produce keys for straightforward things like classroom equipment. The final task was to use it to sort and identify some rocks. This involved looking carefully at each rock, and thinking of questions with yes/no answers which would distinguish them one from another. After class discussion about the sort of features the rocks presented, work began.

The Video Evidence

I hoped that the video recording would reveal the way the children went about deciding together which physical characteristics of the rocks (their colour, hardness, roughness, crystals, and so on) would be best to use in the yes/no questions. Certainly much lively talk was taking place.

The video revealed that disappointingly little useful discussion had gone on. The talk between the children was generally to do with control of the keyboard. Agreement between individuals was reached with no discussion and seemed to relate mainly to friendships and allegiances, or otherwise. The child who took over the job of 'typing' was held responsible for the problems that arose when other children tried to use what the group had created, and those who had not touched the keyboard strongly dissociated themselves from the group. The children were dissatisfied by the experience. They had expected a sort of game, and treated one another accordingly – in a competitive spirit. The quality of the yes/no questions was poor, because no one had really reflected on them. They were the first idea that the 'typist' had thought of.

The main problems revealed by the video recordings were:

- The children understood the idea of classifying the rocks, but they did not understand my aims concerning their talk. They were simply trying to think up questions as quickly as possible, or wait for someone else to do so. They did not know how to negotiate with one another about differing ideas.
- Typically, a 'leader' emerged. The leader usually had a computer at home and could not tolerate the poor keyboard skills of anyone else. They tended to become dictators, and the interest of the rest of the group was soon lost. The group 'leader', usually a boy, imposed an inappropriate game-style approach to the work. This involved trying to whiz through the program, and the content of the yes/no questions became unimportant.
- The children did not function as a group. Less confident children avoided being the person to blame for mistakes or disappointments by not saying anything, or by simply agreeing with things the others said. Friends tended to agree with one another on principle, while other children disagreed not particularly with the content of suggestions, but with whatever was said generally. Difficulty and frustration with the program and each other led some children to abandon the group, saying they were 'going back to work' – confirming the idea that the computer offered a rather unpleasant 'game'.

- 'At the computer' is a coveted place to be, in a classroom. A particular individual's turn may not come round very often. When it does, it is a respite from ordinary classroom activities, which by their nature are things to wrestle with. Using a computer is strongly reminiscent of that other undemanding activity, television viewing. The aim is to spin out the activity till the next bell goes – not an attitude conducive to quality talk.

- The teacher, mostly engaged elsewhere, has very little chance to see the group collaborating or otherwise. Her interventions were sporadic, the screen evidence may offer no indication about the effectiveness of the children's talk, and it is difficult to assess the children's own accounts of their proceedings.

What Could be Done?

The video recordings had revealed that the main function of the children's talk at the keyboard had more to do with the testing and re-establishing of the class pecking order than anything else. The children in my class really did not seem to know how to consult one another properly, and the computer could not encourage useful talk until the children had some idea what that meant. Some of the children could not distinguish a sensible discussion from a more threatening argument, and shied away from talk because of this. Others dictated. Others withdrew, thinking the main point of the activity was to use the keyboard. I decided to organise a topic about talk, not using the computer. I explained to the children that I wanted to develop their awareness of how they talked, so that they could work together more effectively. Over a whole term, in groups, the class took talking lessons. They were learning to talk in a way that was new to most of them, a way that was both impersonal and intimate. It was impersonal because once they had mastered it they could talk like that to anyone, and intimate because it would give them much more access to one another's thoughts. The Talk topic, which involved displays, discussions, artwork, plays, and some recording, was very popular.

The children undertook various activities designed to encourage them to exchange their opinions without fear of dismissal or ridicule, to describe events and pictures to one another, to listen to and relate facts and stories, and, very importantly, to evaluate their own suggestions and contributions, and be able to state the reasons behind them.

Here are three examples of Talking Lessons.

Listening Together (a sharing ideas lesson)

Each group appoints a writer. The class listens to a taped sequence of sounds. The group talks together to decide what the sounds are. The writer records the joint decision, and reports back to the class.

Desert Island (a decision-making session)

The groups are shown a collection of pictures, items and drawings – jam jar, spoon, dog, hat, computer, tent, tin opener, funnel, etc. – and told that they are stranded on a desert island, with plenty of food but no fresh water. They can choose three of the things to have with them. The group talks about which things to choose, and each suggestion they make has to be backed up with a reason. Each member of the group must make a suggestion in turn, and all are expected to comment on one another's ideas. One member of the group acts as reporter, and explains what has been chosen, and why, to the class.

The groups are then told that a ship has appeared on the horizon. They discuss and choose again.

Dog's Home (a critical questioning lesson)

The groups are given pictures and written descriptions of four dogs who are in the Dog's Home. They also have a sheet with pictures and descriptions of three potential owners. Having looked at all the information together, they must match three of the dogs with an owner each, and decide which of the dogs is the unlucky one – to be 'put down'. Each member of the group has to say what they think, and give a reason for their ideas. The questions, 'What do you think?' and, 'Why do you think that?' must be asked of everyone by other members of the group. Complete agreement must be reached before the group reports back to class. (Towards the end of the lesson, a reprieve is granted in the shape of a fourth potential owner.)

By the end of the term, the class were ready to agree on some ground rules for talk in groups, which they could then use when it was their turn to work at the computer. One important idea, a novel one to some of the children, was that if the entire group had talked about a problem, and come to a collective decision, then the whole group must take responsibility for the success, or otherwise, of the outcome. Everyone was expected to contribute and become involved, and everyone 'owned' the work, not just the keyboard operator.

The ground rules were not written down, but were discussed and agreed on by everyone. They were so straightforward that it was easy to remind the children of them before they used the computer, and easy for them to put into practice. These are the rules:

(1) No one in the group could claim credit for successful ideas, and no one could be held solely responsible for errors.

(2) Each member of the group must be asked for their ideas by the others. Everyone's ideas must be given equal consideration.

(3) When a group member suggested an idea, they must be asked to give a reason for it, and given time to state the reason.

(4) The group must have agreed on anything entered into the computer.

(5) Decisions about who will be the 'typist', who makes written notes if required, and so on, must be sorted out before work begins on the computer.

(6) If things become difficult or disheartening, the entire group must seek assistance from the teacher or one of their classmates. No one individual can opt out from the activity.

The Next Stage

At the beginning of the term following the talk topic, the class were studying the Vikings, and using a program called Viking England. The group were raiders, setting off to the English coast and trying to set up camp in the face of many obstacles. The program notes mentioned that this software was designed to encourage discussion. This time, the SLANT videos and transcripts showed that genuine exchanges of ideas were taking place. The children were using the talking skills they had learned to find out what each other's ideas were, and to try to justify their own suggestions. For example, if a suggestion was made, such as, 'I think we should take the Northern sea route', the other group members asked why, or supplied reasons themselves – 'Yes, I think so too, it's shorter'. The more confident children had to justify what they said, and this required them to think more carefully, and not just type in an instant response to the problem. Children not actually operating the keyboard knew that their role was to talk about the decisions to be made, and that this made them vital to the group. The fact that disasters were going to be shared made less confident children more likely to suggest ideas. The more vocal and assertive children were still initiating and leading much of the talk, but there was now much more genuine discussion going on.

The class demonstrated its mixed-ability nature both in the talking lessons and in the computer-based discussions that followed. Almost all the children enjoyed the talking lessons, which contained as little as possible of the 'hard work' tasks of reading and writing. Many of the children liked the idea that there could be a formula for approaching one another – 'what do you think?' and 'why do you think that?' are easy and sensible questions to ask. Some of the children became very skilled indeed in contributing to and supporting exchanges of talk. Some got exasperated with the way it slowed things down, and resorted to the usual work-avoidance strategies. Generally, the children were more satisfied with the outcome of their computer work, and with each other.

The Viking England software is designed for collaborative use, and this was obviously a help. But the success of computer-based activities is not just dependent on the software. The input from the teacher should not be underestimated. It is the teacher who sets the educational aims for the children, and ensures that the children understand the point and purpose of their work in order to achieve those aims. Computers can provide children with some interesting and worthwhile tasks to work on together, but only teachers can help them to work together effectively. One of the best uses of computers is to provide the repetitive practice that learners need. Group work at the computer can be an excellent opportunity to practise the sort of talk which will enable the child to make progress through the National Curriculum levels. For this to happen, the teacher has to make explicit her aims about the quality of the group's talk.

Once the ground rules for talk are established, the skill can be applied to other areas of the curriculum. For example, children are asked to talk about their work together to design and make things, or to investigate a maths or science problem. They may also find their discussion skills useful when trying to sort out more personal problems. The function of the computer-based activity is to be part of the child's wider induction into effective communication practices. Children, talking properly together about which sea-route to use or any other problem, are practising reasoning.

Chapter 15

Scaffolding Through Talk

NEIL MERCER AND EUNICE FISHER

Neil Mercer and Eunice Fisher examine the role of the teacher when children are doing computer-based activities. They argue that contextual factors are very important in encouraging different kinds of discourse, including the way that the teacher has set up the activity and then supported its progress. Taking a number of cases for discussion they look at how teachers 'scaffold' children's learning at the computer, and also at whether computer programs can provide such scaffolding.

This chapter is a companion piece to Chapter 2. Where Chapter 2 introduced the three neo-Vygotskian concepts of 'scaffolding', the 'Zone of Proximal Development' (ZPD) and 'context' this chapter shows how they can be applied to researching teachers interventions around computers in the classroom. Like Chapter 2 this chapter is based on an article written in 1992. The developments described in Chapter 5 and in Neil Mercer's more recent work (e.g. Mercer, 1995) focus on concepts for understanding peer learning and claim to, in some sense, 'go beyond Vygotsky'. However, when looking at the role of the teacher and of active teaching the neo-Vygotskian concepts outlined in Chapter 2 still appear to be, as claimed in this chapter, the best theoretical framework available.

Introduction

The purpose of this chapter is to describe and explain the style and function of the interventions made by teachers when children are doing computer-based activities in their classrooms. We believe that achieving a better understanding of such aspects of teaching is necessary for the most effective use of the new technology in schools and could also contribute to the development of better 'classroom-based' methods for the initial and in-service training of teachers. This chapter also reflects our concern with the adequacy of available theoretical models of learning and instruction, and specifically with the relationship between those theoretical accounts and the practice of teaching and learning as it is actually carried out in schools and elsewhere. We will argue that the 'neo-Vygotskian' approach summarised in Chapter 2 offers the best available basis for the development of a conceptual framework for understanding teaching and learning in classroom settings. We will then use that approach in an analysis of specific examples of teachers' interventions in children's computer-based activity using observational data from the Spoken Language and New Technology (SLANT) research project. In so doing we hope to shed light on the nature of the teaching and learning process and relate theoretical concepts to the realities of classroom education.

Teacher Interventions

In order to identify the contextual factors which encourage different kinds of discourse, it is necessary to examine the total activity, including the way the teacher has set up the task and how she then supports its progress. This understanding has led us to focus on the kinds of intervention that teachers make in pupils' activity in order to help them continue and complete the learning task in hand. In this chapter we are concerned only with teachers' interventions in computer-based activities which are already under way, and not with the ways that teachers 'set up' or initially 'frame' activities before pupils start them (as discussed in Fisher, 1991; Mercer, 1991, 1995).

Relevant here is the work of Emihovich and Miller (1988), who in a small-scale, 'experimental teaching' investigation analysed the discourse of teaching and learning when two pairs of five-year-old children were instructed in the use of LOGO by a teacher (one of the researchers). One of their aims was to demonstrate an effective role for the teacher in LOGO learning, and the nature of the experimentation involved was to design a set of 'cognitive teaching acts' which the teacher–researcher self-consciously employed in attempting to 'scaffold' the children's learning. These acts were 'acts' in the sense that the term has been employed by discourse analysts (Mehan, 1979; Sinclair & Coulthard, 1975); that is, single utterances which initiated verbal exchanges with the pupils. Thus, through the use of a 'meta-elicit' act like 'Remember what those were for?', the teacher elicits from the child information previously learned. Their main finding was that the children became increasingly able to take strategic responsibility for their LOGO activity, and that while the number of teacher-led exchanges remained high throughout, the children's learning was mirrored by an increase over time of verbal exchanges initiated and directed by the children themselves.

Certain distinctive features of computer-based activities in school are important for any analysis of teacher interventions. One is the physical separation of the work done at the computer from the 'mainstream' activity of the class. Even when it is within the classroom (as seems generally to be the case in primary schools), the computer is likely to be at the side (near an electric socket and out of harm's way), with children often seated with their backs to the rest of the class. This makes it easier for an observer to see when the teacher makes contact with the group as well as requiring the teacher to make a definite move if she is to see what the children are doing. The opportunities for teachers to make useful interventions, and relative frequency of different kinds of interventions will certainly vary within the nature of the software and the activities in which it is embedded. For example, Emihovich and Miller (1988) suggest that when tasks and problems (and children's responses to them) are dynamically represented on the screen as in LOGO problem-solving tasks, teachers may more easily be able to make explicit connection between talk, thought and action, than in activities where the effect of children's decisions are not so graphically represented.

Another feature of computer work seems to be that children (and possibly adults also) are prepared to work for longer-than-usual periods of time, even when their work fails to be productive. Consequently the physical separation mentioned earlier, together with the fact that it is not always easy for a teacher to identify what has gone on already, make the timing and nature of intervention even more crucial than it would be with other types of classroom activity. Other researchers have reported on the nature and importance of intervention, and have emphasised the need for strategies which change over time, and in relationship to the complexity of the task with which the pupils are involved. Hoyles and Sutherland (1989) found that whereas pupil requests for teacher intervention decreased as pupils became more experienced in using LOGO, teachers chose to intervene more often as the tasks which they had set became more complex. Their interventions were sometimes aimed at directing pupils, but more often were attempts to encourage pupils to reflect on what they were doing. Similarly, Fraser et al. (1990), also working in mathematics classes, found that teachers gradually relinquished the managing role and took on more of a counselling, fellow pupil, or resource role.

Teaching and Learning in Progress

In this section we will take three transcribed sequences of classroom discourse and, for each, attempt to do the following:

* provide some background information about the educational settings from which it was taken, with special reference to the curriculum goals being pursued and the relationship of the work being done to prior activity and that planned for the immediate future (to the ex-

tent that these were made available to us through discussion with the teachers involved);

- use a conceptual framework based upon neo-Vygotskian theory (as expounded in Chapter 2) to analyse the sequence as a piece of teaching-and-learning.

The sequences have been expressly chosen from our data to illustrate the features of teaching and learning which we wish to discuss. They are taken from actual lessons and embody strategies used by the teachers of their own volition, though sometimes as the result of their reflections during the progress of the project. Our wider observations support the view that these sequences are not odd or atypical examples of teacher activity, but we do not wish to claim them as representative of the 'teaching styles' of particular teachers.

Sequence 1 (below) was recorded in a class in which the children were using computers in pairs to pursue a specific task set by their teacher. In the preceding weeks, the class had spent some time learning different ways of representing the natural environment, including making three-dimensional models and drawing maps on the computer using the software package 'Paintspa' (which enables free drawing on the screen through the use of the 'mouse'). In fact, many of the children in the class found the computer-based part of the activity difficult, probably because it was their first experience of using 'Paintspa' and of using a 'mouse'. It was the stated aim of the teacher that the children should be learning not only how to model and map the village, but should learn about the relationship between alternative modes of representation and how to transpose information from one mode to another. In this sequence, two eight-year-old girls (Louise and Harriet) were trying to reproduce on the computer screen a map of a particular three-dimensional model village which the members of the class had constructed. By the beginning of this sequence, the girls had been working for about 20 minutes. It begins at a point where, having marked out the basic structure of the village, they were putting in some of the buildings. However, they were unsure how to mark each type of building so that it would be identifiable on the map. Although they had had some difficulties (several of which had been observed by the teacher from a distance), Sequence 1 contains the first intervention by the teacher since she gave the girls the initial explanation of what they had to do.

(Note: In all the discourse sequences, the following transcription conventions apply: T = teacher. Simultaneous speech is marked by [. Additional information about observed activities is in parentheses and italics. The talk has been punctuated to make it more comprehensible to the reader.)

Sequence 1: Mapping a village

1 **Louise:** Mrs O_ *(Teacher comes over to the girls)* [Do you have to put
2   'H' now?
3 **Harriet:** [Oh, it's undoing, its
4   undoing.
             (referring to what's happening on screen)
5 **Louise:** Put 'H' in the house
6 **T:**   Well, what other way can you do it?
7 **Louise:** Well, you could, um
8 **Harriet:** It wasn't 'H' anyway, it was a school, weren't it?
9 **T:**   Right. What other way can you think? You need to [have a key.
10 **Louise:** [You can, you
11   can colour it in, what, some colour can't you?
12 **T:**   Right. Well, we're going to be using the colour printer, right, so
13   you could do just that, then.
14 **Louise:** Shall we?
15 **Harriet:** One of the, some of the blocks are too small
16 **T:**   Yeah
17 **Harriet:** And the gaps
18 **T:**   *(Watching as Harriet operates the mouse)* Yeah. That's right.
19   Good. OK. Make sure you don't do them grey otherwise they'll
20   look like roads. Yeah, that's fine.
21 **Harriet:** And what you've got to think about is what colour this *(she*
22   *points to an item on the screen)* is going to be.
23 **Harriet:** I'll do that one yellow.
24 **T:**   Some of it's garden and some of it's grass. *(Teacher walks away)*

The talk in Sequence 1 has many features which are typical of teachers' interventions in children's activity at the computer. The aim of the teacher seems to be to encourage the children's own efforts at solving problems, rather than to offer ready solutions. For example, in line 1, the girls ask the teacher a direct question. Although the teacher has intervened at the request of the pupils, she responds with a question of her own (line 6) in which she asks them to suggest a possible strategy, and so elicits a minimal response from the girls (lines 7 and 8). In performing this elicitation, she does not comment directly on the girls' idea of putting 'H' in the houses to mark them, but elaborates the requirements of the task in hand. She then repeats her question and goes on to suggest a strategy for dealing with their problem (line 9). She confirms Louise's interpretation of her suggestion (that such a key could be based on colours) and adds the additional relevant information that a colour printer is to be used (lines 12–3). So in the latter part of this sequence her talk consists of comments on the quality of pupils' activity and of reiterations and elaborations of the requirements of the task.

With a fairly open-ended task such as this one (in that a variety of mapping styles and formats would be acceptable), there are no single 'right answers'. The teacher's manner of intervention allows the children to explore the software and develop their own strategies for completing the task, but prevents them floundering or getting discouraged by difficulties which are beyond their technical or conceptual expertise. The concept of the Zone of Proximal Development (ZPD) would seem to be relevant to an analysis of this kind of teaching and learning event. The teacher had planned the task as one which would 'stretch' the children but which they should be able to accomplish with some support. Once the activity was begun, she had to make judgements, presumably based on her assessment of Louise and Harriet's competence in general and on the evidence of their progress on this particular task, about how much additional support she needed to provide. Louise and Harriet did go on to produce a satisfactory map, with a colour key.

Having described the teacher's supportive activity, we might now ask: is it appropriate to call this kind of activity 'scaffolding'? The effect of the teacher's interventions is certainly to 'reduce the degrees of freedom' of the task. To go a little further, from what we know of this sequence, it would seem that we can satisfy some of the Maybin et al. (1992) criteria for the use of that term (as set out in Chapter 2). We can satisfy the requirement of knowing that Louise and Harriet 'would not have been quite able to manage on their own' if we accept their own judgement on the matter (the sequence begins with their appeal to the teacher for help). It would seem indisputable that the teacher is offering 'help which is intended to bring the learner(s) to a state of competence which will enable them to complete such a task on their own'. We also have some evidence (in the form of the teacher's stated intention) of 'a teacher wishing to enable a child to develop a particular skill – or achieve a particular level of understanding'. Furthermore, we can satisfy the more stringent criterion requiring 'some evidence of a learner successfully accomplishing the task with the teacher's help'. What we cannot do is satisfy the most stringent criterion of subsequent 'independent competence', because Louise and Harriet did not go on to do an unsupported version of the same kind of task during the period of our observations (the lack of such evidence is, of course, virtually a paradigmatic limitation of naturalistic/observational research: cf. the experimental studies of Newman *et al.*, 1989). Our conclusion, therefore, is that – in the absence of any other apt terminology – 'scaffolding' is indeed an appropriate term to use here.

With some computer-based activities, it might well be argued that the software itself provides an element of 'scaffolding' for the pupils' learning. Certainly, some kinds of software, like adventure games and problem-solving programs, provide structure and guidance for activity, and such programs also often provide feedback to children on their actions (features that are all usually emphasised in the teachers' manuals which accompany most educational software). However, because any educational software that we have observed in use offers, at best, a very limited set of 'feedback' responses to children's input, and since such responses are often a poor match for the problems actually encountered by children in the classroom, we do not feel that the use of the term 'scaffolding' is appropriate. Moreover, we have observed that (a) pupils often get into difficulties in spite of information or guidance offered by a program, and (b) it is precisely at such times that a teacher's supportive intervention is sought and received. This is well illustrated in the next sequence (Sequence 2), which comes from the same class as Sequence 1. On this occasion, a group of three children (aged eight) were playing a game called Nature Park Adventure. This software is highly structured, in that children have to complete successfully a mathematical problem at the end of each stage of the adventure before they can proceed. Just before the start of Sequence 2, they reached a stage which required them to choose from a selection of coins (shown on the screen) so that they had the correct money to purchase two carrots at 12p each. They spent some time selecting a combination of coins, but as they erroneously concluded that they needed a total of 12p, not 24p, the computer informed them that they had the wrong answer. The children reached an impasse and were showing obvious signs of frustration, when the teacher (who has been observing them from a distance) came across and stood behind the group as they faced the computer screen.

Sequence 2: buying carrots

1 **Harriet:** (*to teacher*) What shall we do? We can't (*inaudible remark*)

2 **Tom:** It's only 12p

3 **Harriet:** Last time we pressed 10 and 2 and nothing happened, and then

4   we pressed 5p and 5p and]

5 **T:**   [Right. Read it out, Harriet.

6 **Harriet:** (*Reading from the screen*) If a carrot costs 12 pence which coins

7   would you use to pay for 2 ca– oh, for two carrots, ooh.

(*Teacher laughs and walks away*).

The children then proceeded to solve the problem with ease. Clearly it was not their arithmetical skills which were lacking but, as the teacher immediately realised, they had failed to read the question properly. She did not respond directly to Harriet's question (line 1), but instead she obtained a reiteration of the task by eliciting a response from the child (lines 5–7). In directing them to read the instructions, she made available to them support which was already there, but which in this case was useless to them without her guidance. From her tone of voice, it seemed that this was a kind of mistake which she, and they, had encountered before. She responded by implicitly invoking a simple but golden rule of problem-solving in school: read the question properly!

The teacher's intervention in Sequence 2 meets several of Maybin *et al.*'s (1992) criteria for 'scaffolding'. She is helping the children accomplish a specific task at which they were not succeeding on their own, and they go on to complete it successfully. We do not have evidence that they go on to achieve greater independent capability at such problems, but it is clear that the teacher's help is of a kind intended to help them do so. That is, it is help which does not provide a direct solution to their problem but which instead focuses their attention on the detail of the problem and on an important aspect of dealing with all such problems. She wishes for them not only to correct their mistakes, but also to learn from them. This brings us, in an intriguing way, back to the ZPD concept. Within some paradigms of learning and some educational ideologies, a problem-solving task which can only be done with a teacher's help would be judged as poorly designed or ill-suited to the children's needs. However, from a neo-Vygotskian perspective the necessity of a teacher's support can be seen as a virtue, because it is only when 'scaffolding' is required that we can infer that a child is working in a ZPD. Put more simply, neo-Vygotskian theory suggests that any task which children are able to accomplish without any assistance at all is unlikely to be one which encourages them to work to the limits of their intellectual capabilities!

In both Sequence 1 and 2, we can see a teacher supporting children's learning by not merely helping them, but by providing a structure which enables them to help themselves. In both sequences, the teacher's intervention is a response to a perceived problem on the part of the children: she helps them to 'sort things out' and then leaves them to resume independent activity. In the next sequence (Sequence 3), the teacher's intervention is less reactive, and more directive. The computer-based activity was part of a larger scheme of work on traditional fairy tales, within which the teacher wanted these six-seven-year-old children to develop an understanding of the structure of such stories and how characters in them are typically (and stereotypically) represented. She also wanted the children to develop their understanding of a real audience for such stories, as represented by the young children in the nursery class of the school. The computer-based task which she used to pursue these aims was for the children to design and use an 'overlay' for the keyboard which would transform it into a 'concept keyboard'. The nursery children could use this concept keyboard to select a limited set of words to make sentences and so create their own fairy stories. From our discussions with the teacher, we know that she also intended this computer-based activity to fulfil the aim of developing the computing skills of her pupils, and so to enable them to fulfil National Curriculum targets in Design and Technology.

Eight pupils in the class were working on this task in pairs, and the teacher supported their activity by going round to each pair in turn. With each pair, she would observe the current state of their progress, draw attention to certain features and use them to raise issues related to the successful completion of the activity. With all four pairs, her interventions dealt with the following task-specific issues:

(1) The relationship of the design of the overlay to the computer keys which it was intended to cover.

(2) The need to design an overlay which would generate appropriate sequences of words (so that 'beginning words' were in the left-hand column, with suitable following words in the next column, and so on).

(3) The need to select words which were appropriate for the younger children in terms of difficulty and interest.

Sequence 3 is an example of one such of her interventions with two girls, Carol and Lesley, in which the teacher begins her intervention by asking for information about the task.

Sequence 3: Designing a concept keyboard

1 **T:**   (*Standing behind the pair of pupils*) So what are you going to put

2   in this one? (*points to a blank square on their overlay*)

3 **Carol:**   [(*inaudible mutters*)

 4 **Lesley:** [(*inaudible mutters*)

 5 **T:**   Come on, think about it

 6 **Lesley:** A dragon?

 7 **T:**   A dragon. Right. Have you got some words to describe a dragon?

 8 **Carol:** [No

 9 **Lesley:** [No

   T: (*Reading from their overlay and pointing to the words as she does so*)

10   'There is a little amazing dragon'. They could say that, couldn't

11   they?

12 **Carol:** [Yes

13 **Lesley:** [Yes

(*Carol and Lesley continue working for a short while, with the teacher making occasional comments*)

14 **T:**   Now let's pretend it's working on the computer. You press a

15   sentence and read it out for me Lesley.

16 **Lesley:** (*pointing to the overlay as she reads*) 'Here is a

17   wonderful'

18 **T:**   Wait a minute

19 **Lesley:** 'Princess'

20 **T:**   (*turning to Carol*) Right, now you do one. You read your

21   sentence.

22 **Carol:** (*pointing to overlay*) 'Here is a little princess'

23 **T:**   Good. What do you need at the end of the sentence, so that the

24   children learn about [how

25 **Lesley:** [Full stop

26 **T:**   Full stop. We really should have allowed some space for a full

27   stop. I wonder if we could arrange – When you actually draw

28   the finished one up we'll include a full stop. You couldn't

29   actually do it. We'll put it there. (*She writes in a full stop on the*

30   *overlay*) so that when you, can you remember to put one in? So

31   what are the children going to learn? That a sentence starts with

32   a?

33 **Lesley:** Capital letter

34 **T:**   And finishes with?

35 **Lesley:** A full stop.

36 **T:**   And its showing them (*she moves her hand across the overlay*

37   *from left to right*) What else is it showing them about sentences?

38   That you start? On the?

39 **Lesley:** On the left

40 **T:**   And go across the page (*She again passes her hand from left to right*
                 across the page).

Sequence 3 includes many examples of the kinds of discourse identified by Edwards and Mercer (1987, 1988) as representative of the intellectual relationship between teachers and children. Selecting particular themes, the teacher elicits responses from the pupils which draw them along a particular line of reasoning on that theme (a line of reasoning consonant with her own goals for the activity: lines 1, 2, 5, 7, 10). Moreover she cues some of those responses heavily through the form of her questions (e.g. 'That a sentence starts with a?': lines 31–2) and by her gestures (passing her hand from left to right: lines 36–7). In pursuing this line of reasoning, she has to elaborate the requirements of the activity, and in fact goes on to redefine those requirements (in relation to the inclusion of a 'full stop' on the overlay: lines 26–30). She also defines the learning experience as one which is shared by her and the children through her use of 'we'.

In Sequence 3, we can see how a teacher uses talk, gesture and the shared experience of the piece of work in progress to draw the children's attention to salient points – the things she wishes them to do, and the things she wishes them to learn. The nature of her intervention is to remind pupils of some specific requirements of the task in hand, and so guiding their activity along a path which is in accord with her pre-defined curriculum goals for this activity. It is worth noting that this kind of interaction is very different in style from much of her teaching (as observed elsewhere), when she encourages free-ranging discussion and in which she plays a much less dominant role. We know that she saw this activity as a demanding one for the children (they had spent only one session using a manufactured keyboard overlay before beginning to design their own), and she was anxious that they all did manage to produce workable models. Her teaching style in the interventions she made can be seen as clear attempts to reduce the 'degrees of freedom' of the activity so as to ensure that its demands did not exceed the capabilities of the children and so that the possible directions and outcomes of their efforts were constrained to accord with the specific goals she had set. In fact, we know that Lesley and Carol did produce a satisfactory overlay, and went on to teach the nursery children how to use it.

The prime justification for employing the concept of 'scaffolding' in an analysis of the process of teaching-and-learning must be that it helps distinguish some kinds of teaching-and-learning from others. Sequence 3 shows an adult effectively performing the role of teacher without employing a traditional, didactic 'chalk and talk' pedagogy or using only the kind of non-directive learning support strategies associated with 'discovery learning' and certain 'progressive' approaches to primary education. What we see in that sequence is also clearly not apprenticeship learning of the 'sitting with Nellie' kind, rarely encountered in school but common in craft training, where a novice is expected to acquire skills and understanding simply through observation and working in parallel with an expert. We could describe what we see as 'scaffolded' learning if (following Maybin *et al.* 1992) we are satisfied that (a) Carol and Lesley could not have succeeded without the teacher's interventions, (b) the teacher is aiming for some new level of independent competence on the children's part, and (c) the teacher has the acquisition of some specific skill or concept in mind. For ourselves, we are satisfied that these conditions are met. Furthermore, we also have evidence of the children successfully completing the task in hand and even (though the evidence is not very 'hard') of their success in going on to deal independently with a subsequent related problem (i.e. teaching the nursery children to use the keyboard).

Conclusions and Discussion

On the relevance and applicability of neo-Vygotskian concepts

In Chapter 2 we argued that one of the most attractive features of neo-Vygotskian theory is that it conceptualises the process of cognitive change as one of 'teaching-and-learning' (or 'learning and instruction') rather than dealing with 'learning' as an individualised activity. It is, moreover, a theory which accords significance to the communicative, cultural contexts in which learning takes place. As education is first and foremost a matter of cognitive socialisation (rather than a process of individual discovery), this theory would appear to offer a more appropriate explanatory framework for research into learning in classrooms than other contemporary psychological theories. We accepted, however, that neo-Vygotskian concepts needed to be given more precise formulations if they were to be used to explain classroom events.

For the concept of 'scaffolding' we took up the formulation offered by Maybin *et al.* (1992: 188). Our view is that this definition is sufficiently elaborated to allow researchers to discuss and explain differences in the quality of intellectual support which teachers provide for pairs or groups of learners working at the computer, while sufficiently stringent to exclude some kinds of 'help' provided by teachers. Through applying this formulation of the concept, we have been able to show how teachers use talk to influence children's activities so that the success or failure of those activities does not hinge entirely on the relationship between the children and the computer. More generally, we have used the concept to describe how teachers attempt to support children's problem-solving without taking over complete responsibility for it.

It is probably in making a direct conceptual link between two very different aspects of teacher's involvement with pupils' learning that the concept of 'scaffolding' offers most to educational research. These aspects are firstly, the pursuit of curriculum-related goals for learning, and secondly, the use of specific discourse strategies when intervening in children's' learning. The concept focuses attention on how, and how well, a teacher can actively organise and support children's learning without relying on didactic instruction or mere 'shaping' through feedback. An obvious extension of the research described here would be to relate the relative incidence of the kinds of interventions teachers make to the progress of children through specific tasks.

Our discussion of teachers' cognitive support in this paper deals only with strategic response rather than the planning and design of activity. That is (with the exception of Sequence 3) we have not considered here how cognitive support for an activity may be set up in advance by a teacher in the way a task is defined both in practical terms (e.g. choice of software), organised (e.g. which children should work together), related to other learning experiences (e.g. to other work on a particular topic, or to children's broader interests) and how the task is introduced and explained by the teacher to the children. Aspects of such planning should probably be considered as part of 'scaffolding', as it may well be that some of the more profound aspects of pedagogical decision-making (e.g. what curriculum goals are actually to be pursued through a task, and how these goals may be adapted to the needs of particular children) are made at that stage.

The second concept, the Zone of Proximal Development, also embodies a view of the developing child or learner as someone whose learning achievements are situationally determined. We have offered observational data which illustrates how teachers attempt to provide a supportive contextual framework, and to do so in ways which reflect their judgements about how much help the children need to perform to the limits of their capabilities. For the psychology of learning and cognitive development, this concept challenges views of problem-solving ability or 'cognitive level' as something abstract and non-task specific. It invites us to consider how learning tasks as social events constrain or extend the cognitive potential of learners. For educational psychologists, classroom researchers and teachers, it also encourages an approach to the monitoring of individual children's capabilities which focuses on supported development rather than 'decontextualised' individual performance. In practice, children's development might be gauged as they progress through a series of related activities, carried out in the continuity of shared classroom experience, in terms of the extent to which the children become increasingly able to function with diminishing amounts of teacher support. Where special diagnosis is required owing to a child's learning difficulties, an approach such as this could be very useful.

However, the ZPD seems to us to have limited applicability in research directly concerned with the quality of teaching and learning in classrooms. One obvious reason is that practical circumstances force most teachers to plan activities on the scale of classes or groups, not individuals. The notion of any group of learners having a common ZPD seems problematic. Perhaps classroom researchers and teachers need instead a conceptualisation of the ways that the organising actions and interventions of a teacher are related to the creation of a learning culture in the classroom, and hence to the cognitive advancement of the members of a group or class as a whole. If we shift focus from the strengths and weaknesses of individual learners and instead consider how well a class or group of pupils and their teacher function as a 'community of enquiry' (as Prentice, 1991, puts it) as they progress through a series of curriculum-based activities, we may be more able to identify in what directions members of that class or group could be collectively expected and encouraged to advance. We believe that the conceptualisation of what might be called the synergy of a learning group should be an important theoretical goal for research into learning and instruction.

On the nature of computer-based activity in the classroom

A common view, held by teachers, software designers and many education technology researchers, is that the nature of any computer-based learning activity is almost entirely defined by the software. Teachers typically attribute the future or success of any activity to 'good' or 'poor' programs. Although software is of course a defining influence on activities (to greater or lesser extents for different kinds of programs: compare, say, some adventure games with word-processing packages), our observations show that in practice the procedures and outcomes of any computer-based activity will emerge through the talk and joint activity of teacher and pupils. That is, the same software used by different combinations of teachers and pupils on different occasions will generate distinctive activities. These distinctive activities will operate to different time scales, generate different problems for pupils and teachers and will almost certainly have different learning outcomes. Apart from the software itself, the main defining influence on the structure and outcomes of a computer-based activity will be that of the teacher, through any initial 'setting up' of the activity, through the nature of the interventions he or she makes during the activity, and through the ways (before and after the time spent at the screen) that pupils are enabled to relate the activity to other educational experience. As Crook (1991) suggests, there is a need for the computer to:

> become a topic of classroom discourse such that the experience can be interpreted and blended into the shared understanding of the participants. This is a more demanding and perhaps more intrusive role for the teacher than has otherwise been identified. (Crook, 1991: 87)

We should not decry or attempt to diminish the powerful influence of the teacher on computer-based learning activities, for the teacher's responsibility is to ensure that children's computer-based experience contributes to their education. That responsibility cannot be delegated to even the most sophisticated software, or to the children themselves. If we can describe and evaluate the ways that teachers attempt to 'scaffold' children's learning with computers, we might then be able to help teachers to perform that role more effectively and also contribute to the design of more 'classroom-friendly' software.

Chapter 16

Improving Group Work at Computers

MADELINE WATSON

Madeline Watson describes how she developed an intervention to improve the quality of the interactions between children working together at the computer. The features of her intervention were particularly influenced by sensitivity to the gender differences in interaction styles and response to computers which she reported in Chapter 11. Madeline Watson also shows how her intervention relates to the recent history of educational interventions in Britain at both national and classroom level.

Introduction

It was through addressing the issues of gender that have arisen around the use of computers in the classroom that I became aware of the need to take into account a wider perspective of group work and the nature of collaboration. This awareness led me to focus on the talk, and the social interaction that it supports, in group work at computers. Girls and boys tend to behave in different ways when working together in mixed gender or same gender groups and analysing the talk they use can give insights into how they are constructing the task in hand and the social relationships that they have with each other.

Although new technology is now an established part of the primary classroom, evidence suggests that equality of opportunity for access and successful educational outcome from its use is still not available for all pupils. It has been established by researchers such as Hoyles (1988), Lee (1993) and Sutherland (1985) that a pupil's gender may lead to disadvantage when working at computers. Pozzi *et al.* (1993) summed up their study of children working in groups at computers by concluding that '... pupils' perceptions of gender and ability do have an effect on the functioning of the group'. Pryor (1995) comments that in our society, the computer is associated with male-ness and this makes 'information technology use in the classroom a gender-sensitive area'.

There have been a number of interventions at national and classroom level in Britain addressing the issue of gender and technology. I give a brief review of some of these interventions so that my own work can be seen in the context of the range that have been made. Intervening in classroom activities is something which reflexive practitioners do as part of their work, but in my own research, I wanted to investigate and detail the talk in groups at the computer so that I could try out a programme with the class teacher that would enhance the collaborative nature of the group.

Talk, Gender and Computers

As Joan Swann points out in *Girls, Boys and Language* (1992: 4) different values in a culture are attached to being male or female, and one way these values are communicated is through language usage. If the talk used by teachers or pupils is reinforcing gender stereotypes or supporting working practices which are detrimental to one gender, then it is important to be aware of this and employ strategies and interventions which can address the issue.

In Chapter 11 I surveyed some of the research findings about gender and group work. Here is a brief recapitulation of some of the main points with extra findings relevant to developing an intervention.

In the classroom

- Girls have a more collaborative style of working than boys, who tend to be more competitive (Underwood *et al.*, 1990).
- Evidence shows a strong tendency for boys to dominate verbally in the classroom by taking up more 'verbal space' than girls (Swann, 1992).

In groups

- The social system of a group has a strong influence on the 'nature and extent of learning' (Pozzi *et al.*, 1993)
- The issue of dominance is crucial to the style of working and the experience of the children in a group (Beynon, 1993; Culley, 1993; Siann & Macleod, 1986).
- In mixed groups boys are more likely to be afforded a higher status both situationally and socially and be expected to be more competent (Berger *et al.*, 1980).

Using a computer at home

- Helps children at school (NCET, 1993).
- Most computers in the home have been bought for boys (Culley, 1988).

When working around a computer

- Girls are less assertive when it comes to having access and control (Culley, 1988; Sutherland, 1985).
- Boys see computers and technology as being their domain (Underwood, 1994).
- Girls are most likely to make frequent positive socio-emotional interactions and ask questions and receive help from group members (Lee, 1993).
- When boys work in all-boy groups they interact less frequently and have lowered levels of 'total verbal activity' (Lee, 1993).
- Boys together in a group receive more task-related help, although they ask questions and receive inadequate task-related help more frequently than when they are in mixed groups (Lee, 1993).
- Both boys and girls may be as likely to give direction and support for a group engaged in a problem solving process (Pozzi *et al.*, 1993).
- When fragmented, unsuccessful styles of learning are taking place, gender related antagonism may well be the cause (Pozzi *et al.*, 1993).

The Effect of the Social Structure of a Group

Children in a primary classroom work and play together throughout the school day. The way children relate to each other is constantly developing and changing and will be reflected in their choice of partners to work with in a group. For children, working in a group is more than an intellectual activity for the sharing of ideas; it is a time to discuss feelings, compare television viewing, gossip about other children and adults, and generally share their world with one another.

When children work together at a computer, it frequently happens that the resolution of 'who does what' can dominate a group's time to the extent that the program task becomes subordinated to arguments. Pozzi *et al.* (1993) note that the least successful style of group working could be attributed to cross-gender antagonism. Any child attempting to dominate a group can impoverish the experience for the other members by denying them access to the hardware or a role in the decision making. If boys see the computer as their domain but the girls are less assertive about having access and control, boys can dominate the keyboard and control what goes into the program being used. The girls can become resentful at not being allowed to have a turn or having their ideas listened to, and arguments ensue.

It has been proposed (Dawes *et al.*, 1992; Pozzi *et al.*, 1993) that the social system of a group has a strong influence on the way in which children learn and that teacher intervention in the form of showing children how to construct and use their talk and behaviour collaboratively, can make a difference to the way in which children work together in front of a computer screen. If then, there are gender dissimilarities in working in groups at a computer, as I have detailed above, it is possible to conceive that teacher intervention to address gender and the social organisation of a group could have an effect on the experience of children.

Kruger (1993) suggests that in collaborative work, what is important for learning is not a matter of agreement or disagreement, but the 'engaged discussion of the issues, including explanation, clarification or revision of ideas' and the opportunity each child has to compare their understanding and ideas with others in a group. 'Thus it was the critical discussion of the ideas of both participants that predicted cognitive change.' If 'engaged discussion of the issues' is to take place around a computer, the children have to be able to share the space and the equipment and concur as to what is going to appear on the screen and ultimately (when appropriate) be printed out. There has to be agreement as to the next 'move' and who is using the mouse or the keyboard.

Pozzi *et al.* (1993: 239) suggest that one reason why the social processes of group work are not given more prominence in research activities is that 'cognitive theories of peer facilitation are considered complex enough without taking on board what may seem secondary social effects'. I would argue, however, that no cognitive theories of peer facilitation should disregard the social process of a group, as it is in the social negotiations that patterns of group dominance and of collaboration and peer facilitation are laid down. Berger *et al.* (1980) showed that gender can function as a status attribute and influence the processes of interaction in small groups. In mixed-gender groups, males were afforded a 'competence' status, both socially and situationally, that had considerable influence on the problem-solving and social process within a group.

Webb (1989) reviewed a range of social skills and peer interaction which influenced working in small groups. She points out that effective communication of the need for help in solving a problem and its responses will influence the learning experience of each individual in a small group and that in many cases 'the group's *response* to a student's behaviour is the most critical predictor of his or her learning'. The findings of this study of small-group work supports the evidence from Lee (1993), who found that gender composition of a group influenced the amount of task-related help that was given. More frequent task-related help occurred in groups where members of the same gender were the majority and that girls were more likely to ask questions and receive help from group members regardless of group composition.

Lee (1993: 572) recommends caution when mixed-gender groups are being organised to work collaboratively, and suggests that the way to achieve 'appropriate cognitive and social educational objectives' effectively is through the development and practice of students' social and co-operative skills with an emphasis on gender integration.

Gender and Technology: British Initiatives

The low percentage of applications for courses in technology and computing by female students led to a series of initiatives in the 1980s whose aims were to encourage girls and women into science and technology (Delamont, 1990).

In the UK, in the late 1970s and the 1980s, purposive interventions about gender and technology took the form of equal opportunities initiatives to encourage girls and women into Science and Technology careers. (e.g. GIST – the Girls Into Science and Technology initiative). The principal aim was to encourage girls in secondary schools and women in industry to 'go into' technology-focused further studies and careers. Collaborative partnerships between schools and industry were one of the outcomes. Particular emphasis was placed on computer use because it was felt that computers could be seen as a boys' or male domain. 'Toys for the boys' is a phrase frequently used to describe this assumption.

At the same time as the equal opportunities initiatives, there was a government funded scheme (GEST – Grants for Educational Support and Training) to encourage primary schools to buy computers for use in classrooms. However, the government did not encourage, nor provide, any guidance on the gendered aspects of computer use that had been highlighted by the GIST initiative. Indeed, in 1988 Somekh comments that, 'There is clearly still a need to ensure that girls are encouraged to use micros and shown positive models of women teachers using them effectively' (quoted in Beynon, 1993: 162).

During the late 1970s and 1980s, there were interventions in British schools to encourage exploratory and collaborative talk (e.g. the National Oracy project, see Norman, 1992).

Despite the fact that equal opportunity of access to technology and the importance of collaborative talk were thus both being promoted in British primary schools in the 1980s, no direct link was made between them and so no direct link was made between gender and group collaboration when working at a computer.

Classroom Interventions

In 1990 the NCET (National Council for Educational Technology), NCC (National Curriculum Council) and NOP (National Oracy Project) document *Talking IT Through* raised many questions about talk and learning around the computer. Although the conclusion notes the importance of structuring and planning for talk (p. 72), there are no specific guidelines for intervention but rather a report of the ways in which teachers found they had to 'think about the learning that they wanted to take place ... changing the ways in which pupils inter-related between and in groups...' In the INSET (In-Service Training) advice one of the ideas for group work suggests 'Experiment with the way that groups are organised to explore issues – for example, gender, home language.' (p. 77).

'Ideas for further research' (p. 74) at the end of *Talking IT Through* do acknowledge the links between gender, talk and computers by asking how it may be possible to counteract the associated problems. The question is also asked about how and in what way teacher intervention could 'improve the quality of talk at and away from the computer?'.

The recurring theme in discussions at the end of many papers on group work and gender differences at the computer (Beynon 1993; Dawes *et al.*, 1992; Fitzpatrick & Hardman, 1993; Kruger 1993; Lee, 1993; Pozzi *et al.*, 1993; Underwood 1994), is the need to address the social process of the group. There is also speculation that intervention in the form of teaching children how to collaborate and engage with each other in a socially co-operative way, will enhance the learning experience of the children involved.

Interventions may be seen as falling into two categories: either as the situation requires or as part of a planned programme.

- Teacher interventions listed by Mercer (1995) and Edwards & Mercer (1987) are situationally dependent and concerned with cognitive processes and the construction of knowledge.
- Interventions as part of a planned programme are exemplified by the prior coaching proposed by Dawes *et al.*, (1992) whereby children are given ground rules for group discussion and collaboration as illustrated in Chapter 17 of this book.

Although it has been acknowledged that intervention could have an important impact on working in groups at a computer, and studies suggest that intervention would be a 'good thing', none of them detail the role of talk and social behaviour in the assessment and intervention process.

A Programme of Intervention in a Primary Classroom

Group work is a social experience for children and social practices are brought into a group. My experience as a teacher confirms that cross-gender and within-gender antagonism occurs between children when working in groups, and so in my own research I looked to see if there were interventions that had been carried out which specifically addressed social behaviour in the classroom.

Peter Kutnick (1994) carried out one such programme in primary classrooms, to integrate the development of social skills with that of communication and joint problem solving. Kutnick points out that studies have shown that teachers need to provide 'appropriate interpersonal "goal structures", learning tasks and a supportive classroom context'. Kutnick's developmental model emphasises the importance in close social relationships of trust/dependence, increased communication skills and the promotion of problem solving skills. Kutnick and Brees (l982) used exercises in trust and sensitivity to promote closer peer relationships and co-operation.

One point that is not addressed by 'cognitive coaching' nor by Kutnick, is the sharing of space and equipment. It is quite possible for good, constructive discussion to go on in a group, but for one child to dominate the use of the keyboard or mouse and from this position of strength to sit themselves squarely in front of the screen and effectively marginalise others in the group. The feeling of being marginalised and not being allowed access to the keyboard or mouse, is a frequent cause of discord when children work in groups.

When developing my own programme of interventions, I worked as a participant/observer with a class of Year 5 mixed ability children, in a middle school in Milton Keynes. I decided to go into my chosen school, video-record the children working in groups at the computer and then devise a programme of interventions based on an analysis of the talk and behaviour captured on tape.

These short extracts from pre-intervention transcripts illustrate the problem that interested me: how talk and action can be used to achieve dominance of a group or a particular situated context.

The group consists of Jenny, Katy, Annie and Colin. The three girls have arranged themselves around the computer in such a way that Colin cannot sit with them and has had to go and get a stool to sit behind them and lean over the girls' shoulders.

Sequence 1

Jenny:	No	*Katy goes to press*
Annie:	Now delete. Yeh. That's it.	*DELETE.*
	And then nuh *(sounds out the letter n)*	*Jenny pushes her hand out of the way.*
		Colin pushes over and goes to press the key.
Colin:	For God's sake	*Jenny pushes Colin's hand out of the way*
Katy:	Stop it Colin	
Colin:	You're not doing any of mine	*Colin gets off stool*
	(speaks in aggressive high voice to Katy)	
Annie:	Now space	*Raises hand towards keyboard*
Katy:	*(high pitched – arguing with Colin)* I know. She's just doing the title	
Annie:	No a bit – delete one of those spaces. There you have to	*Annie leans across Jenny at keyboard to press DELETE*
Katy:	*(Still arguing with Colin)* ... We're meant to be doing the title. It's the title	*Katy points to screen*
Annie:	Hang on	*Jenny pushes Annie's arm up off the keyboard*

In this sequence, Jenny is dominating the group and will physically remove someone's hand from the keyboard if she does not agree with them. She is tending to dominate the input to the word-processing program and the organisation of the group, throughout this session. It is Jenny's behaviour that triggers Colin's aggressiveness. However, it has to be said that Colin has been regarding the rest of the group as lacking in computer expertise and in need of being told what to do.

Sequence 2

Annie: Can I sit in your place?

Jennie:	Oh oh yes	*Gets up and changes places with Annie*
Colin:	No	*Puts his face close to Annie's*
	You didn't do that to me did yuh	
Jennie:	You [didn't ask	
Annie:	[That's 'cos you're a boy	
Katy:	You didn't ask	*Smiles at the other girls*
		Girls shifting and adjusting chairs but still keep Colin out of the group behind them

Here, the girls exclude the boy. The grounds given are gender related, whereby the girls form a half circle and smile at each other in a social context and give sex as the basis for exclusion.

Sequence 3

Annie:	Are falling Where am I	
Colin:	Children all around	
Annie:	Shut up Don't boss me about	*Colin knocks her headband off so it falls over her face*
	Get off	
Colin:	Whoops a daisy	*Colin holds up hands protectively*
	Whiiipsh	*Colin pretends to try to do the same again*
Katy:	What did he just do	
Annie:	He knocked (…) he just hit my head	*Katy keys in a letter*
Colin:	Whoops	*Flaps hand at head again*
Annie:	He hit me	
Katy:	We've just gone onto a new line	
Colin:	Annie (…) you must space	
Annie:	Are falling	

Sequence 3 shows the discord which had built up in the group over seating arrangements, turn-taking and the content of the poem being word-processed.

Reviewing all the video-tapes, and in discussion with the class teacher, I came up with the following list of 'needs for intervention':

- to learn how to *share* ideas;
- to learn to *value* each child's ideas;
- to *help* each other with work and understand the nature of working with someone;
- to *teach* children how to take turns, to negotiate and support the work that they are doing when they are around a computer;
- to take *gender* into account and as part of the valuing of ideas to bring out the concept that girls and boys have an equal right to have their ideas and contributions valued;
- to learn that computers *are not just a male domain*.

The programme of interventions was planned to cover a total time of 13 hours spread over seven weeks. The class teacher intervention took the form of a Personal and Social Education programme for primary children called 'Circle Time', for 30 minutes once a week for seven weeks. A total time of three-and-a-half hours. My own intervention programme was twice a week; a morning session of 90 minutes and an afternoon session of 60 minutes; a total of two-and-a-half hours a week and 10 hours overall, running concurrently with the 'Circle Time'.

Circle Time

The class teacher would sit the children in a large circle and share and discuss such topics as bullying, sharing ideas and learning to listen. There was a 'talking stick' and only the child holding the stick was allowed to speak.

The enhancement programme

Eight children (four girls and four boys) chosen by the class teacher as being representative of the spread of personalities and abilities of the children in her class.

The interventions consisted of:

- trust games such as being blindfold and led through an obstacle course;
- pairs of children sharing 'good' and 'bad' things that had happened to them recently;
- discussion of what it means to 'work together'. Eliciting from the children why it is considered important to value ideas from other people.

(Related this to Circle Time work);
- the children worked out and recorded guidelines on how to share ideas and equipment at the computer. Listed which words helped when working together in a group and which words would not be helpful;
- discussion and trying out talk and physical sharing of tasks when working together in a group;
- setting the children the task of dividing themselves into two groups with an equal number of boys and girls and then setting the groups the task of writing a story about two girls and two boys who have to work together to get something important done;
- asking the children to write down or record everybody's ideas and then to discuss them and choose the ones that they thought would help to tell the story most effectively;
- getting each group to plan and discuss how they are going to put their stories into the word-processing program. They had to discuss turn-taking at the keyboard, seating arrangements and access to the screen. An important point was ensuring that the girls were not 'pushed out' by the boys.

My field notes make it quite clear that all the interventions did not progress smoothly:

> Boys came in first and sat squarely in front of the screen. I had to remind them to let the girls have room to sit down.

> I asked the groups to behave in such a way that I could show the recording to other groups as an example of how to work together. A's group couldn't do this. They just carried on without due regard for the rest of the group. I had to intervene and remind them.'

> When I asked how they are going to organise the turns, A (a girl) says K (a boy) always uses it first then it's whoever's next ...

When I analysed the talk of the children, I looked for evidence of a change of the way in which they addressed each other and negotiated the collaborative activities of the group.

Dominance can be achieved by taking up the majority of verbal 'space' available (Swann, 1989) as well as being selfish and 'hogging' all the available equipment. Giving bald directives rather than mitigative ones, also lends authority to the speaker, in that a polite form may not be seen as necessary due to the dominance position within the group (Coates, 1993) and (Harness-Goodwin, 1990).

The class teacher's assessment of the intervention programme

After the intervention programme, I discussed the results with the class teacher and recorded our conversations. The class teacher was using a program called the 'Crystal Rainforest', an adventure-cum-modelling program which the children work through in groups. The children who had participated in the concentrated intervention program with me were sometimes working together, and were sometimes mixed into new groups around the computer. It is fair to say that all the children in the class had been aware of the interventions and had frequently asked both myself and the 'intervention' children what we were doing. We always told them quite clearly and on more than one occasion children had watched the groups working at the computer with me.

I asked the class teacher to tell me just what changes had taken place after the intervention programme that we had both been running. She found that:

- once the children had been taught how to set up the program for themselves, they could be left to run it;
- there had not been any arguing at the computer;
- 'without fail' every group had been sitting helping each other;
- they were sharing the mouse, taking turns on the keyboard;
- when someone tried to jump their turn, the others had intervened;
- they had been aware of sharing space and turns;
- the children were consciously trying to collaborate together.

Although the class teacher ascribes most of the success to '... the fact that you had talked to children and used the computer with them and talked to them about collaborative working', she also points out that 'Some of it may be to do with the program' and 'Some of it I feel is to do with the fact that ... they are that little bit older, they're that little more mature'.

Here are two post-intervention transcripts which illustrate the change in the style of talk and non-verbal communication between the children in Sequences 1, 2, and 3. Jenny had left the school by this time and so there are only three in the group. Annie and Katy sit close to each other and Colin is sitting back in his chair, next to Annie, with arms folded and looking at the screen.

Sequence 4

Katy:	Now we've got to get him down there	
Annie:	Hang on	
	Spacebar? Oh we've got to use these	
	So he wants to guide him through the maze	*Katy touches mouse and Annie puts her hand over Katy's*
	We have to use that to go	*Annie has one hand on the mouse*
	We have to use that button to go that way	*and the other hand on the screen*
	that's it	
	And spacebar to jump	
	Colin do you want to do the jump	
Colin:		*Presses a button*
Annie:	No, wrong way	
	It needs to go that way	*Touches point on the screen*
	Down there	
Colin:	A jump	*Presses spacebar several times*
Annie:	You can't get /	*Katy laughs in sympathy as the figure on the screen turns the wrong way*
Colin:	That's it.	
	All done	
		Colin smiles too
Annie:	That's it	
	Turn him.	

Sequence 5

Annie:	Change the instructions before you start the robot	*Clicks the mouse*
		Points to the screen
	OK right, what you do	
	There's Carlos /look	
Katy:	Where	
Colin:	Where's Carlos	
Annie:	There's Carlos and he needs to get through there but that robot's got to ... touch that	*Annie is touching the screen with her finger and pointing to relevant points on the screen*
	So how many steps do you think you'll need to take to get to there /	*Annie touches a point on the screen*
	so he jumps down there?	*Annie touches a point on the screen*
Colin:	Err 2	*Leans over towards Annie*
	No 3	

Katy and Annie have been part of the intervention programme and Colin has not. The situation is very different from that in the pre-intervention sequences, with a subdued and slightly dejected looking Colin sitting on the edge of 'the group'. Annie and Katy sit very close. However, there is none of the pre-intervention antagonism and Colin creeps closer to the screen without being rebuffed. Colin is asked by Annie if he would like a turn and his question is answered rather than ignored. Annie uses a greater number of mitigated directives such as 'We've got to ... ' and 'We have to ... '. Colin is directly addressed for his opinion and does not exhibit such an aggressive, hostile attitude towards the two girls.

Conclusions

The class teacher's comments after the programme emphasise the temporal and cumulative nature of effective interventions. They are not 'quick fixes' to be tried out for a couple of weeks and then dropped if there are not any instant results. Instead, a successful intervention programme has to be incorporated into an ethos of sharing of ideas and the valuing of each child's contributions that will become an accepted working practice of the classroom. The teacher needs to listen to the talk in groups and tailor the interventions to meet the needs of the children in the class. Within that social context, the computer has to be seen as an essential part of life in the classroom rather than a special treat or the domain of one gender who lets others 'into' that domain. Children need to be taught how to share physical space and equipment, whilst listening to the nature of children's talk, teaching them to communicate and develop ideas and share verbal and physical space, will help children build up trust between them. The teacher and the children can develop an internal model of what collaborative group work will look and sound like, and in this way, enhance the learning experience of all those working in a group at a computer.

Chapter 17

Computers, Talk and Learning: An Intervention Study

RUPERT WEGERIF AND LYN DAWES

The research projects reported on in Section 2 of this book were largely descriptive with the focus on understanding the factors influencing children's talk around computers. This chapter, by contrast, reports on a project which took some of the theory that emerged from those more descriptive studies, particularly the principles expressed in Chapter 13, and applied it to developing a classroom intervention programme designed to improve the quality of work at the computer. This intervention combined the kind of coaching in 'exploratory talk' described by Lyn Dawes in Chapter 14 with the use of software specially designed to support the kind of educational exchanges between computers and children described by Wegerif in Chapter 8. The findings of this study illustrate a benign cycle joining classroom research to the improvement of classroom practice.

Introduction

One of the main conclusions to emerge from the research reported in the preceding chapters of this book is that the software alone does not determine the nature of the activity around the computer. The role of teachers was found to be crucial and, related to this, perhaps the most important factor affecting the quality of children's talk around computers was the expectations of the children as to how to work together. When we set out to design an intervention programme that would illustrate a way to make effective use of computers within the classroom context we took this conclusion into account by designing the software and the pedagogy together.

Our intervention combined a series of lessons coaching the practice of 'exploratory talk', the sort of lessons already described by Lyn Dawes in Chapter 14, with software designed to encourage 'exploratory talk' within the curriculum. On the one hand, putting the emphasis on the use of computers in education, this could be seen as a way of improving the quality of talk at the computer by giving children a clear model of how to collaborate when working together. On the other hand, putting the emphasis on the pedagogy, this could be seen as incorporating the use of computers into an educational approach which focused on improving the quality of children's spoken language across the curriculum. Work around the computers was used, in this programme, to support small group practice in exploratory talk applied to the curriculum.

The practical side of the educational programme incorporating computers which we developed responded to the findings of the research described in Section 2 of the book, making use of the findings reported in Chapter 8 and Chapter 13 in particular. However, the study as a whole and its evaluation was also designed to be an exploration and assessment of the sociocultural theoretical framework developed in Section 1 of this book and articulated most clearly in Chapter 5. The claim made in Chapter 5 and in Wegerif and Mercer (1996) is that much that is meant by the term 'cognitive development' can be translated as learning how to participate in 'exploratory talk' which is a way of reasoning together with others. To evaluate this claim, the intervention explored the relationship between the use of exploratory talk and ability to solve the problems in Raven's progressive matrices – a widely used measure of 'non-verbal' reasoning which has been shown to correlate well with academic achievement (Raven *et al.*, 1993).

This study depended on a close 'research partnership' (Mercer, 1995) between a classroom teacher and researcher, Lyn Dawes, and a full-time university researcher, Rupert Wegerif. The 'research partnership' method has several advantages. Working closely with a classroom teacher ensured that the intervention was developed with sensitivity to a specific context, something which much academic research has been accused of lacking (Carr & Kemmis, 1986) On the other hand, the involvement of a professional educational researcher ensured that the research did not suffer from the weaknesses, such as a lack of specialist knowledge of research methods and of the relevant background literature, for which pure action research has been criticised (Edwards & Westgate, 1994; Hammersley, 1993).

The Intervention Programme

The target class were a mixed-ability group of 33 children aged 9 and 10 years (Year 5), in an English state middle school. They were organised into 11 groups of three, to include mixed ability and mixed gender. The educational programme was made up of two components which we will describe in turn.

The talk lessons

The children were given a series of weekly off-computer lessons, each lasting one-and-a-half hours, to teach them the sub-components of exploratory talk such as effective listening, giving explicit information, providing reasons, and co-operating as a group. Some of the lessons involved the children talking together in their groups, and some were whole-class discussions. In Chapter 14 Lyn Dawes gave a description of some of these 'Talking Lessons'.

A key part of this coaching programme was that the children were made aware of the importance of their talk with one another, and were aware of the teacher's aim to encourage a particular sort of talk. Once the first few weeks of term were over, class discussion led to agreement on the ground rules needed for talking together. The list was added to the 'Talk Display' prominent in the classroom.

Ground rules for talk

(1) Everyone should have a chance to talk.

(2) Everyone's ideas should be carefully considered.

(3) Each member of the group should be asked
     – what do you think?
     – why do you think that?

(4) Look and listen to the person talking.

(5) After discussion, the group should agree on an idea.

The computer work

Two items of software were specifically designed and developed to support talk among groups of students and to direct it towards particular curriculum areas. (Design principles were derived from the study reported in Chapter 13.)

The base of the software developed to stimulate talk in the area of science was a simple simulation of plant growth, showing how this is affected by temperature and by the amount of light and water available. This basic design is similar to software simulations commercially available. To support exploratory talk two extra dimensions were added. First, the simulation was embedded in an overall narrative frame in which the children 'role-played' scientists trying to find the formula to help a friend win the local flower show. Second, what amounted to a 'talk-support module' was added. This module interrupted the users as they tried to run the simulation prompting them to talk to each other, asking them to make explicit predictions, relate these predictions to outcomes and explain why the predictions were either right or wrong.

The design of the 'talk support' module was based on research done at Strathclyde University on computer-based collaborative learning in science (Howe *et al.*, 1996; Tolmie *et al.*, 1993). This research indicates that significant learning gains follow if children are encouraged first to discuss predictions before conducting experiments and then relate the outcomes to those predictions (see Figure 17.1).

Computer software was designed to integrate with the area of 'citizenship' as an extra activity after whole-class discussion about the issue of stealing from shops. The software takes the form of a branching narrative about a girl called Kate divided between loyalty to her friend and pressure to tell others about his theft. In the course of the story Kate meets the shopkeeper and others involved in the crime and they give their points of view. The group of children using this software have to make decisions as to what Kate should do or say at key junctures in the story, and these decisions determine how the story continues. The aim is not to direct the children towards a particular conclusion but to encourage genuine and wide-ranging debate about the

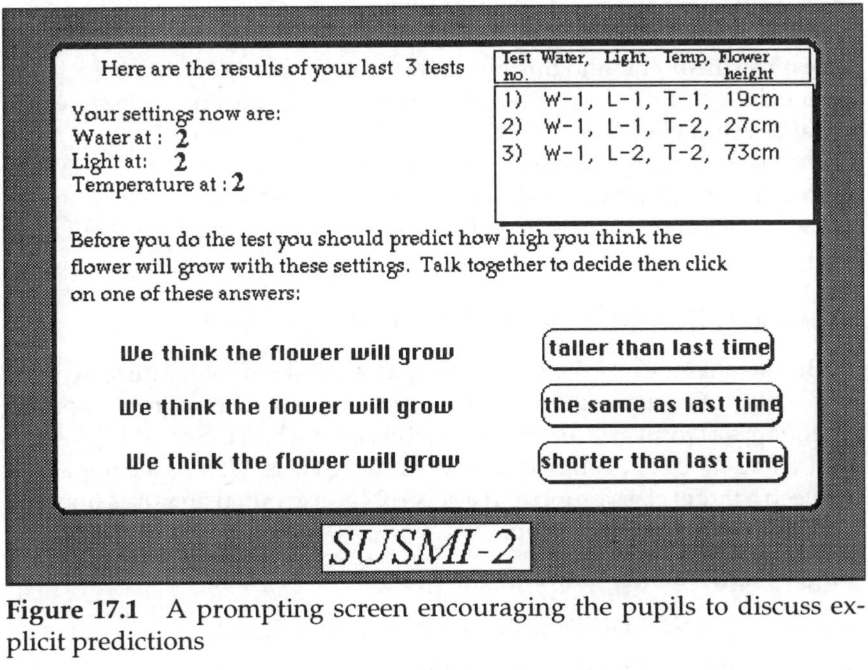

Figure 17.1   A prompting screen encouraging the pupils to discuss explicit predictions

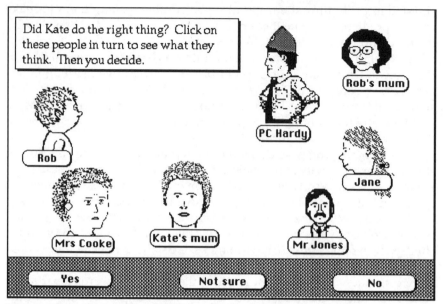

Figure 17.2   Near the end of the story the users have to decide collectively whether they made Kate do the right thing or not

issues. The theory behind this is that the capacity to 'de-centre' sufficiently to take the point of view of others into account is the core component of moral development (Rowe, 1992; Rowe & Newton, 1994).

The two areas of citizenship and science were chosen to illustrate an approach to using educational software that could be applied, for maximum impact on learning, across all core subjects of the curriculum (see Figure 17.2).

Assessing the Role of the Computer

The effectiveness of the programme as a whole in integrating exploratory talk into curriculum areas was explored through comparing video-tapes of focal groups in the target class who had the coaching lessons with video-tapes of groups in a neighbouring class. Here is a comparison between a target class group and a control class group using the same software in the area of citizenship.

Target class. Natalie, Jane and George

> *(Natalie reads the instructions from the screen.)*

Jane: Right we'll talk about it now.

Natalie: Shh *(reads)* 'talk about what Kate should do. When you have decided click on one of the buttons'.

Jane: Well what do you think?

George: Doesn't tell.

Jane: What do you think Natalie?

Natalie: Well I think she should tell because its wrong to steal – but it's her friend.

Jane and George
(together): It's her friend.

Natalie: It's her friend as well.

George: He knows it's wrong.

Natalie: Yes but he's not doing it for her, er, for him, he's doing it for his mother. So I reckon she doesn't tell.

Jane: Yes, I agree.

George: Agreed, agreed.

Natalie: Doesn't tell then? One, two, three – *(clicks)*.

George: Here we go, here we go.

Jane: *(reads)* 'Have you all talked about it?'

All: Yes.

Natalie: *(Clicks)*

Commentary

These children respond immediately to the cue on the screen which says 'Talk together'. They obviously know what this means and they sit back from the screen a little and turn to look at each other. Jane takes on a discussion facilitator's role asking the others what they think and encouraging a consensus. Through this everyone is involved. Reasons are given and questioned. Both Natalie and George give reasons against their original positions. Natalie appears to change her view. All children reach agreement before the mouse is clicked.

Control class. Mary, Cathy and Brian

(Cathy reads instructions from the screen.)

Mary: Doesn't tell or tells? What should we do? Does she tell or doesn't she?

Cathy: We've got to guess.

Brian: Tells *(in a loud and authoritative voice).*

Mary: Tells *(clicks).*

Cathy: *(Reads from screen)* 'Do you all agree?'

Brian: Yes *(again in a loud and authoritative voice).*

Cathy: Yes.

Commentary

The group does not know what to do despite the cue on the screen to 'Talk about what Kate should do' and the teacher's prompt before they use the software suggesting that they should talk together. Cathy says 'We've got to guess', implying perhaps that she thinks that there is a right answer and that they just have to guess which of the two it is. The one boy in the group decides for everyone with a single authoritative exclamation. No reason is given for his decision. No one questions it.

The differences between these two transcripts were typical of the differences between the target class groups and other groups of same-age children, both in the area of citizenship and that of science. The following features were exhibited in the talk of most of the target-class groups observed:

- Asking each other task-focused questions.
- Giving reasons for statements and challenges.
- Considering more than one possible position.
- Drawing opinions from all in the group.
- Reaching agreement before acting.

These five features were all explicitly coached in the intervention programme as 'ground rules' for talking together. These features were found less or not at all in the talk of non-target groups. Most non-target groups observed moved forward through the story in one of the following ways:

- Unilateral action by the child with the mouse.
- Accepting the choice of the most dominant child without reasoning together about it.
- Drifting together to one or other choice without debating any alternatives.

The impact of the coaching lessons could also be seen in the response of the children to the simple cues put up on the screen to 'talk about what Kate should do'. The non-target groups were baffled and did not know how to proceed. The target groups clearly knew what to do.

Computer-based Text Analysis

In Chapter 8 the idea of searching an electronic text to count key usages was introduced. A key usage is not simply a key word but a key word being use to serve a particular function. The use of a specialist electronic concordancer (Wegerif & Mercer, in press) to look at a word in its immediate context, facilitates the ascribing of a function to that word. In the talk of the children in this study the following list of key usages were found to be indicative of exploratory talk:

'if' used to link a reason to an assertion;

'because/'cos' used to link a reason to an assertion;

Questions used to support debate, including challenging 'why' questions, and more socially inclusive 'what do you think?' and 'do you agree?' questions.

Applying this 'key usage' analysis to the full transcripts of two target (coached) groups and two control (uncoached) groups working on the citizenship software produced the results shown in Table 17.1.

Table 17.1   Key usage count for target and uncoached control groups.

	Uncoached control	Target
Questions	4	13
Because/'Cos	0	7
If	0	2
Total words	496	942

The first 20 minutes talk of two groups in the target class was transcribed and compared to the first 20 minutes talk of two groups in the uncoached control class. These groups were selected by the teachers involved as typical of the range of ability and motivation in their classes. Applying the same 'key usage' analysis as was applied in Chapter 8 and above to the results of the citizenship software produced Table 17.2.

Table 17.2   Key usage count for target and uncoached control groups.

	Uncoached control	Target
Questions	15	30
Because/'Cos	4	6
If	2	2
Total words	1211	1640

Assessing the Coaching of Exploratory Talk

To evaluate the effectiveness of 'group-cognition' a set of graphical puzzles widely used in education to assess the 'non-verbal' aspects of general reasoning ability were used. The 60 problems in Raven's standard progressive matrices were converted into two similar tests so that the target and control classes could be tested in two modes: working as individuals and working in groups. These tests are described by their originators as tests of 'clear thinking' and of 'educive ability' which is an aspect of problem solving.

One of these tests was given to both the target class and the control class, divided up into groups of three, at the beginning of the intervention programme and again at the end. There was one question sheet and answer sheet per group and children were encouraged to talk together in reaching a joint solution. The other test was given to both the target and the control class but this time working as individuals. This was done at the beginning of the intervention period, two days after the group tests had been conducted, and again at the end, two days after the group tests. As has been mentioned earlier, the target class consisted of a class of 33 Year 5 (nine-year-old) children in a state middle school in Milton Keynes, England. The control class consisted of a class of 17 Year 5 children in a neighbouring state middle school. Other than this pre- and post-testing the control class had no special lessons either with or without the computer.

All the group scores in both target and control classes increased over the period of the intervention programme. The target class group scores increased by 32% while the control class group scores increased by 15%. (See Figures 17.3 and 17.4.)

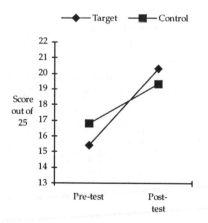

Figure 17.3 Comparing target and control class means from the group reasoning tests

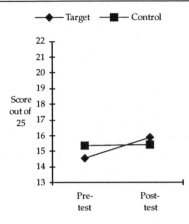

Figure 17.4 Comparing target and control class means from the individual reasoning tests

Both these differences are statistically significant. The differences between the group means was strongly significant ($Z = -1.87$ $p = 0.031$. One-tailed Mann-Whitney test, corrected for ties) while that between the individual means was just on the borderline of what is normally taken as the measure of significance, a probability of one in 10 that the results were due to chance alone ($Z = -1.65$, $p = 0.05$. One-tailed Mann-Whitney test).

Transcript evidence

The test results suggest that group effectiveness in problem solving has increased as a result of the coaching of exploratory talk. However to demonstrate this connection it is necessary to look at the change in quality of the interactions of the groups. Video-tapes of focal groups were taken at both in the initial pre-test task and at the post-test task after the intervention programme. From these it was possible to isolate the talk of the groups as they solved problems the second time that they had failed to solve the first time. The following two transcripts give an illustration of this type of analysis.

Natalie, Jane and George

Pre-test talk on problem E1

Jane: E1.

George: We've only got three more to do.

Jane: I know what it is.

Natalie: That, that *(rings number 3, a wrong answer, on the answer sheet).*

(sound of page turning)

Post-test talk on problem E1

Natalie: E1.

            (pause)

Natalie: Right I know. Wait a minute – look, that and that and that and that and that and that together – put it all together and what do you get you get that.

George: Yeh, cos' they've all got a dot in the middle.

Natalie: Wait a minute.

Jane: I actually think it's ...

Natalie: I think it's number 6.

George: Or number 7?

Natalie: Who agrees with me?

George: No it's number 7 cos' that and that makes that. Number 7 yeh.

Natalie: Yeh.

Jane: Number 7. E1 *(rings number 7, the right answer, on the answer sheet)*.

Commentary

In the post-test the group articulated what they were doing much more than in the pre-test. They took longer over each problem and produced more utterances. In the pre-test George was largely ignored by the two girls. He could be heard on the recording complaining about this. After the coaching programme the focal group asked many more questions, 33 compared to eight. Many of these were in the form: 'What do you think George?' The effect of this was to draw George into the decision-making process. On his own in the individual test George scored slightly less than either of the two girls, but here we can see his contribution moves the group forward. This illustrates the close relationship between the 'social' and the 'cognitive' aspects of group performance. All the children give reasons for their claims. On the video the two girls can be seen pausing to think about George's suggestion, which he backed up with arguments, before agreeing with it. This illustrates how, in the post condition, all are involved in thinking about each answer and agreeing to it before the group moves on. This was not the case in the pre-condition where some children took a back seat while others took charge and decided what the answers should be on their own.

It was generally found to be the case that problems which had not been solved in the pre-test and were then solved in the post-test, leading to the marked increase in group scores, were solved as a result of group interaction strategies coached in the intervention programme.

Abstracting linguistic features for all the data

Table 17. 3 shows counts of the key usages for the talk of the three focal groups when doing the standard group test together. The children here were working on exactly the same task but Table 17.3 shows that their talk after the intervention programme was markedly different from their talk before the programme. The total amount of talk increased and all the key usages indicative of exploratory talk increased dramatically. This shift in language use was paralleled by an increase in group reasoning test scores.

Table 17.3 Key usage count for the pre- and post-intervention tests of the focal groups

	Pre-test				Post-test			
	Gp1	Gp2	Gp3	Total	Gp1	Gp2	Gp3	Total
Test score	15	18	19	52	23	22	22	67
Questions	2	8	7	17	9	33	44	86
Because/'Cos	13	18	9	40	23	34	40	97
If	1	1	0	2	13	8	14	35
Total words	1460	1309	715	3484	2166	1575	2120	5761

Conclusions

This intervention study had a number of positive results:

(1) Teaching exploratory talk led to a change in the language used by groups working together which helped them to solve the problems involved in tests of the kind used to predict educational success. This suggests that, as was claimed in Chapters 3 and 5, exploratory talk is indeed a valuable kind of talk for education.

(2) The explicit teaching of exploratory talk as a way of working together led to improved individual scores on reasoning tests. This gives a tangible demonstration of the value of sociocultural model of intellectual development put forward in Section 1 by showing the close link between social interaction and cognition.

(3) A computer with a simple and even directive interface was shown supporting sustained exploratory talk between children – talk which

realised curriculum aims. This justifies the claim made in Chapter 8 about the distinctive educational potential of group work around computers.

This chapter, together with the previous chapter by Madeline Watson, represents the culmination of a research cycle illustrated in this book as whole. The first section of the book developed a framework for the analysis of classroom talk, in Section 2 this framework was applied and refined in largely descriptive studies of classroom talk around computers, and in this final section the findings of the Section 2 studies have been applied to developing and evaluating interventions aimed at improving classroom practice. Of course, there are other ways in which the research described in this book could have been applied to classroom practice. We have tried to show that the research cycle illustrated is an open and flexible one. Each stage – the development of theory, the descriptive research and the application to practice – is subject to differences and debate. The cycle itself is never finished or closed off but continues indefinitely, uniting teachers and researchers in the work of theorising and improving classroom practice in the light not only of changing circumstances such as the advent of new technologies but also of reflexive questioning of provisional theories, methods and findings.

References

Anderson, A., Tolmie, A., McAteer, E. and Demisne, A. (1993) Software style and interaction around the microcomputer. *Computers and Education* 20 (3) 235–50.

Baker, M. (1992) Modelling negotiation in intelligent teaching dialogues. In M. Elsom-Cook and R. Moyse (eds) *Knowledge Negotiation* (pp. 199–240). London: Paul Chapman Publishing.

Barbieri, M. and Light, P. (1992) Interaction, gender and performance on a computer-based task. *Learning and Instruction* 2, 199–213.

Barnes, D. (1976) *From Communication to Curriculum*. Harmondsworth: Penguin.

Barnes, D. (1988) The politics of oracy. In M. Maclure, T. Phillips and A. Wilkinson (eds) *Oracy Matters*. Milton Keynes: Open University Press.

Barnes, D. and Todd, F. (1978) *Discussion and Learning in Small Groups*. London: Routledge & Kegan Paul.

Barwise, J. and Perry, J. (1983) *Situations and Attitudes*. Cambridge, MA: MIT Press.

Bereiter, C. and Scardamalia, M. (1987) *The Psychology of Written Composition*. Hillsdale, NJ: Laurence Erlbaum.

Berger, J., Rosenholtz, S. and Zelditch, M. (1980) Status organizing processes. *Annual Review of Sociology*, 6.

Beynon, J. (1993) Computers, dominant boys and invisible girls: or 'Hannah, it's not a toaster it's a computer!' In J. Beynon and H. Mackay (eds) *Computers into Classrooms: More Questions than Answers*. London: Falmer Press.

Bhatia, V. (1993) *Analysing Genre: language Use in Professional Settings*. London: Longman.

Bruner, J. (1962) *Introduction to Vygotsky, Thought and Language*. Cambridge, MA: MIT Press.

Bruner, J. (1978) The role of dialogue in language acquisition. In A. Sinclair, R. Jarvella and W.J.M. Levelt (eds) *The Child's Conception of Language* (pp. 241–56). New York: Springer-Verlag.

Bruner, J. (1985) Vygotsky: a historical and conceptual perspective. In J. Wertsch (ed.) *Culture, Communication and Cognition: Vygotskian Perspectives*. Cambridge: Cambridge University Press.

Bruner, J. (1986) *Actual Minds: Possible Worlds*. Cambridge, MA: Harvard University Press.

Button, G. (1992) Answers as interactional products: two sequential practices used in job interviews. In P. Drew and J. Heritage (eds) *Talk at Work*. Cambridge: Cambridge University Press.

Cameron, D. (1992) *Feminism and Linguistic Theory*. London: Macmillan.

Cameron, D. (1995) Rethinking language and gender studies: Some issues for the 1990s. In S. Mills (ed.) *Language and Gender: Interdisciplinary Perspectives*. London: Longman.

Carr, W. and S. Kemmis (1986) *Becoming Critical.* London: Falmer Press.

Cavalli-Sforza, V., Moore, J.D. and Suthers, D.D. (1993) Helping students articulate and criticise scientific explanations. *Proceeding of Artificial Intelligence in Education 1993, Edinburgh.*

Cavalli-Sforza, V., Weiner, A. and Lesgold, A. (1995) Software support for students engaging in scientific activity and scientific controversy. *Science Education 78,* 577–99.

Claire, H. (1986) Collaborative work as an anti-sexist process. In Inner London Education Authority (ILEA) (ed.) *Primary Matters: Some Approaches to Equal Opportunities in the Primary School.* London: ILEA.

Clarricoates, K. (1983) Classroom interaction. In J. Whyld (ed.) *Sexism in the Secondary Curriculum.* London: Harper & Row.

Coates, J. (1993) *Women, Men and Language: A Sociolinguistic Account of Sex Differences in Language.* London: Longman.

Cochran-Smith, M., Paris, C.L. and Kahn, L. (1991) *Learning to Write Differently: Beginning Writers and Word Processing.* Norwood, NJ: Ablex Publishing.

Cole, M. (1985) The zone of proximal development: where culture and cognition create each other. In J.V. Wertsch (ed.) *Culture Communication and Cognition* (pp. 146–61). Cambridge: Cambridge University Press.

Collins (1996) *The Quiet Child.* London: Cassells.

Collins, A., Brown, J.S. and Newman, S. (1990) Cognitive apprenticeship: teaching students the crafts of reading, writing and mathematics. In L.B. Resnick (ed.) *Knowing, Learning and Instruction: Essays in Honour of Robert Glaser* (pp. 121–36). Hillsdale, NJ: Lawrence Erlbaum.

Collins, J., Littleton, K., Longman, J., Mercer, N., Scrimshaw, P. and Wegerif, R. (1996) *CD-Roms in Primary Schools: An Independent Evaluation.* Coventry: NCET.

Crawford, M. (1995) *Talking Difference: On Gender and Language.* London: Sage.

Cromer, R. (1979) The strength of the weak form of the cognition hypothesis for language acquisition. In V. Lee (ed.) *Language Development.* London: Croom Helm.

Crook, C. (1987) Computers in the classroom: Defining a social context. In J. Rutskowska and C. Crook (eds) *Computers, Cognition and Development.* London: Wiley & Sons.

Crook, C. (1991) Computers in the zone of proximal development: implications for evaluation. *Computers in Education* 17 (1), 81–91.

Crook, C. (1994) *Computers and the Collaborative Experience of Learning.* London and New York: Routledge.

Culley, L. (1988) Girls, boys and computers. *Educational Studies,* 14 3–8.

Cumming, G. (1993) A perspective on learning for intelligent educational systems. *Journal of Computer Assisted Learning* 9, 229–38.

Cummings, R. (1985) Small-group discussion and the microcomputer. *Journal of Computer Assisted Learning* 1, 149–58.

Daiute, C. (1985) *Writing and Computers.* Reading, MA: Addison-Wesley.

Daiute, C. (1986) Physical and cognitive factors in revising: insights from studies with computers. *Research in the Teaching of English* 20 (2), 141–59.

Dawes, L., Fisher, E. and Mercer, N. (1992) The quality of talk at the computer. *Language and Learning,* October 1992, 22–5.

Delamont, S. (1990) *Sex Roles and the School.* London: Methuen.

Department for Education (DFE) (1995) *Statistical Bulletin.* London: HMSO.

Department for Education and Employment (DfEE) (1995) *The National Curriculum for England and Wales*. London: HMSO.

Dillon, J.T. (1990) *The Practice of Questioning*. London: Routledge.

Dillon, J.T. (1994) *Using Discussions in Classrooms*. Buckingham: Open University Press.

Doise, W. and Mugny, G. (1984) *The Social Development of Intellect*. Oxford: Pergamon Press.

Donaldson, M. (1978) *Children's Minds*. London: Fontana.

Draper, S. and Anderson, A. (1991) The significance of dialogue in learning and observing learning. *Computers and Education* 17 (1), 93–107.

Drew, P. and Heritage, J. (1992) Analysing talk at work: an introduction. In P. Drew and J. Heritage (eds) *Talk at Work: Interaction in Institutional Settings*. Cambridge: Cambridge University Press.

Driver, R., Guesne, E. and Tiberghien, A. (1985) *Children's Ideas in Science*. Milton Keynes: Open University Press.

Dudley-Marling, C. and Searle, D. (1989) Computers and language learning: misguided assumptions. *British Journal of Educational Technology* 20 (1), 41–6.

Edwards, A. and Westgate, D. (1994) *Investigating Classroom Talk*. London: Falmer Press.

Edwards, D. (1991) Classroom discourse and classroom knowledge. In C. Rogers and P. Kutnick (eds) *Readings in the Social Psychology of the Primary School*. London: Croom Helm.

Edwards, D. and Mercer, N. (1987) *Common Knowledge: The Development of Understanding in the Classroom*. London: Routledge.

Edwards, D. and Mercer, N. (1988) Discourse, power and the creation of shared knowledge: how do pupils discover what they are meant to? In M. Hildebrand-Nilshon and G. Ruckriem (eds) *Proceedings of the 1st International Congress on Activity Theory* (Vol. 3) (pp. 9–36). Berlin: CIP.

Edwards, D. and Potter, J. (1992) *Discursive Psychology*. London: Sage.

Elbers, E., Derks, A. and Streefland, L. (1995) Learning in a community of inquiry: teacher's strategies and children's participation in the construction of mathematical knowledge. Paper read at 6th EARLI Conference, at Nijmegen, Netherlands.

Emihovich, C. and Miller, G. (1988) Talking to the turtle: a discourse analysis of Logo instruction. *Discourse Processes* 11, 182–201.

Fairclough, N. (1989) *Language and Power*. London: Longman.

Fairclough, N. (1992) *Discourse and Social Change*. Cambridge: Polity Press.

Farish, D. (1989) Computer as catalyst. *Talk: The Journal of the National Oracy Project* 2, 17–9.

Fisher, E. (1991) The teacher's role in teaching with the computer. Unit 8 of *EH232 Computers and Learning*. Milton Keynes: The Open University.

Fisher, E. (1993) Distinctive features of pupil–pupil talk and their relationship to learning. *Language and Education* 7 (4), 239–58.

Fisher, E. (1996) Identifying effective educational talk. *Language and Education* 10 (4), 237–53.

Fisher, E., Dawes, L. and Moyse, L. (1992) Discussion in the primary school: teachers developing their strategies for encouraging investigative talk amongst children using computers. Paper presented to the British Educational Research Conference, Stirling, August 1992.

Fitzpatrick, H. and Hardman, M. (1993) Boys, girls and the classroom computer: an equal partnership? Paper presented at the BPS Developmental Section Conference, University of Birmingham.

Foot, H.C., Morgan, M.J. and Shute, R.H. (1990) (eds) *Children Helping Children*. London: Wiley & Sons.

Fraser, R., Burkhardt, H., Coupland, J., Phillips, R., Pimm, D. and Ridgeway, J. (1988) Learning activities and classroom roles with and without the microcomputer. In O. Boyd-Barrett and E. Scanlon (eds) *Computers and Learning* (pp. 205–30). Milton Keynes: The Open University.

Gergen, K. (1994) *Towards Transformation in Social Knowledge* (2nd edn). London: Sage.

Gilmour (1994) Interfaces for supporting learning. Technical Report 13. Dept. of Psychology, University of Nottingham.

Graddol, D. and Swann, J. (1989) *Gender Voices*. Oxford: Blackwell.

Grice, H.P. (1975) Logic and conversation. In P. Cole and J. Morgan (eds) *Syntax and Semantics, 3: Speech Acts*. New York: Academic Press.

Groundwater-Smith, S. (1993) Beyond the individual: collaborative writing and the microcomputer. In M. Monteith (ed.) *Computers and Language*. Oxford: Intellect Books.

Habermas, J. (1970) Towards a theory of communicative competence. *Inquiry* 13, 372.

Habermas, J. (1979a) *Communication and the Evolution of Society*. London: Heinemann.

Habermas, J. (1979b) What is universal pragmatics? In *Communication and the Evolution of Society*. London: Heinemann.

Habermas, J. (1990) *Moral Consciousness and Communicative Action*. Cambridge: Polity Press.

Habermas, J. (1991a) *The Theory of Communicative Action. Vol. 2*. Cambridge: Polity Press.

Habermas, J. (1991b) *The Theory of Communicative Action. Vol. 1*. Cambridge: Polity Press.

Habermas, J. (1993) *Justification and Application*. Cambridge: Polity Press.

Halliday, M.A.K. (1978) *Language as Social Semiotic*. London: Edward Arnold.

Hammersley, M. (ed.) (1993) *Educational Research – Current Issues. Vol. 1*. Milton Keynes: Paul Chapman Publishing.

Harness-Goodwin, M. (1990) *He-Said-She-Said*. Bloomington and Indianapolis: Indiana University Press.

Harre, R. and Gillet, G. (1994) *The Discursive Mind*. London: Sage.

Hermans, J.M., Kempen, H.J.G. and van Loon, J.P. (1992) The dialogical self. *American Psychologist* 47 (1), 23–31

Hill, A. and Browne, A. (1988) Talk and the microcomputer: an investigation in the infant classroom. *Reading* 22 (1), 61–9.

Holmes, J. (1992) Women's voices in public contexts. *Discourse and Society* 3 (2), 131–50.

Howe, C. (1991) Information technology and group work in physics. *Journal of Computer Assisted Learning* 7, 133–43

Howe, C., Tolmie, A. and Mackenzie, M. (1996) Computer support for the collaborative learning of Physics concepts. In C. O'Malley (ed.) *Computer-supported Collaborative Learning*. Berlin: Springer-Verlag.

Hoyles, C. (1988) *Girls and Computers*. Bedford Way Papers, 34. London: Institute of Education, University of London.

Hoyles, C. and Sutherland, R. (1989) *Logo Mathematics in the Classroom*. London: Routledge.

Hoyles, C., Healy, L. and Pozzi, S. (1994) Groupwork with computers. *Journal of Computer Assisted Learning* 10, 202–15.

Hoyles, C., Healy, L. and Sutherland, R. (1991) Patterns of discussion between pupil pairs in computer and non-computer environments. *Journal of Computer Assisted Learning* 7, 210–28.

Hymes, D. (1972). On communicative competence. In J.B. Pride and J. Holmes (eds) *Sociolinguistics*. Harmonsworth: Penguin.

Johnson, R.T., Johnson, D.W. and Stanne, M.B. (1986) Comparison of computer-assisted co-operative, competitive and individualistic learning. *American Educational Research Journal* 23, (3), 382–92.

Jones, A. (1996) The use of computers to support learning in children with emotional and behavioural difficulties. In M. Kibby and J. Hartley (eds) *Computer Assisted Learning: Selected Contributions From the CAL 95 Symposium*. Oxford: Pergamon.

Keppler, A. and Luckmann, T. (1991) Teaching: conversational transmission of knowledge. In I. Markova and K. Foppa (eds) *Assymetries in Dialogue* (pp. 143–65). Hemel Hempstead: Harvester-Wheatsheaf.

King, A. (1989) Verbal interaction and problem solving within computer aided learning groups. *Journal of Educational Computing Research* 5, 1–15.

Kruger, A. (1993) Peer collaboration: conflict, cooperation or both? *Social Development* 2, 3.

Kutnick, P. (1994) Developing pupils' social skills for learning, social interaction and cooperation. In H.C. Foot, C.J. Howe, A.K. Tolmie, D.A. Warden and A.Anderson (eds) *Group and Interactive Learning* (pp. 283–88). Ashurst: Computational Mechanics Publications.

Kutnick, P., and Brees, P. (1982) The development of cooperation: explorations in cognitive and moral competence and social authority. *British Journal of Educational Psychology* 52, 361–5.

Lakoff, R. (1981) Persuasive discourse and ordinary conversation. In D. Tannen (ed.) *Georgetown University Roundtable on Language and Linguistics*. Washington, DC: Georgetown University Press.

Laurillard, D. (1993) *Rethinking University Teaching: A Framework for the Effective Use of Educational Technology*. New York and London: Routledge.

Lave, J. (1992) Word problems: a microcosm of theories of learning. In P. Light and G. Butterworth (eds) *Context and Cognition* (pp. 74–93). Hemel Hempstead: Harvester-Wheatsheaf.

Lee, M. (1993) Gender, group composition and peer interaction in computer based cooperative learning. *Journal of Educational Computing Research* 9 (4), 549–77.

Levinson, S.C. (1992) Activity types and language. In P. Drew and J. Heritage (eds) *Talk at Work*. Cambridge: Cambridge University Press.

Light, P. (1993) Collaborative learning with computers. In P. Scrimshaw (ed.) *Language, Classrooms and Computers*. London: Routledge.

Light, P. and Littleton, K. (1996) Situational effects in children's computer-based learning. Chapter to appear in L. Resnick, R. Saljo, and C. Pontecorvo (eds) *Discourse, Tools and Reasoning*. Springer-Verlag.

Light, P., Littleton, K., Messer, D. and Joiner, R. (1994) Social and communicative processes in computer-based problem solving. *European Journal of Psychology of Education.* 9 (1), 311–24.

Lipman, M. (1991) *Thinking in Education.* Cambridge: Cambridge University Press.

Malone, T.W. (1981) Towards a theory of intrinsically motivating instruction. *Cognitive Science,* 4, 333–69.

Maltz, D. and Borker, R. (1982) A cultural approach to male–female miscommunication. In J.J. Gumperz (ed.) *Language and Social Identity.* Cambridge: Cambridge University Press.

Martin, A. (1988) An adaptable microworld for the history classroom. *Computers in Education* 12, 1.

Martin, J.R., Christie, F. and Rothery, J. (1987) Social processes in education: a reply to Sawyer and Watson (and others). In I. Reid (ed.) *The Place of Genre in Learning: Current Debates.* Deakin University, Australia: Centre for Studies in Literary Education.

Martin, J.R. (1984) Language, register and genre. In F. Christie (ed.) *Children Writing* (pp. 21–9). Geelong, Victoria: Deakin University Press.

Maybin, J. (1994) Children's voices: talk, knowledge and identity. In D. Graddol, J. Maybin and B. Stierer (eds) *Researching Language and Literacy in Social Context.* Clevedon: Multilingual Matters.

Maybin, J., Mercer, N. and Stierer, B. (1992) Scaffolding in the classroom. In K. Norman (ed.) *Thinking Voices: The Work of the National Oracy Project* (pp. 165–95). London: Hodder & Stoughton.

Mehan, H. (1979) *Learning Lessons: Social Organisation in the Classroom.* Cambridge, MA: Harvard University Press.

Mercer, N. (1991) Learning through talk. In *Talk and Learning 5–16: An In-service Pack on Oracy for Teachers* (pp. A5–A10). Milton Keynes: The Open University.

Mercer, N. (1992) Culture, context and the construction of classroom knowledge. In P. Light and G. Butterworth (eds) *Context and Cognition* (pp. 28–46). Hemel Hempstead: Harvester-Wheatsheaf.

Mercer, N. (1994) Neo-Vygotskian theory and education. In B. Stierer and J. Maybin (eds) *Language, Literacy and Learning in Educational Practice.* Clevedon: Multilingual Matters.

Mercer, N. (1995) *The Guided Construction of Knowledge: Talk Between Teachers and Learners in the Classroom.* Clevedon: Multilingual Matters.

Mercer, N. and Fisher, E. (1992) How do teachers help children to learn? An analysis of teachers' interventions in computer-based tasks. *Learning and Instruction* 2, 339–55.

Mercer, N. and Scrimshaw, P. (1993) Researching the electronic classroom. In P. Scrimshaw (ed.) *Language, Classrooms and Computers.* London: Routledge.

Middleton, D. and Edwards, D. (1990) *Collective Remembering.* London: Sage.

Mills, S. (ed.) (1995) *Language and Gender: Interdisciplinary Perspectives.* London: Longman.

Murphy, P. (1991) Gender and assessment practice in science. In L. Parker, L. Rennie and B. Fraser (eds) *Gender Science and Mathematics: A Way Forward.* Oxford: Pergamon.

Murris, K. (1993) *Teaching Philosophy with Picture Books.* London: Infonet Publications.

National Council for Educational Technology (NCET) (1990) *Talking IT Through.* Coventry: NCET.

National Council for Educational Technology (NCET) (1993) *Evaluation of IT in Science.* Coventry: NCET.

Newman, D., Griffin, P. and Cole, M. (1989) *The Construction Zone: Working for Cognitive Change in School.* Cambridge: Cambridge University Press.

Norman, K. (ed.) (1992) *Thinking Voices: The Work of the National Oracy Project.* London: Hodder & Stoughton.

O'Malley, C. (1992) Designing computer systems to support peer learning. *European Journal of Psychology of Education* 1 (4), 339–52.

O'Neill, B. and McMahon, H. (1991) Opening new windows with bubble dialogue. *Computers in Education* 17 (1), 29–35.

O'Shea, T. and Self, J. (1983) *Learning and Teaching with Computers.* Brighton: Harvester Press.

Papert, S. (1980) *Mindstorms: Children, Computers and Powerful Ideas.* New York: Basic Books.

Potter, J. and Wetherell, M. (1994) *Discourse Analysis and Social Psychology.* London: Sage.

Pozzi, S., Healy, L. and Hoyles, C. (1993) Learning and interaction in groups with computers: when do ability and gender matter? *Social Development* 2 (3).

Prentice, M. (1991) A community of enquiry. *In Talk and Learning 5–16: An In-service Pack on Oracy for Teachers* (pp. A28–A31). Milton Keynes: The Open University.

Pryor, J. (1995) Gender issues in groupwork - a case study involving work with computers. *British Educational Research Journal* 21 (3), 277–88.

Raven, J., Raven, J.C. and Court, J. (1993) *Manual for Raven's Progressive Matrices and Vocabulary Scales* (1993 edn). Oxford: Oxford Psychologists Press.

Rogoff, B. (1990) *Apprenticeship in Thinking.* New York: Cambridge University Press.

Rogoff, B. and Wertsch, J.V. (eds) (1984) Children's learning in the zone of proximal development. In W. Damon (ed.) *New Directions in Child Development,* No. 23, March 1984. Jossey-Bass.

Rommetveit, R. (1992) Outlines of a dialogically based social-cognitive approach to human cognition and communication. In A. Wold (ed.) *The Dialogical Alternative: Towards a Theory of Language and Mind.* Oslo: Scandinavian Press.

Rowe, D. (1992). The citizen as a moral agent: The construction of a continuous and progressive conflict-based citizenship curriculum. *Curriculum* 13 (3), 178–87.

Rowe, D. and Newton, J. (1994) *You, Me, Us: Citizenship Materials for Primary Schools.* London: The Citizenship Foundation.

Rysavy, S. and Sales, G. (1991) Cooperative learning in computer-based instruction. *Educational Technology Research and Development* 39, 70–9.

Sacks, H., Schegloff, E.A. and Jefferson, G. (1974) A simplest systematics for the organisation of turn taking in conversation. *Language* 50 (4), 696–735.

Sadker, M. and Sadker, D. (1985) Sexism in the schoolroom of the '80s. *Psychology Today* March, 54-7.

Sampson, E. (1993) *Celebrating the Other: A Dialogic Account of Human Nature.* Hemel Hempstead: Harvester.

Scardemalia, M. and Bereiter, C. (1991) Higher levels of agency for children in knowledge building: a challenge for the design of new knowledge media. *The Journal of the Learning Sciences* 1 (1), 37–68.

Scardemalia, M., Bereiter, C., McLean, R., Swallow, J. and Woodruff, E. (1989) Computer-supported intentional learning environments. *Journal of Educational Computing Research* 5 (1), 51–68.

Schegloff, E.A. (1982) Discourse as an interactional achievement: Some uses of 'uh huh' and other things that come between sentences. In D. Tannen (ed.) *Analyzing Discourse: Text and Talk*. Georgetown University Roundtable on Languages and Linguistics. Washington DC: Georgetown University Press.

Scrimshaw, P. (ed.) (1993) *Language, Classrooms and Computers*. London: Routledge.

Sewell, D. (1990) *New Tools for New Minds: A Cognitive Perspective on the Use of Computers with Young Children*. London: Harvester-Wheatsheaf.

Sherwood, C. (1991) Adventure games in the classroom: a far cry from 'A says apple'. *Computers in Education* 17 (4), 309–15.

Shotter, J. (1993) *Cultural Politics of Everyday Life*. Buckingham: Open University Press.

Siann, G. and Macleod, H. (1986) Computers and children of primary school age: issues and questions. *British Journal of Educational Technology* 17 (2), 133–44.

Simon, H.A. (1980) Cognitive science. The newest science of the artificial. *Cognitive Science* 4, 33–46.

Simon, H.A. (1981) *The Sciences of the Artificial*. Cambridge, MA: MIT Press.

Sinclair, J. and Coulthard, R. (1975) *Towards an Analysis of Discourse: The English Used by Teachers and Pupils*. London: Oxford University Press.

Smith, L. (1989) Changing perspectives in developmental psychology. In C. Desforges (ed.) *Early Childhood Education*. BPS Monograph Series No. 4. Edinburgh: Scottish Academic Press.

Solomon, C. (1987) *Computer Environments for Children*. Cambridge, MA: MIT Press.

Spender, D. (1982) *Invisible Women: The Schooling Scandal*. London: Writers and Readers Publishing Cooperative.

Spender, D. and Sarah, E. (eds) (1988) *Learning to Lose: Sexism and Education*. London: Women's Press.

Stanworth, M. (1983) *Gender and Schooling: A Study of Sexual Divisions in the Classroom*. London: Hutchinson.

Steadman, S., Nash, C. and Eraut, M. (1992) *CD-Roms in Schools*. Evaluation Report. Coventry: NCET.

Straker, A. (1989) *Children Using Computers*. Oxford: Blackwell.

Stubbs, M. (1983) *Discourse Analysis: The Sociolinguistic Analysis of Natural Language*. Oxford: Blackwell.

Sutherland, M. (1985) Classroom interaction and sex differences. *British Journal of Educational Psychology*. Edinburgh: Scottish Academic Press, Monograph Series No. 2.

Swales, J. (1990) *Genre Analysis: English in Academic and Research Settings*. Cambridge: Cambridge University Press.

Swann, J. (1992) *Girls, Boys and Language*. Oxford: Blackwell.

Swann, J. and Graddol, D. (1995) Feminising classroom talk? In S. Mills (ed.) *Language and Gender: Interdisciplinary Perspectives*. London: Longman.

Swann, J. and Graddol, D. (1988) Gender inequalities in classroom talk. *English in Education* 221, 48–65.

Tannen, D. (1996) *Gender and Discourse*. Oxford: Oxford University Press.

Thompson, C. and P. Martinet (1980) *A Practical English Grammar*. Oxford: Oxford University Press.

Tolmie, A., Howe, C., Mackenzie, M. and Greer, K. (1993) Task design as an influence on dialogue and learning: primary school group work with object flotation. *Social Development* 23, 183–201.

Tracy, K. and Baratz, S. (1993) Intellectual discussion in the academy as situated discourse. *Communication Monographs* 60, 300–20.

Tracy, K. and Carjuzaa, J. (1993) Identity enactment in intellectual discussion. *Language and Social Psychology* 123, 171–94.

Tracy, K. and Muller, K. (1994) Talking about ideas: academics' beliefs about appropriate communicative practices. *Research on Language and Social Interaction* 274, 319–49.

Tracy, K. and Naughton, J. (1994) The identity work of questioning in intellectual discussion. *Communication Monographs* 61, 281–302.

Uchida, A. (1992) When 'difference' is 'dominance': A critique of the 'antipowerbased' cultural approaches to sex differences. *Language in Society* 21, 547–68.

Underwood, J. (ed.) (1994) *Computer Based Learning*. London: David Fulton.

Underwood, J. and Underwood, G. (1990) *Computers and Learning*. Oxford: Blackwell.

Underwood, G., McCaffrey, M. and Underwood, J. (1990) Gender differences in a cooperative computer-based language task. *Educational Research*, 32 44–9.

van der Veer, R. and Valsiner, J. (1991) *Understanding Vygotsky: A Quest for Synthesis*. Oxford: Blackwell.

van der Veer, R. and Valsiner, J. (eds) (1994) *The Vygotsky Reader*. Oxford: Blackwell.

Volosinov, V.N. (1986) *Marxism and the Philosophy of Language*. Cambridge, MA: Harvard University Press.

Vygotsky, L. (1978) *Mind in Society*. Cambridge, MA: Harvard University Press.

Vygotsky, L. (1991) The genesis of higher mental functions. In P. Light, S. Sheldon and B. Woodhead (eds) *Learning to Think*. London: Routledge.

Vygotsky, L.S. (1986) *Thought and Language*. Cambridge, MA: MIT Press.

Walkerdine, V. (1984) Developmental psychology and the child-centred pedagogy: the insertion of Piaget into early education. In J. Henriques, W. Hollway, C. Urwin, C. Venn and V. Walkerdine (eds) *Changing the Subject* (pp. 153–201). London: Methuen.

Webb, N. (1989) Peer interaction and learning in small groups. *International Journal of Educational Research* 13, 21–39

Webb, N.M., Ender, P. and Lewis, S. (1986) Problem solving strategies and group processes in small groups learning computer programming. *American Educational Research Journal* 23 (2), 243–61.

Wegerif, R. and Mercer, N. (1996) Computers and reasoning through talk in the classroom. *Language and Education* 10 (1), 47–64.

Wegerif, R. and Mercer, N. (1997) Using computer-based text analysis to integrate quantitative and qualitative methods in the investigation of collaborative learning. *Language and Education* 11 (3).

Wertsch, J.V. (ed.) (1985a) *Culture, Communication and Cognition: Vygotskian Perspectives*. Cambridge: Cambridge University Press.

Wertsch, J.V. (1985b) *Vygotsky and the Social Formation of Mind*. Cambridge, MA: Harvard University Press.

Wertsch, J.V. (1991) *Voices of the Mind*. New York: Harvester.

Wertsch, J. (1996) The role of abstract rationality in Vygotsky's image of mind. In A. Tryphon and J. Voneche (eds) *Piaget – Vygotsky: The Social Genesis of Thought*. Hove: Psychology Press.

Whyte, J. (1986) *Girls into Science and Technology: The Story of a Project*. London: Routledge & Kegan Paul.

Wishart, J. (1990) Cognitive factors related to user involvement with computers and their effects upon learning from educational computer games. *Computers in Education* 14, 1–3.

Wold, A. (ed.) (1992) *The Dialogical Alternative: Towards a Theory of Language and Mind*. Oslo: Scandanavian Press.

Wood, D. (1992) Teaching talk. In K. Norman (ed.) *Thinking Voices: The Work of the National Oracy Project*. London: Hodder & Stoughton.

Wood, D., Bruner, J. and Ross, G. (1976) The role of tutoring in problem solving. *Journal of Child Psychology and Psychiatry* 17, 89–100.

Young, R. (1991) *Critical Theory and Classroom Talk*. Clevedon: Multilingual Matters.

Index

Name Index

Subject Index

DATE DUE
